SEX STRATIFICATION

Children, Housework, and Jobs

QUANTITATIVE STUDIES IN SOCIAL RELATIONS

Consulting Editor: Peter H. Rossi

UNIVERSITY OF MASSACHUSETTS
AMHERST, MASSACHUSETTS

In Preparation

Ann D. Witte and Peter Schmidt, **THE ECONOMICS OF CRIME:** *Theory, Methods, and Applications*

Peter H. Rossi, James D. Wright, and Andy B. Anderson (Eds.), **HAND-BOOK OF SURVEY RESEARCH**

Published

Joan Huber and Glenna Spitze, **SEX STRATIFICATION:** *Children, Housework, and Jobs*

Toby L. Parcel and Charles W. Mueller, **ASCRIPTION AND LABOR MARKETS:** *Race and Sex Differences in Earnings*

Paul G. Schervish, **THE STRUCTURAL DETERMINANTS OF UNEMPLOYMENT:** *Vulnerability and Power in Market Relations*

Irving Tallman, Ramona Marotz-Baden, and Pablo Pindas, **ADOLESCENT SOCIALIZATION IN CROSS-CULTURAL PERSPECTIVE:** *Planning for Social Change*

Robert F. Boruch and Joe S. Cecil (Eds.), **SOLUTIONS TO ETHICAL AND LEGAL PROBLEMS IN SOCIAL RESEARCH**

J. Ronald Milavsky, Ronald C. Kessler, Horst H. Stipp, and William S. Rubens, **TELEVISION AND AGGRESSION:** *A Panel Study*

Ronald S. Burt, **TOWARD A STRUCTURAL THEORY OF ACTION:** *Network Models of Social Structure, Perception, and Action*

Peter H. Rossi, James D. Wright, and Eleanor Weber-Burdin, **NATURAL HAZARDS AND PUBLIC CHOICE:** *The Indifferent State and Local Politics of Hazard Mitigation*

Neil Fligstein, **GOING NORTH:** *Migration of Blacks and Whites from the South, 1900–1950*

Howard Schuman and Stanley Presser, **QUESTIONS AND ANSWERS IN ATTITUDE SURVEYS:** *Experiments on Question Form, Wording, and Context*

The list of titles in this series continues on the last page of this volume

SEX STRATIFICATION
Children, Housework, and Jobs

JOAN HUBER
Department of Sociology
University of Illinois
Urbana, Illinois

GLENNA SPITZE
Department of Sociology
State University of New York at Albany
Albany, New York

ACADEMIC PRESS
A Subsidiary of Harcourt Brace Jovanovich, Publishers
New York   London
Paris   San Diego   San Francisco   São Paulo   Sydney   Tokyo   Toronto

ACADEMIC PRESS, INC.
111 Fifth Avenue, New York, New York 10003

United Kingdom Edition published by
ACADEMIC PRESS, INC. (LONDON) LTD.
24/28 Oval Road, London NW1 7DX

Library of Congress Cataloging in Publication Data

Huber, Joan, Date
   Sex-role ideologies.

   Includes index.
   1. Sex role. 2. Sex discrimination against women.
3. Marriage. 4. Sex discrimination in employment.
I. Spitze, Glenna D.   II. Title.
HQ1206.H79   1983   305.3   82-18407
ISBN 0-12-358480-9

PRINTED IN THE UNITED STATES OF AMERICA

83 84 85 86   9 8 7 6 5 4 3 2 1

To William Form and Robert Franklin

Contents

CHAPTER ONE
Sex Stratification Theory   1

CHAPTER TWO
Data and Methods   52

CHAPTER THREE
Husband–Wife Reporting Consistency   59

CHAPTER EIGHT
Religion and Sex-Role Issues 167

CHAPTER NINE
Conclusions 209

APPENDIX
University of Illinois Survey Research Laboratory: Attitudes toward Women and Work Main Questionnaire 222

List of Tables

Preface

This book proposes and begins to test a theory about how Americans respond to social and economic changes that affect sex stratification. This theory assumes that in all societies people who produce have more power than people who consume and that the most power and prestige accrue to those who control distribution of valued goods beyond the family. The theory's central proposition holds that patterns of sex stratification are shaped by the way a given subsistence technology enables women to combine pregnancy and lactation with valued work. We explicate the theory by showing how different technologies in foraging, horticultural, herding, agricultural, and industrial societies affect women's prestige and power relative to men's.

A macrotheory of change during industrialization enables us to develop, in turn, a microtheory to interpret our findings, primarily based on telephone survey data for a national probability sample of U.S. residents in 1978. The main variables in the macrotheory are mortality, education, fertility, and women's labor-force participation. During the nineteenth century, decreasing mortality and rising education levels led to a long fertility decline that permitted, in turn, a massive increase in the rates of women's labor-force participation when economic conditions became favorable. As more women became producers as well as consumers, their political status improved. But women are still underrepresented in the top positions of power and prestige. Women's attainment of social equality now hinges significantly on the division of household labor. In the last chapter we explain why we expect change in aggregate levels of this variable in coming decades.

A macrotheory of social change can inform a microtheory by indicating which variable should most effectively predict traditional versus nontraditional attitudes and behaviors at the individual level. The most effective micropredictor should be the variable that most recently changed substantially at the aggregate level. Populations are still adjusting to the ripple effects of the change. In contrast, variables whose levels changed earlier tend to be taken for granted, mortality, for example. We therefore expected women's labor-force participation to be the most effective predictor of the traditionality of sex-role behaviors and attitudes because, of all the variables in our macrotheory, women's labor-force participation has most recently experienced dramatic change.

We then compare our microtheory with a well-known economic theory of household organization. Interdisciplinary comparisons, however rough, force one to look at the world in new ways. New Home Economist Gary Becker stresses the wife/husband wage ratio as the primary determinant of household organization. Unlike the rates of women's labor-force participation, the wife/husband wage ratio has resisted change. It is central to Becker's theory of household organization because it explains why women do housework and men do market work. The wage-ratio hypothesis derives from a theory whose key assumption is that nearly everyone wants at least two children. Someone must therefore stay home to care for them. If one grants the key assumption (and several others), the theory makes some sense. From a sociological perspective, however, the main problem with the theory is that its major assumption needs to be examined empirically rather than taken as given. If people are as rational as Becker supposes, then it seems likely that their behavior would be affected by the costs and benefits of childrearing.

A comparison of the effects of women's labor-force participation and the wife/husband wage ratio on the traditionality of household-related attitudes and behaviors shows that women's labor-force participation is a better predictor. This does not prove that Becker is wrong. We do not test his theory. But it does suggest that an adequate economic theory of household organization should test the extent to which the economic costs and benefits of rearing children should affect the preference for having zero, one, or two or more children.

This book was written for students and scholars interested in the problems of sex stratification, demographic change, and the family, areas that cross the boundaries of a number of disciplines in the social sciences and humanities. In the last decade, scholars in these disciplines have unearthed a wealth of data. However, integration is difficult. Researchers run the risks of instant scholarship, rediscovering wheels long since buried in a neighbor's field. Writers run the risk of assuming that readers from a variety of disciplines can follow arguments framed in the terminology of a particular discipline. Many of the chapters here, for example, employ quantitative techniques out of reach of persons untrained in the statistical methods that are a standard analytic technique in sociology. However, we have tried to present the arguments in such fashion that they will be understandable to persons who are interested in knowing about the trends that raise or lower women's status relative to men's in developed societies.

The first three chapters address issues of theory and methods. In Chapter 1 we give a historical account of sex stratification in various societies in order to develop the theory that guides the data analysis in the rest of the book. Chapter 2 describes the sample and data-collecting procedures. In Chapter 3 we take advantage of the presence in the sample of a large number of husbands and wives married to one another to examine the usefulness of individual versus couple data for measuring household attitudes and behaviors.

In Chapter 4 we test alternative hypotheses regarding variation in the division of household labor among couples. Chapter 5 extends Becker's economic theory of marital instability by examining predictors of husbands' and wives' thoughts on divorce. Chapter 6 examines individual-level predictors of attitudes regarding fertility and fertility-related policies and then assesses the future of pronatalism. In Chapter 7 we test the effect of wives' work attachment, current employment status, and earnings on perceptions of household decision-making, the household division of labor, and on sex-role attitudes. In Chapter 8 we examine the effect of religious affiliation on attitudes relating to women's employment, race, and the family. Finally, in Chapter 9, we summarize our findings and speculate about the future of sex equality.

Acknowledgments

We are coauthors. Our names are listed alphabetically. We collaborated fully on every aspect of this research.

We are grateful to a number of agencies and persons who helped to make this research possible. We are indebted to the National Science Foundation for awarding Joan Huber a grant (SOC 78-18015) that supported the data collection and much of the writing. Additional support was provided by the University Research Board, the Social Science Quantitative Laboratory, the School of Social Science, and the Research Committee of the Department of Sociology of the University of Illinois at Urbana-Champaign. Support was also provided by a National Science Foundation grant (SES 80-23646) and by Grant 320-7472A from the Research Foundation of the State University of New York to Glenna Spitze. The views expressed in the book are those of the authors. They do not necessarily reflect the views of the agencies that so generously permitted us to conduct the research.

Several editors graciously permitted us to include materials published in their journals. An early version of some of the ideas in Chapter 1 appear in Social Problems and Sociological Quarterly. Chapter 5 is a revision of an article that appeared in the American Journal of Sociology; Chapter 7 of an article in Social Forces. Three of the tables in Chapter 8 first appeared in Work and Occupations.

A number of persons contributed to the research in various ways. Kenneth Land and Joe L. Spaeth encouraged and advised us at the stage of formulating the proposal. Seymour Sudman gave us advice on sampling; the idea of including husbands and wives married to one another was his. Patricia Ulbrich helped to design the questionnaire and worked as a research assistant on the project.

Personnel of the Survey Research Laboratory of the University of Illinois, then under the capable direction of the late Robert Ferber, performed with their usual reliability and speed: Johnny Blair, head of Sampling; Jutta Sebestik, Head of Field work; Dorothy Nemanich, Head of Data Analysis; Chris Rust, Data Reduction Coordinator; Sue Lewis, Research Data Analyst. Our connecting link with the world of SRL was Linda Lannom, Project Coordinator and administrator par excellence.

With her customary precision, Carolyn White analysed trends on church attendance, using NORC data.

Useful comments on various chapters were provided by Jan Gorecki, Robert Alun Jones, James Kluegel, Steven Rytina, Robert Schoen, Seymour Sudman, Linda Waite, and Mary Jo Weaver. William Form commented usefully on every chapter.

We have benefited from excellent clerical assistance at all stages of the research. We are especially grateful to Eileen Crary, Gloria Swigert, Linda Schroll, and Debbie Neuls at SUNY Albany and to Margaret Quinn, Sheila Welch, Bonnie Wilhite, and especially to Trudy Thiede at the University of Illinois at Urbana-Champaign.

Last, we give heartfelt thanks to Debbie Bell, Christopher Franklin's daytime mother and to Alice Huber, who helped out in ways that are hard to count.

SEX STRATIFICATION

Children, Housework, and Jobs

CHAPTER ONE

Sex Stratification Theory[1]

This book is about what contemporary Americans do, think, and feel about the interrelationships of men, women, children, and work. The primary data are based on a national sample survey of American adults conducted in 1978. The questions primarily concerned attitudes, but respondents were also asked to report certain household behaviors. Because the basis for women's status has been called into question only in the last decade, the materials for a historically based theory are scattered. Because feminist scholarship takes place in the real world, some of the observations that contribute to our perspective are drawn from personal experience. The materials for this chapter therefore come from a variety of sources. Our purpose is to present a historical evolutionary perspective on sex stratification in order to provide a basis for predicting the future of women's status in industrialized countries.

The way childrearing meshes with subsistence work is critical to collective survival. Like other forms of life, human beings tend to produce more children than their environment can support. Hence main-

[1]We are grateful to Social Problems for permission to adapt material that appeared in Joan Huber, "Toward a sociotechnological theory of the women's movement," Social Problems 23 (April 1976):371–388 and to Sociological Quarterly, for permission to adapt material from Joan Huber, "Will U.S. fertility decline toward zero?", Sociological Quarterly 21 (Autumn 1980):481–492.

taining the delicate balance between having enough babies to ensure survival but not too many for the food supply has been a perennial problem. Therefore, in all societies a web of beliefs supports customs that adapt fertility to subsistence: when to marry, whom to marry, how many children to have, and what kind of work to do. Because these beliefs so strongly affect collective survival, they are deeply rooted, hard for individuals to change.

Yet, natural forces and human ingenuity can create new environments that induce new behaviors and erode even the strongest beliefs. In the last 2000 or 3000 years, the most important environmental changes probably have been those that resulted from human inventions that increased the production of material goods, especially food. Since human life is a collective response to the practical problems of earthly existence (Harris, 1980), knowing how subsistence technology changes over time is basic to understanding what people do, think, and feel.

The insight that human beings respond to environmental change is hardly new. The grand social theories of past and present, whether of class struggle, the formation of bureaucratic elites, or agrarian revolution, draw on historical materials that take subsistence technology into account. But women appear only as shadows in these theories about men and their work. Women's work was taken for granted as being part of family life. Family sociologists, however, tended to ignore both men's and women's work. Instead, they focused primarily on personal interaction, assuming that the major contribution of the modern family was to its members' happiness. Until feminist sociologists noted the connections, work and family were studied as separate topics (Rossi, 1980:26).

In sum, the grand social theorists tended to focus on men and their work; family sociologists, on the interaction of men, women, and children. Why did the interrelationships of men, women, children, and work remain invisible for so long?

First, until feminist thought began to affect academic research, the work of most social scientists had the net effect of regarding women's status as stemming from unchangeable biological factors. Childbearing and childrearing were seen as inextricably intertwined. Hence women's responsibility for childrearing was taken for granted despite sociologists' abiding interest in the division of labor.

Yet, of the biological differences relevant to the division of labor, only one categorically separates women and men: No man can bear a child. Other differences are of degree rather than kind. We shall argue in this chapter that the effects of sex on the division of labor primarily result from men's inability to reproduce rather than from the characteristics, natural or nurtured, that overlap between the sexes. We briefly discuss such overlapping physical and mental characteristics. Their effect on sex stratification patterns can then be contrasted with the effect of women's childbearing capacity under various subsistence conditions.

Several characteristics statistically differentiate men and women. Men tend to be larger and stronger; women tend to live longer (Bayo and Glanz, 1955; Madigan, 1957; Johnson, 1977). In preindustrial societies, men's size and strength gave them an advantage in such tasks as throwing rocks, subduing large animals (including humans), and managing draft animals. Today these characteristics give men an edge in playing football and shoveling snow, but such advantages are now less important. In developed societies, the best rewarded tasks require brains, not brawn. Women's durability advantage over men increased from 1930, when the effects of reduced maternal mortality began to appear (Riley, 1980). But greater longevity gives women no status advantage in societies that pay no special respect to age.

The psychological characteristics of men and women also overlap. The extent to which these characteristics result from socialization, biology, or their interaction remains a question that is probably unanswerable (Lambert, 1978:117), at least by current research techniques. Socialization demonstrably affects character (Whiting and Edwards, 1973; Maccoby and Jacklin, 1974). Biological differences, in hormone levels, for example, may also play a part (Baker, 1980; Rossi, 1980).

Although the existence of such statistical differences is beyond dispute, they are socially important only to the extent that they imply a division of labor by sex. Van den Berghe (1979), for example, argues that an innate drive to reproduce fitness defines women forever primarily as childrearers. The existence of such a factor is logically possible. Yet, even if research evidence conclusively demonstrated the existence of a female drive to reproduce fitness that was empirically separable from the sex drive, one must still question its strength. Whether a woman were driven to reproduce once or many times would affect her time for other tasks. Moreover, social patterns could make childrearing so costly that an innate drive could provide too little incentive to rear even one child. Van den Berghe does not address such questions using data concerning the factors that have been related to declining fertility in developed countries. His argument is therefore not convincing. It is not enough to assert that biology constrains culture. Of course it does. Culture can also alter biological constraints. Today men can fly although they have no wings. They can feed babies although they have no breasts.

The second reason that theories about men, women, and work are rare is that many social scientists have long been more concerned with the ideal than with the material aspects of human life (Harris, 1980). This is perhaps another reason (cf. Rossi, 1981) that sociologists remain so ambivalent about doing research on practical problems. In the 1950s, Talcott Parsons and his followers mesmerized sociologists with an idealist theory that posited value consensus as the glue holding societies together. The theory was so abstract that it concealed the daily realities of human life. It yielded little insight into potential sources of change.

More recently, scholars concerned with critical theory have tended to neglect material problems in order to bemoan the epistemological inadequacy of much current research. Critical theorists (as well as some feminist theorists) argue, correctly, that research findings can legitimate particular political interests. Their solution is to reject "positivism" and to raise their own vague and inoperational values to the level of science. They do not grasp that the charges they raise against positivism apply also to their own research (van den Berg, 1980; McCormack, 1981).

Third, Marxists concerned with empirical data have not applied a materialist perspective to the study of women's work because they did not understand the long-term implications of declining fertility. Marxists have long opposed Malthus owing to the conservative implications of his view that overpopulation causes poverty. They hold, instead, that malapportionment of resources is the main cause. They attribute women's problems to capitalism. They ignore similar problems in fully developed countries that are not capitalist. Male Marxists disregard early radical feminist claims that both capitalism and state socialism are patriarchal (Carroll, 1980:457). Nor do Marxists recognize that the revolution was intended to free only men. Women would have to wait for the end of a revolutionary period of unspecified length (Weinbaum, 1978:52). As former Chairman Mao remarked, it would take perhaps a few thousand years, or at least several hundred, for the family to disappear (Levy, 1975:98). Even feminist Marxists have tended to ignore the effect of fertility on women's status. In the early 1970s, they assumed that industrial capitalism was the major cause of women's labor market problems. Later, they became aware that the social relations of patriarchy were also involved. Marxist literature showing this awareness, however, is scattered and new. Feminist Marxists still have not resolved the question as to why women became responsible for child care under both state socialism and capitalism (Sokoloff, 1980:114, 196).

Thus did social theorists and family sociologists fail to relate changes in the material conditions of urban industrial life to women's work. They therefore failed to observe a relative decline in women's status that would leave women susceptible to rising resentment. In the last century, the status of women's work decreased relative to men's. Nineteenth century Americans typically worked in unpaid or low-wage dirty jobs, in the factory, on the farm, or at home. "Head work" was the prerogative of a small group of elite men whose wives assumed ornamental or childbearing roles, as Veblen noted. The daily work of rearing elite babies was done by poor women.

By the 1950s, however, the proportion of men working in dirty, unskilled jobs had declined. A growing proportion of men worked in clean and well paid white-collar jobs. But the wives of these white-skinned, white-collared husbands were spending as much time doing housework as their grandmothers had (Vanek, 1974). A dramatic rise in standards offset the effect of improvements in household technology. The discrepancy in the kind of daily work performed by middle-class men and women set the stage for an increase in women's sense of unfairness.

So far as we have been able to discover, no family sociologist analyzed the changes in the material conditions of husbands' and wives' daily work or noted that the improvement in the conditions of men's work had altered the status balance of market and housework. Had they done so, they might have asked how such a division of labor came into being, whether it would ever change, and if so, what might bring change about.[2]

Today, an apparent instability in family life makes many people uneasy. Indeed, by the twenty-first century, as we shall soon show, it is probable that a continuing fertility decline will be inextricably intertwined with trends in marriage, divorce, remarriage, cohabitation, women's and men's labor-force participation, and the division of household labor. These aggregate trends concern the way women and men earn a living, divide household labor, and rear (or avoid rearing) children. In sum, they affect the most intimate details of family life.

---

[2]In contrast to family sociologists' neglect, Caplow's (1954:230–280) seldom-cited analysis of women's work seems ahead of its time. Housewives' maladjustment results from imposing the same job requirements on morons and geniuses, on young girls and old women. Women's progress to occupational equality is merely a change in the form of inequality, guaranteed by women's discontinuous careers, lower pay, geographic immobility, the presence of a reserve labor force of nonemployed women, and a vast network of special rules, some designed for protection, some, to reduce women's competition, and some adroitly contrived for both purposes.

The purpose of this book is therefore to show the current relationships of behavior and beliefs about work and family in order to assess what people are likely to do and to believe 20 years hence. This chapter will outline a theory of sex stratification in order to show how these factors are related to one another.

We begin by discussing the basis for our approach, Harris's (1980) analysis of cultural materialism. Second, we review the few analyses of sex stratification in evolutionary perspective (Friedl, 1975; Blumberg, 1978; Lenski and Lenski, 1978). Third, we analyze nineteenth century trends in labor-force participation and fertility in order to show how industrialization affected women's status. Last, we analyze economic, demographic, and social trends of the twentieth century in order to predict relationships in our data and to assess how these factors may affect behavior and belief by the end of the century.

NEEDED INGREDIENTS

An adequate theory of gender stratification must consider four factors. The most basic is ecological, the environmental constraints on human organization. Until quite recently, ecological factors tended to be taken for granted by citizens in industrial societies—climate, rainfall, soil fertility, energy. The world energy shortage now throws the importance of ecology into relief.

Second, an adequate theory must consider subsistence technology in evolutionary perspective. The types of energy (tools and techniques) that societies use to produce food determines a range of organizational forms. In prehistoric times, for example, 85% of the energy expended to maintain a family was used to provide food, in contrast to 16% in the United States today (Pimentel and Pimentel, 1979). Placing the study of subsistence technology in an evolutionary framework makes sense because, historically, energy budgets, economic productivity, and population size have tended to increase together, with a resulting increase in the material surplus (Harris, 1980:67). Furthermore, similar technologies applied to similar environments tend to produce similar arrangements of labor in production and distribution. In turn, these call forth similar kinds of social groupings that justify and coordinate their activities by means of similar systems of values and beliefs (Harris, 1980:4).

The evolutionary perspective of contemporary social science differs from that of the nineteenth century, which fell from favor because it was mostly dataless speculation combined with moral evaluation. Today, evolutionary theory is based on mountains of data collected by anthropologists and it avoids moral judgments (Lenski, 1976).

Third, an adequate theory must examine the mode of generational replacement, the arrangements intended to insure that enough babies will be born and will live to rear their own children. In all societies, most women and men must do some work each day to survive. Hence the problem is to see how women's varied work patterns mesh with childbearing and childrearing. Anthropologists have typically examined how childrearing practices determine the kind of work that women do. Friedl (1975:8) notes that this view fails to consider the large number of societies in which women regularly cultivate crops or engage in trade many miles from home, nor does it consider the common practice of assigning baby-tending to young children or old people, nor the use of foods that supplement mother's milk. Friedl therefore suggests that it may be more fruitful to examine how the kind of work that women do affects child spacing and childrearing.

Fourth, an adequate theory must consider how people attain power and prestige. In any society, those who produce valued goods tend to have more power and prestige than those who consume them. But the right to distribute and exchange valued goods and services to those not in a person's domestic unit confers the most power and prestige (Friedl, 1975:8). It is better to give than to receive. In modern societies the key factor is control of wealth, not ownership alone (Tickamyer, 1981:478).

In sum, an adequate theory of sex stratification must consider ecology, subsistence, reproduction, and power and prestige. We now turn to the concrete examination of some societies to see how these factors help to explain systems of sex stratification.

SEX STRATIFICATION IN EVOLUTIONARY PERSPECTIVE

Our view of sex stratification in evolutionary perspective will be that of a bird, a small bird at high altitude. We shall cover most of human history in a few pages. For this brief foray into the past, we have been most influenced by Gerhard Lenski in the use of the evolutionary perspective. In using this perspective to explain sex stratification we have been influenced by Ernestine Friedl, an anthropologist, and by Rae Lesser Blumberg, who was herself influenced by Lenski.

Following upon the outline of an evolutionary perspective on social organization (Lenski, 1966), the theme was fully developed in the first introductory textbook in macrosociology (Lenski and Lenski, 1978/1973). This important work made data on a wide range of societies accessible to sociologists (Moseley and Wallerstein, 1978:262). The usefulness of the work stems from its basic proposition: If technology, then social organization. Knowledge concerning subsistence technology permits the shape of the general stratification system to be predicted.

The Lenski approach stems from an eighteenth-century tradition of classifying societies by their subsistence technologies (e.g., hunting, herding, farming) and the nineteenth-century Thomsen typology that groups societies by the dominant materials used for tools and weapons in an evolutionary sequence of stone, bronze, and iron. Archaeologists later divided the Stone Age into the Paleolithic, Mesolithic, and Neolithic periods. Lenski and Lenski (1978:454) expand and modify G. Lenski's (1966) presentation according to a classification and developed by Goldschmidt (1959) and influenced by V. Gordon Childe (1951). The advantage of the Lenski typology is that, unlike Thomsen's, it permits rather accurate predictions about the size and shape of the stratification system.

The Lenskis classify societies into 10 types according to their primary mode of subsistence: hunting and gathering, simple horticultural, advanced horticultural, simple agricultural, advanced agricultural, fishing, maritime, simple herding, advanced herding, and industrial. The four categories of horticultural and agricultural societies comprise an evolutionary sequence that depends on plant cultivation. Simple horticultural (garden) societies rely on a wooden hoe or digging stick; advanced horticultural, on a wooden hoe with a metal blade, following the invention of metallurgy. Simple agricultural (field-tending) societies rely on plows whose shares are made of bronze or copper. In advanced agricultural societies, the plowshare is made of iron, as are other tools and weapons. Iron is so much more plentiful than tin or copper that it can be used for ordinary tools as well as weapons. However, it is so much harder to reduce iron ore to metal that iron use was the last to develop.

Fishing, herding, and maritime societies, environmentally specialized, are distinguished from societies at comparable technological levels not so much by the technological repertoire they possess as by what parts of it they use. Fishing societies parallel the technological levels of hunting and gathering or simple horticultural societies. Maritime societies are at about the level of simple and advanced agrarian societies. Simple herding societies parallel the level of simple and advanced horticultural societies. Advanced herding societies are at the level of advanced horticultural societies.

Hunting and Gathering Societies

The classification of societies begins with hunting and gathering societies, which alone span all of human history (Lenski and Lenski, 1978:107–141). Hunters and gatherers obtained food by killing large animals like giraffes or bears with sticks, spears, and rocks, living on nuts, berries, small animals, and insects between kills. Hunting and gathering societies continued to flourish after more advanced societies emerged. One hundred years ago, many still existed in the New World, Australia, Southwest Africa, parts of Central Africa, certain remote areas of Southeast Asia, and Arctic Asia.

Primitive subsistence technology made a nomadic life necessary because groups moved when they exhausted food in an area. Hence group size was small, averaging 40 persons. The family was the only important form of economic organization. Kinship ties comprised a web of reciprocities that provided lifetime social insurance. However, the conjugal unit was loose because spouses could part without jeopardizing their own or their children's food supply. Almost all hunting and gathering societies permitted divorce, which varied from being easy to more difficult to attain (Friedl, 1975:14).

The degree of social inequality was low because the pickings were lean. Hoarding was limited to what people could carry when the group moved. Men hunted large animals. Women and children gathered nuts and berries. Hunters distributed the meat from a large animal to the entire group because the supply was large enough to permit sharing and because meat spoils so fast it cannot be hoarded. In contrast, gatherers distributed nuts, berries, small animals, and insects only to their own families. The amount of food was too small to permit wider distribution. Because hunters could distribute food to the entire group, they had more prestige and power than gatherers did. But why did not women hunt, and why did not men gather? Or why did not women and men hunt and gather together?

Our answer to these questions follows Friedl's (1975:16–17) materialist analysis. The usual explanation is that men's larger size, greater muscular strength, and better running ability make men better hunters. Yet, the considerable overlap by sex in these characteristics makes one question why a statistical difference in physical traits should result in a categorical difference in behavior. The question can be answered by examining the interrelated functional requirements for hunting and gathering and those of bearing children and carrying them around at the breastfeeding age. Hunting and gathering require two skills: scanning the ground and horizon for large animal traces and recognizing clues to the existence of roots, plant foods, and small animal hiding places. Both men and women can acquire such skills. But what no one, regardless of sex, can do while hunting is to gather and carry enough plant foods to supply those left in camp. Carrying burdens makes running long distances harder and interferes with the physical coordination needed to throw spears or release arrows. Hence no one can hunt and gather simultaneously. In principle, men and women could hunt alternate days, but the unreliability of the hunt makes such a division unlikely—hunts can require many days. No orderly rotation of hunting and gathering is feasible.

Since women cannot both hunt and gather, they gather. Their childbearing functions interfere less with gathering than with hunting. At later stages of pregnancy and for the first 2 years of the baby's life, women's hunting ability is decreased by the physical awkwardness resulting from carrying the fetus and, later, the nursling. The burden of the child is great even for gathering. Study of a Kalahari desert group reports that women provided two-thirds of the food eaten in camp. Each women gathered 2 or 3 days a week, walking from 2 to 12 miles a day. On her return, she carried from 15 to 33 pounds of vegetable foods and any of her children who were under age 4.

Nonpregnant women whose children are over 4 cannot form a pool of potential hunters because it would be too small. In the typical group, only 7–10 women are in childbearing years. Women are constantly pregnant or lactating during most of their reproductive years to offset infant mortality rates of 30–50%.

Hunting and gathering societies therefore illustrate how the level of technology constrains patterns of social inequality and how the requirements of subsistence tasks, interacting with the need for population replacement, result in a particular division of labor by sex. The principle that those who distribute valued goods have the most power explains why men's status is higher than women's. During the 9000 years that hunters and gatherers competed with technologically more advanced societies for land and resources, they had only one defense: to retreat to lands that other groups regarded as worthless or hard to reach. By the end of this century or before, the last true hunting and gathering society will probably have vanished (Lenski and Lenski, 1978:141).

Horticultural Societies

The invention of horticulture about 7000 B.C. has been called the first great social revolution in human history because of its profound consequences for human organization and culture. The change to horticulture enabled people to settle in one place and thus to accumulate more possessions. Dwellings became more substantial, settlements became larger and more dense, and the creation of a stable economic surplus made occupational specialization common. Advanced horticultural societies typically include priests, artisans, and craftworkers as well as common laborers. The advent of hoe technology marks the beginnings of a modern system of social stratification.

In simple horticultural societies, the main subsistence tool is a wooden digging stick (Lenski and Lenski, 1978:142–176). It cannot penetrate the soil deeply enough to bring needed nutrients to the surface, nor can it easily get rid of weeds. Hence every few years simple horticulturists must move, using some form of the slash-and-burn method to replace plots that have lost fertility. Yet, a technology for even semisettled plant culture so increases the food supply that these societies can support up to several hundred persons. They typically live in self-sufficient, politically autonomous villages. Extremely complex kin relationships provide social security.

By about 4000 B.C., metal tools and weapons were common enough that some societies could be classified as advanced horticultural. At one time, such societies appeared in North and South America (the Mayas, Aztecs, and Incas), Asia, and Europe. Today, almost all remaining advanced horticultural societies are in sub-Saharan Africa, with a few in Southeast Asia. The invention of metallurgy had two important effects. First, using metal to make tools vastly increased their efficiency, and thus the food surplus. These societies were therefore about 60 times larger than their predecessors, the simple horticultural societies. The food surplus also led to a greatly increased division of labor that, in turn, resulted in a marked increase in social inequality through a complex and often hereditary class system. For example, slavery occurred in only 14% of the societies that used wooden hoes, but in 83% of the ones that used metal tools.

Second, the invention of metallurgy made waging war a profitable means of obtaining a food surplus. For the first time in history, the conquest, control and exploitation of other societies became a possible and profitable alternative to technological innovation (Lenski and Lenski, 1978:151). China illustrates this change. It became an advanced horticultural society about 1000 B.C. During its simple horticultural era,

Northern China had been covered with many small, autonomous villages. With the invention of bronze weapons, urban centers emerged as a result of the military success of village leaders.

The sexual division of labor consists of the male monopoly over initial clearing of new land in simple horticultural societies and in male responsibility for fighting wars in advanced ones (Friedl, 1975:53–60). The male monopoly on clearing land meant that women could never initiate the process of clearing new land. Yet men's land-clearing monopoly failed to give them the advantage of a male monopoly on hunting. Preparing soil does not give men the opportunity to distribute a highly favored food outside the domestic group. Furthermore, the work of cultivation tended to be shared. There was no simple division of labor with men producing one kind of food and women another, and no universal pattern in which women produced one type of craft object and men another, except that routine domestic cooking was most often done by women and metal working by men. Hence great variation marked patterns of domestic exchange in these societies.

Theoretically, women's relatively high contribution to subsistence tasks should be reflected in the extent to which these societies were matrilineal or matrilocal. Although tracing descent through the woman's line or moving in with the wife's parents do not make women more powerful than men, these customs do diminish male advantage. If women are not movable, it is harder to treat them as male property. Data from George Murdock's *Ethnographic Atlas* support this view. About one-quarter of simple and advanced horticultural societies are matrilineal, in contrast to 10% of hunting and gathering societies and 4% of agricultural societies. Moreover, when horticultural societies are divided by the extent to which subsistence is also obtained by hunting and herding, matrilineality and matrilocality relate even more strongly to use of the hoe as major subsistence tool (Lenski and Lenski, 1978:162).

In principle, the more women share in subsistence tasks, the higher should be the divorce rate. Husbands and wives who come to dislike one another can more readily part if the separation has little effect on either spouse's daily subsistence. This expectation is borne out. Although information is sketchy, divorce rates among horticulturists appear to be very high compared to contemporary United States rates (Friedl, 1975:93). The divorce rate for parents with children is only slightly lower than for couples with no children. When uxorlocality prevails, the husband instead of the wife may be anxious about the possiblity of separation from the children. That this possibility is not a more powerful deterrent probably results from cultural patterns that often separate young children from their parents. In some societies, for example, children of sexually active parents are sent to sleep with relatives.

Agricultural Societies

The invention of the plow greatly affected social stratification because it so greatly increased the food supply. Use of the plow reduces weeds and turns over the soil at a level deep enough to bring back to the surface the nutrients that had washed in with successive rains. The plow also paves the way for harnassing animal energy. Men and women supply the energy for the digging stick and the hoe. The plow can be pulled by animals. Use of the ox was the first step to the steam engine and the motor (Childe, 1951:100). Use of oxen led, in turn, to stall feeding and to the use of manure as fertilizer, which greatly improved soil fertility. The shift to agriculture was soon followed by the invention of writing, because a food supply large enough to be stored could be better managed with the use of a notational system. Historians usually call this period the dawn of civilization because of the emergence of urban communities and the beginnings of empire building (Lenski and Lenski, 1978:177–230).

The use of the plow dated from about 3000 B.C. in Mesopotamia and Egypt. It spread by diffusion, or borrowing, until agrarian societies covered most of Europe, North Africa, and Asia. So far as we have been able to discover, use of the plow never became widespread in sub-Saharan Africa for ecological reasons. Goody (1976) claims the soil was too infertile. Historian William McNeill (1976:19) argues that the reason Africa remained backward in the development of "civilization" in comparison to temperate lands was because of malaria and, especially, sleeping sickness. The tse-tse fly transfers the trypanosome that causes it from one host to another. The tse-tse fly prefers to dine upon cattle, but if it is hungry enough, it will dine on humans. The parasite, which is stable and well-adjusted, produces no signs of sickness in the tse-tse fly or in the cattle that play host to it. In humans, however, it drastically debilitates or kills within a few weeks. It was therefore imprudent for humans to live near cattle in tse-tse fly country. Since the ox is the draft animal par excellence, the complex life cycle of the trypanosome tended to preclude agriculture south of the Sahara.

In simple agricultural societies, plows were made of wood. Although these societies could make bronze, it was rarely used for tools because tin, one of its constituents, was scarce. Bronze was therefore used primarily for military or ornamental purposes. Although food production benefited little from the invention of metallurgy, group cleavages in these societies clearly foreshadowed patterns that developed fully when the use of iron became common. Cleavages occurred between the small governing class and the masses who were forced to turn over most of their surplus, between the urban minority and the vast majority of peasant villagers, and between a tiny literate minority and the illiterate masses.

These cleavages reduced the rate of technological innovation (Lenski and Lenski, 1978:186). Before the agricultural revolution, poor and nonliterate communities had invented artificial irrigation using canals and ditches, the sailboat, wheeled vehicles, bricks, the arch, and glazing. Even though agricultural populations were larger, communications improved, and the store of knowledge had increased, innovation decreased because of the social transformation resulting from the use of the plow. Since peasants could produce much more than they needed for bare survival, a steady flow of taxes, tithes, and rents supported the host of specialists catering to the governing classes and the army. The governing classes turned to warfare and conquest as the most promising way to increase wealth. The peasants who did the daily work of production were gradually reduced to barest subsistence and kept that way by their powerful superiors. Hence they lost incentive for innovation. Inventions occur most often when the persons whose daily work makes them aware of problems can also reap the profit of solving the problem. Peasants, serfs, and slaves lose incentive to invent better ways of doing things. The surplus would simply be taken away. Landholding patterns in India today also depress innovation in this way (Myrdal, 1968: Volume II, Part III).

One important aspect of the rate of innovation in the years preceding the agricultural revolution has gone almost unnoticed. Women's status declined as a result of technological innovation. The new inventions tended to result in a male monopoly on the use of the most productive tools. These facts were noted but, until recently, their implications were not analyzed. Childe (1951), for example, observed that the use of oxen enabled a man to cultivate in a day a far larger area than could a woman with a hoe and that "incidentally, men replaced women as principals in cultivation [p. 100]." A few pages later (Childe, 1951:102), we read that the potter's wheel was invented about 3500 B.C.—and that men then took over pot making. We shall resume this topic shortly.

Advanced agricultural societies appeared about 1000 B.C. when people discovered how to smelt iron, a common mineral that is easy to obtain. Such societies survive today, in hybrid form, in much of Asia, the Middle East, and Latin America, where they comprise the majority of the less developed countries. Egypt was the largest of the simple agricultural societies in the latter half of the second millennium B.C. but several advanced agricultural societies built empires later that far surpassed it. The Spanish Empire in the eighteenth century covered 5 million square miles. The Chinese Empire at various times since the first century B.C. covered up to 4 million square miles, and the Roman Empire in the second century covered 2 million square miles. These later populations were therefore much larger, whereas Egypt had fewer than 15 million persons. By the mid-nineteenth century. China had about 400 million persons (Lenski and Lenski, 1978:192).

As in simple plow societies, the coercion of peasants, who were defined as subhuman, slowed the rate of innovation. The newly emerging proprietary theory of the state held that the ruler could use any property for personal advantage. Peasants, serfs, and slaves in the agricultural kingdoms of Eurasia were probably less well off than were their hunter and gatherer ancestors (Lenski and Lenski, 1978:206).

Compared to men's, women's status probably declined to a historic low in plow cultures. Our analysis draws on Boserup's (1970) research showing how the introduction of the plow in contemporary sub-Saharan Africa worsened women's status, and on Goody's (1976) research showing how the use of the hoe (as in most of sub-Saharan Africa) versus the plow (as in most of Eurasia) affects marriage and family. It is important to understand why women's status was so low in plow societies, because these are the progenitors of contemporary industrial societies, and many of their norms are with us still, although in attenuated form.

Boserup's (1970) basic proposition is that women do more of the productive work in hoe than in plow cultures. Goody (1976) supports the proposition with data from the Human Relations Area Files. Men monopolize the use of the plow wherever it is introduced, probably because using a plow requires managing heavy draft animals and because the much larger fields, further from home, make it harder to arrange a schedule to suit a nursing baby (Blumberg, 1978:50). Where women do little work producing food, they are valued only as mothers (Goody, 1976:34). We would therefore expect women's status to decline as the use of the plow spread.

However, differences between hoe and plow cultures affect women's status in other ways as well. In plow societies, land becomes the chief form of wealth. This stems from the plow's higher productivity, the specialization this permits, the scarcity of land created, and the differential holdings of land and capital that then become important (Goody,

1976:97). In Africa, productivity was low, full-time specialization was rare, and most craft workers also grew crops. Land, as distinct from labor, was rarely a scarce resource; hence its exclusive ownership was not the basis for local or national stratification.

In plow cultures, land ownership becomes the basis for social stratification. The scarcer land becomes and the more intensively it is used, the greater the tendency to retain it in the basic productive and reproductive unit, the nuclear family (Goody, 1976:97). The greater volume of production the plow affords can support an elaborate division of labor and a variety of life-styles. To maintain one's own style of life and that of one's children, one must marry a spouse similarly endowed, and one must marry monogamously lest the land become dispersed among too many heirs. The higher a woman's status, that is, the more land she may be endowed with, the more her premarital and marital behavior will be controlled (Goody, 1976:14). Men's behavior need not be similarly controlled. Concubinage typically occurs wherever monogamy is the mode of marriage, since children of concubines have little legal claim to property.

Different strategies of heirship in Africa and Eurasia also stem from the importance of land in agrarian societies. In Africa, personal continuity was important but, since economic differentiation is slight and there is little shortage of land, there is less pressure to provide an heir to a specific estate (Goody, 1976:97). Also, a daughter's marriage little affected her economic position since women, married or not, typically grew crops or did craft work. Hence daughters did not need an endowment to maintain their status. In contrast, in Eurasia a man had to provide for both male and female offspring, the male at death and the female at her marriage in order that they not fall in the social hierarchy. Men were also concerned with the future of the estate. The concern with women's sexual purity derives from their status as transmitters of male property (Goody, 1976:15).

In sum, women's low status in agrarian societies apparently stems from two factors. First, their productivity is lower, relative to men's, than in horticultural societies. Second, complex consequences follow from the fact that use of the plow makes land the chief form of wealth. Land, unlike money or other forms of property, is impartible. Barring technological innovation, a given piece of land supports only a given number of persons. Divorce therefore becomes difficult or impossible. Monogamy prevails. It constrains men less than women because men's out-of-wedlock children cannot inherit property. Wealthy Eurasian men can in effect practice polygyny by keeping mistresses or concubines whose children have few inheritance rights.

The customs of footbinding, suttee, and clitoridectomy indicate women's status in agrarian societies in Asia and Africa. They are worth noting because few scholars recognize their affinity with agrarian subsistence technology. The Chinese custom of footbinding has attracted little scholarly attention. It is not referenced in the *International Encyclopedia of Social Science*, 1968, or in the *Encyclopaedia Britannica*, 1974. According to Levy (1966:41), whose report is most detailed, the custom arose about 1000 A.D. An emperor admired a dancer's feet. Loosely bound in linen cloths, they resembled those of a modern ballerina. This occurred in a period marked by change in the direction of greater control over women's behavior. Hence the custom took root. The rationale was that footbinding produced a heavier thigh, tightening the genital region so that sleeping with a women with bound feet was like sleeping with a virgin. Western physicians deny that this belief is true.

The severity of the binding increased as girls ascended the social scale. For girls from rich families, binding began at age 3. The goal was to attain the 3 inch lotus foot, so called for its resemblance to that flower. The daughters of workers and peasants escaped binding till age 5 and attained only a 4 or 5 inch foot, big enough to permit walking (Levy, 1966:281). They could do housework and cooking but their efficiency was impaired. Rich women and prostitutes were so crippled that they could not walk at all. The chief source of pain was the result of bending the four smaller toes underneath the foot, tightening the bindings progressively until the toes were broken. They would then atrophy. During this period the feet often became infected and the pain was constant. The desired lotus shape was attained in about 10 years.

The custom was apparently widespread. One nineteenth century writer whom Levy (1966:52) cites reported that from 50 to 80% of Chinese women's feet were bound. The one area where women escaped was in the south, where rice was the main crop. It required wet cultivation. Working in the rice paddies would have increased the risk of foot infection. More important, rice is much more labor intensive than wheat, the main crop in the drier region of North China. Hence women's labor was needed much more in the south (Blumberg, 1978:51). Gamble (1943) reports that in the northern village he studied, almost all women born before 1890 had bound feet. The Manchus tried to eradicate the custom but failed. Widespread opposition appeared only in the twentieth century when, after a series of decrees that reflected an increasing need for women's labor, the custom died. Wives with bound feet were deserted and divorced. When the Japanese forbade footbinding in Formosa, the women objected and cried (Levy, 1966:210,

284). Social change is hard on those with high investment in the old ways.

Westerners who are surprised that a custom causing so much pain to so many women lasted so long should ponder the high-heeled shoe. It permits the foot to attain an instant lotus shape. It throws women's back awry and prevents their running easily and walking gracefully. But it can be taken off at night.

More information is available concerning suttee, the Hindu custom that requires a widow to be burned alive on her husband's funeral pyre. The orthodox Hindu rationalization was that a widow, by sinning in a previous life, was responsible for her husband's dying first (Stein, 1978:255). Some widows climbed willingly upon the pyre. Others had to be tied down. The widow's death assured guardianship and un-disputed influence over her children to the husband's male relatives and also kept her from enjoying lifetime rights in her husband's estate. The incidence of suttee was low compared to that of footbinding. From 1815 to 1824, for example, "only" 6632 suttees were reported in Bengal, Bombay, and Madras (Stein, 1978). It was most common in Bengal, especially from 1680 to 1830, due, indirectly, to an inheritance system that gave rights to widows (Micropaedia VIII, 1974:931). To date, no one has analyzed the interrelationships of suttee, child marriage, and ill-treatment of widows in India (Mazumdar, 1978).

A third custom that indicates women's status as a transmitter of male property is clitoridectomy, apparently widespread in Moslem Africa today, primarily in regions where the use of the plow is important. It is common in Egypt, Yemen, and other Persian Gulf States (El Saadawi, 1982:33), in Ethiopia and Somalia, the Sudan, in Kenya, and in Moslem West Africa (Hosken, 1979: Introduction, 4). Clitoridectomy is usually called *female circumcision*, but this is a euphemism. Physiologically, it is equivalent to slicing off the glans penis or the entire penis. The purpose of the operation, practiced on prepubertal girls, is to prevent sexual pleasure so that women will find it easier to remain chaste, according to a former Director of Public Health in Egypt (El Saadawi, 1982:33). The incidence of clitoridectomy shows the immense signifi-cance of protecting a daughter's reputation for chastity (Paige, 1982:36).

There are three types of operation (Hosken, 1979: Part I, 2). In tradi-tional (Sunna) circumcision, the clitoral prepuce and tip of the clitoris are removed. In excision, the entire clitoris is removed. Infibulation (*fibula* means 'clasp' in Latin) involves removal of the clitoris, the labia minora, and part of the labia majora. The two sides of the vulva are partially sliced or scraped raw and then sewn together, obliterating the entrance to the vagina except for a tiny posterior opening to allow urine and, later, menstrual blood to drain. Primary fatalities result from hemorrhage, shock, and septicemia. Long-term consequences include urinary disturbance due to chronic infection, difficulties in childbirth and in coitus (El Saadawi, 1982:33).

The thread connecting footbinding, suttee, and clitoridectomy is that they tend to control women's behavior in areas where the plow is a major subsistence tool. The plow makes land the chief form of wealth. Land is impartible. The number of heirs must be controlled to balance the food supply and the number of mouths to be fed. The paternity of the heirs must be controlled because men prefer not to leave their wealth to another man's child.

Fishing, Maritime, and Herding Societies

Lenski and Lenski (1978) define three specialized societal types that are out of the mainstream of evolutionary history because of their less typical environments. One type has had effects on contemporary societies. We briefly discuss all three.

Two types of societies depend on the presence of rivers, lakes, or seas. Fishing societies, technologically similar to early hoe cultures, are most common today in the northwestern United States and western Canada. They appeared about 1000 years before the first hoe cultures. They are relatively advanced socially, however, because fishing can support a larger sedentary population than can hunting and gathering. Fish have such high reproductive rates compared to land animals that fishers usually work only a small part of the food-producing territory.

Maritime societies are rarest. Not one survives. Technologically, they resembled agrarian societies. They were located on large bodies of water at a time when it was cheaper to move goods by water than by land. They were probably developed by the Minoans on Crete late in the third millenium B.C. and included the Phoenicians, Carthaginians, Athenians, and Corinthians. These societies were usually republics rather than monarchies because commerce, rather than warfare and peasant exploitation, was the ruling group's chief economic interest. Such societies therefore had less need for a strong centralized state to wage war. An oligarchy of merchants could do as well. Since their primary task was to regulate commercial competition and to provide naval forces to defend access to foreign ports, civilian leaders were plagued less by military forces than were leaders of agrarian states because navies are usually in places far from the seat of government. This reduces the risk of military takeover. Because the main type of work, commerce, could not be delegated to illiterate peasants, these societies lacked the anti-work ethic of agrarian societies. In the long run, as Bertrand Russell observed, the functional needs of commercial societies lead to deemphasizing military power and emphasizing peaceful means of settling disputes.

Herding societies occur where crops cannot grow because of low rainfall, too short a growing season, or mountainous terrain, as in much of Central Asia, the Arabian Peninsula, and parts of Europe and sub-Saharan Africa (Lenski and Lenski, 1978:235). Their range of technological development resembles that of hoe and simple plow societies. Animals were domesticated about the same time that plants were first cultivated. Because herding requires a nomadic or semi-nomadic life-style, the average community has only about 55 persons. The size of the societies is larger, averaging about 2000, according to the *Murdock Atlas*. About 1800 B.C. herders learned to harness horses to chariots, and then, in 900 B.C., to ride horses, setting off a wave of conquests that lasted till 1500 A.D., as a succession of herding societies attacked rich agrarian societies from China to Europe, often conquering them. Politically important herding societies included the Arab Muslim Empire, which covered a wide area from Spain across Central Asia to India by the ninth century; the great Mongol Empire founded by Ghenghis Khan; and the Mogul, Manchu, and Ottoman Empires.

Herding societies contributed to women's status today because Hebrew constraints on women became part of the Christian religion and early Arab constraints became part of Islam. Owing to the accidents of history, major world religions as well as contemporary legal systems have tended to perpetuate norms that originated in herding societies.

Women were probably more subordinated in herding than in hoe cultures but less subordinated than in agarian ones. In herding societies, women tended to work in groups rather than in isolated households, leading them to participate more in community life (Boulding, 1976:Chapter 7). Women's subordination resulted from the importance of fighting in determining water and grazing rights and from the lack of fit between the functional requirements of lactation and tending animals away from home over long periods of time. Martin and Voorhies (1975:337ff) concluded from a study of 44 contemporary pastoral societies that women's subordination varied with the type of plant cultivation that was ecologically possible. Women were most subordinated when the herds had to be pastured away from the group for long periods of time. Almost all the economically productive activity, including dairying, was then done by men.

In this brief review of women's status in evolutionary perspective, we have tried to show how childbearing interacted with subsistence technology to shape patterns of sex stratification. We now examine the effects of industrial development on women's status in the nineteenth and twentieth centuries.

INDUSTRIALIZATION

Industrialization undermined the basis for agrarian patterns of sex stratification by changing environmental constraints on production and reproduction. The effect of decreasing mortality, increasing levels of education, decreased childbearing and, finally, a massive increase in women's labor-force participation was to diminish the male/female status gap compared to that in agrarian societies. We discuss these events separately in rough order of their occurrence, but the events, of course, interacted with one another and did not order themselves so neatly over time as our discussion may imply.

The major effect of nineteenth-century changes in developing countries was to increase the importance of an individual's market relations and decrease the importance of other social and economic ties. Scholars have described the rapid changes variously as a shift from community to society, from status to contract, from organic to mechanical solidarity. They saw preindustrial men and women as working, marrying, rearing children, and dying, involved in a network of rather stable social and economic reciprocities. Industrialization tore the web. Individuals were linked, instead, to the market by the impersonal tie of money.

Whether favoring individual (rather than collective) good is good or bad depends on whose ox is being gored. Individualistic values support the notion of marrying for love, for example, instead of marrying to satisfy family economic interests after the fashion of peasants and princes. Yet, marrying for love seriously undermines marital stability. Love is a thin glue for a lifetime contract. Similarly, paid work and city living free individuals from the petty tyrannies of small communities. At the same time, city living increases the risk of feeling isolated, lonely, or anomic.

Loosening community ties set the stage for new political ideologies more suited to contract relations. Indeed, it was industrialization that spawned the idea of ideology, the notion that stratification systems are explained and justified by a comprehensive myth. In most preindustrial societies, God was held more or less responsible for the stratification system, however inscrutable His ways might appear to humans.

In the words of the popular Victorian hymn, "The rich man at his castle, the poor man at his gate, God made them high and lowly, and ordered man's estate."

Two ideologies concerning the causes and justice of reward distribution appeared during industrialization. First is the belief that the owners of the means of production tend to control rewards. Hence those who live by selling their labor must engage in a little class conflict to get a fair share. Appearing in many forms, this ideology undergirds the theoretical perspectives of the socialist, communist, liberal, and labor parties. It represents the central core of ideas that conservatives oppose.

Yet class theory has little to say about sex stratification. Class theorists, assuming that women's economic interests were identical to those of their husbands, showed little awareness of employed women's double burden of house and market work. Marx and Engels recognized the stultifying effects of household drudgery and urged that women become "productive" workers instead. But they never came to grips with the question as to who would clean the house when the state withered away.

Wherever it appeared, the labor movement has therefore been a men's movement. Women have had little part in it. The countries most dominated by class theories, the socialist and communist countries of Europe, Asia, and Africa, have been least likely to produce a women's movement. The double burden of market and housework that the state assumes to be nonexistent indicates that socialism has not yet liberated women (Scott, 1974).

A second ideology spawned by industrialization holds that the reward system is just because each person has equal opportunity to get ahead. The political driving force of such individualist doctrines arose in part from middle-class opposition to aristocratic claims to rights based on descent (Parkins, 1979:64) and in part because such ideologies make for political stability in all developed societies, capitalist or socialist. Individuals must feel responsible for their own fates (Ossowski, 1963). Yet this ideology, paradoxically, can be invoked by the privileged to justify their rewards and also by the underprivileged to justify their claims for a fair share. Since the 1960s, women's groups have invoked the ideology of equal opportunity to justify their claims for equal pay, for equal opportunity to hold the best paid jobs, and for equal opportunity to receive rewards for their education and training that equal men's. These ideologies comprise a climate of opinion that people use to interpret the social trends they experience. We now discuss the first of these trends that ultimately came to have a profound effect on sex stratification patterns: the increase in educational attainment that is the *sine qua non* of industrialization.

Compulsory Education

Although some analysts hold that public schools evolved to serve the needs of capitalist employers (Bowles, 1972:1), this explanation seems too simple. Compulsory education serves the interests of many groups because it serves so many different functions: it removes children from direct wage competition with men. It shields children from the worst horrors of industrial work. It serves entrepreneurial interests by producing a class of literate wage workers—nowhere has industrialization occurred without the widespread attainment of third-grade literacy. It keeps the children off the streets, thereby reducing juvenile mischief— how to keep children, especially boys, from annoying urban adults, especially rich ones, is always a problem. It deprives poor parents of the benefits of their children's labor but at the same time it prepares lower-class children for upward mobility.

In the sixteenth and seventeenth centuries, the stimulus to develop schools was religious (Dobbs, 1919/1969:104). Martin Luther himself had argued that the state could compel people to support schools (Adams, 1875:45). The objective of establishing state schools in England, Prussia, and Scotland was to increase religious uniformity (Barker, 1944:85, 86; Armytage, 1970:1). A Protestant effect also appeared in the United States. In Puritan Massachusetts, a 1647 law required towns of 50 or more families to pay for a teacher (Butts and Cremin, 1953:103).

Opposition to schools came mainly from two sources. Some men of means disliked paying school taxes (Carlton, 1908/1965:39), but this kind of opposition was short-lived (Adams, 1875:80). The poor often opposed compulsory education because they needed their children's earnings (Rich, 1970:ix) or because they failed to understand the value of schooling for the child (Adams, 1875:80).

The nineteenth-century public education movement stemmed from rational arguments derived from eighteenth-century philosophy (Counts, 1937:417), according to the received view (Cremin, 1968, 1970). However, some reformers thought education solved the problem of juvenile delinquency (Katz, 1971:2), which had become especially noticeable in the 1820s (Carlton, 1908/1965:39). As the *Ohio School Journal* noted in 1845, it was far better to pay taxes that would rise like vapors to descend in refreshing showers than to build jails and almshouses to relieve wretchedness and punish crime that a wholesome education might have prevented (Carlton, 1908/1965:63). By 1880, compulsory attendance laws had been enacted in most developed countries (Steinhilber and Sokolowski, 1966:2).

An added advantage of public education, according to Woody's (1929) account, was that it helped to solve the problem of surplus women, noticeable in the eastern United States after 1790. In the early 1700s, men had been defined as the natural and most desirable teachers. By the Civil War, women became more popular. Their wages were about one-half of men's. Furthermore, schoolteaching was alleged to give splendid training for marriage. As Catherine Beecher remarked, men had many roads to wealth and honor and few would choose the humble and unhonored toils of the schoolroom and its penurious rewards. What was needed was young, unmarried women teachers whose souls burned for some channel into which they could pour their benevolence, who would teach 2, 3, or 4 years and then marry and become firm pillars to hold up their successors. Thus, the economic facts of life melded with feminist desires to obtain better education and professional employment for women (Woody, 1929:8, 321, 460, 462, 492).

Compulsory education affected women's lives in two main ways. First, a substantial portion of their task of socializing children shifted to the schools, leaving the mother at home to perform services that would enable the children to do well in school. Household technology improved, standards rose, and children needed to be scrubbed and starched lest they lose an opportunity for upward mobility. By the middle of the twentieth century, women's seclusion at home seemed so natural that many people were unaware that it was a comparatively recent innovation (Rossi, 1964). Thus, women's maternal duties justified excluding them from high-wage jobs and later justified their being paid less since, according to economists, they were less productive than men.

Second, compulsory education prepared women for labor market opportunities. Indeed, as much as any factor, the rise in women's level of education prepared the way for the several women's movements that erupted in the last two centuries. If one wants to keep a class of creatures in their place, it is always a mistake to educate them. But the mistake did not become obvious until the 1970s. After 1950, women were massively induced to participate in the labor market by the joint occurrence of a relatively high level of education, relatively low fertility, and a high demand for women workers. This led to the eruption of the women's movement. But we are getting ahead of our story. Let us examine women's labor-force participation during the nineteenth century, taking the story up to about 1940.

Women's Labor-Force Participation before 1940

Our theory suggests that, all else equal, women's social status hinges on the level of their economic productivity. The historical research of Tilly and Scott (1978) supports this view. The European historical record, especially for Britain and France since 1700, suggests a U-shaped pattern for women's economically productive activity: relatively high in the preindustrial household economy, lower in industrial economies, and higher again with the development of the modern tertiary sector (Tilly and Scott, 1978: 229). The entire family, including children, was economically productive in the preindustrial and protoindustrial period—the latter occurs when manufacturing is expanded outside the factory system by increasing the number of producing units rather than through technological change or a shift in the scale of production (C. Tilly, 1978:2).

Although the industrial revolution affected working- and middle-class women differently, it reduced both groups' economic productivity. Working-class women tended to be excluded from skill training (Abbott, 1913:254; Clark, 1919:300), or their products and skills were defined as inferior (Sturmingher, 1979). Bourgeois wives, who had earlier kept books and tended to business details, became ornaments, suited only for childbearing because their work had been assigned to male employees (Stern, 1944:444).

Women factory workers—typically in textiles—comprised only a small part of the female labor force. Most women worked in traditional "female" occupations such as, for example, domestics, dressmakers, in laundering or tailoring (Tilly, Scott, and Cohen, 1976:18, 16). The typical British woman employee was young and unmarried. Some evidence suggests that French women more often engaged in wage work after marriage. In nineteenth-century Lyon, for example, many married women worked in the silk industry, owing to the need for their wages. Hence a majority of Lyonnais infants were sent out to nurse (Garden, 1975:122, 351). However, much female employment was episodic, largely cleaning and laundering, and never appears in the census. Female wage work declined with the lowering of rural migration and the growth of new manufacturing and service sectors that tended to be dominated by urban-born men (Tilly, 1978). Throughout industrialization, however, and especially today, an apparently large number of women have worked in the so-called underground economy, in establishments whose activities do not appear in any tax records. (Berger and Piore, 1980).

During industrialization, whenever unemployment was high—often, in the nineteenth century—working men agitated to eliminate women and children from job competition. The history of women's exclusion from high-wage industrial jobs goes back a century. The goal was to keep them out of machine-intensive (and therefore higher wage) jobs. Excluding women from such jobs was not hard. Most groups approved. Middle-class women saw such restriction as being motivated by humanitarian concern. The entrepreneurial class favored restricting women's work because it created a low-wage industrial reserve to be drawn on as needed. Working-class men feared that economic opportunities for women might undermine men's authority in the family (see Smelser, 1959: Chapter 9), and they also feared scab competition from creatures who would work for such low wages. From 1840 to 1890, almost all American women workers, but only one-fourth of men, were in the lowest wage group (Abbott, 1919:300). Late in the nineteenth century, women's wages were less than three-fifths of men's; children's were slightly more than one-third (Long, 1960:104).

The main mechanisms for excluding women from high-wage jobs were the unions' refusal to admit women members or to organize them and the enactment of legislation designed to protect women's maternal status. By the 1880s, the frontier had closed and recurrent depressions made agriculture risky for men. Factory jobs were therefore more attractive than they had been earlier in the century. Furthermore, European immigration was heavy and massive unemployment plagued urban areas. Skilled workers feared low-wage competitors for good reason. Women were just one of a number of groups that unions excluded from high-wage jobs.

The literature dealing with women's exclusion from unions is slender. The mainstream view is based on men's interest, a legacy of nineteenth-century class politics. In an annotated bibliography covering women's part in the American union movement from 1825 to 1935 (Soltow, Forché, and Massre, 1972:22–49), of the 112 items under the rubric "Trade Unions," only 12 deal with the unions' refusal to organize or admit women members. Yet by Chafe's (1972) account, the American Federation of Labor treated women workers with open hostility and did almost nothing to organize them. Both Samuel Gompers and his successor, William Green, attacked the presence of married women in the work force. They said that women should care for families. When the Executive Council of the Federation was accused of prejudice, Gompers replied that the Federation discriminated against any nonassimilable race (Chafe, 1972:78). Even when women organized themselves, they were denied recognition.

In addition to union exclusion, women were also restricted by protective labor legislation that protected their maternal status at the expense of their economic status. This legislation stemmed from the desire to obtain higher wages and better working conditions for factory workers. It dates from the English Health and Morals of Apprentices Act of 1802, inspired by humanitarian motives, before workers could vote and before unions had much influence. This act limited child labor in the mills to 12 hours a day. The first labor law for women, in 1844, similarly restricted them to 12 hours a day (Witte, 1944:658). United States protective legislation appeared much later.

The politics of protective legislation in the United States was complicated by the constitutional issue, as we soon show, and by the failure to perceive that a fertility decline might permanently affect women's status. This failure may be attributed in part to liberal and radical reaction to Malthus, whose analysis of population growth implied that higher wages would induce higher fertility. In turn, this would reduce the average subsistence of the working class. Employers tended to approve this doctrine because it justified keeping wages low. Class analysts therefore took the opposite view, that poverty resulted not from overpopulation but from malapportionment of resources. By the twentieth century, the Roman Catholic Church and assorted socialist parties agreed that relatively high fertility levels posed no great threat to human well being. It is therefore understandable that liberals and radicals failed to consider the possible impact of lowered fertility on women's status.

The constitutional issue involved whether individual rights to make contracts with employers could be restricted by federal law. By 1896, only 13 states had restricted women's hours of employment, and the constitutionality of these was doubtful (Brandeis, 1935). In 1908, however, the Supreme Court unanimously established the constitutionality of legislation covering women's health. A liberal Court exempted women from the freedom-of-contract doctrine on the grounds that they needed special protection. Those who objected to women's being singled out were therefore accused of being antilabor. The liberal trend (during which the Court approved almost all labor legislation it examined) peaked in 1923 when Justice Sutherland, a conservative, held that the nineteenth amendment (giving women the vote) had established sex equality; special legislation for women was therefore unconstitutional.

The issue of protective legislation split the women's movement in the 1920s. In 1923, the National Women's Party (NWP) proposed an Equal Rights Amendment (ERA) to the constitution to eliminate special protective legislation for women. The Equal Rights Amendment was opposed by the League of Women Voters (LWV), a direct descendant of the National American Women's Suffrage Association. The National Women's Party favored legislation that would enable women to compete more effectively in the labor market. The League of Women Voters favored legislation that would make it easier for women to stay home with their children. The National Women's Party claimed that protective legislation would exclude women from high-wage jobs. The League of Women Voters, following the standard liberal line, held that protective legislation improved working-class women's lives (see also Deckard, 1975; Boles, 1979).

The extent to which protective legislation eased women's double burden or excluded them from high-wage jobs is unclear. Most of the literature on this topic is based on deductive argument rather than empirical research. A few women scholars (Breckinridge, 1906) claimed that restricting women's hours of employment ensured that their already low wages would be even lower. Others (Goldmark, 1905), taking the standard labor line, held that the arguments for restricting men's hours of work applied even more to women. The United States Department of Labor 1928:22) tended to maintain that restrictions on women's hours of employment had not harmed them (see Huber, 1976:379).[3]

A rare empirical study argued against the Department of Labor viewpoint. Baker (1925), in a Columbia University economics dissertation, investigated the effect of protective labor legislation in New York State. Her examination of specific jobs in specific industries showed that within a few years after the enactment of such legislation, women were nearly excluded from high-wage jobs. The process typically worked as follows: After women's hours of employment were restricted, the unions would require workers to take the night shift for a specified time to acquire seniority. Since women were excluded from night work, they were thereby cut from the seniority system. The law penalized skilled women most, but the result was felt by all women workers because it

[3]The United States Department of Labor's optimism about the effects of protective legislation can still be seen in Eastern Europe. Biryukova (1980:60) claims that it enables Soviet women to create a cosy home atmosphere. Gömöri (1980) reports it has no negative effects on Hungarian women.

drove them into already crowded occupations, into competition with less skilled women rather than with skilled men (Baker, 1925:427, 433).

The 1940s therefore found blue-collar women excluded from the most highly skilled, capital-intensive jobs. They were concentrated, instead, in "feminized" occupations; that is, in jobs whose wages were too low to attract men qualified to do the work.[4] The 1940s similarly found women excluded from the most highly paid professional and managerial white-collar jobs, whereas the lower paid white-collar occupations were feminized. Relatively few women were physicians (Walsh, 1977:xvi), lawyers (Patterson and Engelberg, 1978:276), or college professors (Graham, 1973). A sizable body of evidence documents the mechanisms, including direct discrimination, by which women were excluded from these occupations (Epstein, 1970a, 1970b; Coser and Rokoff, 1971; Rossi and Calderwood, 1973; Kanter, 1977; Walsh, 1977).

Women professionals were concentrated in the so-called college women's ghetto, as teachers, nurses, social workers, and librarians (Blau, 1978). These are nonladder jobs that enable a wife to move in pursuit of her husband's job opportunities and to enter and leave the labor force freely since the cost of doing so is low. Women also dominated the "lower" white-collar occupations as clerical and sales workers. In the latter part of the nineteenth and the early twentieth centuries, clerical occupations expanded rapidly with the rise of large national companies (Glenn and Feldberg, 1982:204).

In sum, in the United States from 1800 to 1940, women's labor-force participation gradually increased. By 1900, 20% of women between the ages of 18 and 64 were employed. They were typically young, unmarried, or poor. They would work a few years, then marry and leave the labor force never to return unless a husband's death, unemployment, or low wages made the wife's employment a necessity. By 1940, women's labor-force participation had increased only to 30%, and the life-course pattern was unchanged. Before discussing why the pattern changed, let us first examine how technological change had affected women's other major role, motherhood. We shall argue that fertility responds in the long run primarily to economic factors. Cultural factors may be important in the short run. The first attempt to explain how industrialization affected fertility is the theory of the demographic transition. We discuss it and then turn to new work that recasts some of the arguments.

[4]Actually, more women than men use machines on the job. Women are more likely to use unmoveable machines with mechanical controls, the most alienating kind. If Marxist theory were correct, women should be the most alienated workers in the United States (Form and McMillen, in press).

The Demographic Transition

Theory of the demographic transition is the term used to describe the relation of birth and death rates during European industrialization. It shows how reproductive behavior responded to complex incentives. Fertility patterns result from complex social arrangements that induce people to have enough children to ensure societal replacement but not too many for the environment to support. Historically, this has represented a delicate equilibrium. Primitive people thought in Malthusian terms long before Malthus (Himes, 1970:2). During periods when the potential of an organizational advance had been fully used up, populations might even have to unlearn methods of controlling fertility that were not needed when the food base expanded sufficiently (Wrigley, 1969:187).

Individuals could limit fertility through contraception. The principal folk methods were *coitus interruptus* and the douche (Tietze, 1968:383). Population was also limited through infanticide, which occurred in all cultures (Sauvy, 1961:36). Societies could try to control population size through a variety of social arrangements such as age at marriage and heirship patterns that balanced the incentives to marry and have children with the carrying capacity of the environment (Hajnal, 1965; Tilly, 1978:335). In preindustrial Europe, for example, a large minority of households probably experienced excess demand for children throughout most of history. But other households had too many. The balancing occurred through such institutions as arranged marriage, farming out of excess children, and temporary sharing of housing. Those groups that adopted such institutions survived while others destroyed themselves through over- or underpopulation. However they were formed, such institutions constituted a group rationality that strongly constrained individual rationality (Wrigley, 1978:135–137).

The background to the demographic transition was a slow rise in European productivity. Modern European states evolved from agrarian kingdoms whose subsistence technology was based on the use of the plow and iron metallurgy. During the ninth century, wilderness had given way to plowed land. The revival of industry that occurred between the eleventh and thirteenth centuries involved an immense extension of arable land through the use of better farming methods, breeding of horses, an improved harness, the iron horseshoe, windmills, and watermills. In turn, extending the agricultural base increased the population. Thriving town life originated in agricultural improvement (Mumford, 1938:22).

After the fourteenth century, the rate of innovation increased rapidly, owing to the stimulus of the discovery of gold in the New World. As economic conditions improved, demographic growth accelerated. The demographic transition occurs in three stages. First, mortality declines because of improved living conditions while fertility remains high, resulting in rapid population growth. In the second stage, the onset of a fertility decline is accompanied by a continued mortality decline. But, the age structure—a higher proportion of young people as a result of the first stage—helps to maintain a high birth rate and marked population increase. In the third stage, the transition is completed. The birth rate declines to a level nearly as low as that of the death rate, and population increases slowly. Because death rates fell slowly and the level of living rose more rapidly, population increase could be accompanied by an increased standard of living.

The primary demographic event was the decline of married women's fertility from about seven to fewer than three children at progressively earlier marital durations (United Nations, 1973:68). The reduction was achieved by using the technique of *coitus interruptus*. Later, the condom was used (Kirk, 1968:344).

France became a country with low fertility in the 1830s; Ireland, the 1840s; Switzerland and Belgium, the 1880s; Sweden, Denmark, the United Kingdom, Australia, and New Zealand, the 1890s; the Netherlands, Norway, Germany, and the United States, the 1900s; Canada, Finland, Austria, Hungary, and Czechoslovakia, the 1910s; Italy, Spain, and Portugal, the 1920s; Poland, Bulgaria, and Rumania, the 1930s; the Soviet Union, the 1940s; Japan and Yugoslavia, the 1950s (United Nations, 1973:65). No one has ever related these dates to a comparative study of women's status.

Why did the decline occur? The primary reason was the perception that children were no longer economic assets. By the second half of the nineteenth century, this perception had become increasingly common in Western Europe (United Nations, 1973:89). Yet, recent investigation reveals a more complicated situation. The transition represents not just decreasing demand for children but a demand for higher quality (better educated) children. Industrialization creates upward mobility options for more educated lower- and middle-class children. Middle- and upper-class children must be educated in order to maintain their parents' position in the status order. Men may have been more aware of the need for fewer but higher quality children than women were (Banks and Banks, 1964). Yet historically, women's education is by far the most important factor in the fertility decrease (Kasarda, 1979; see also

Rindfuss, Bumpass, and St. John, 1980). The greater the perceived need to advance or maintain one's place in the system, the more likely is fertility to decline.

Fertility rates may also be linked to economic dependency (Tilly, 1978:3). Faced with declining mortality, peasant families limit their fertility earlier than proletarianized ones because peasants have something to leave their children. They want to avoid breaking up their landholdings into packets so small that no family can live on one (Braun, 1978). An impartible inheritance system slows the creation of new households by maintaining a fixed number of openings on the land. It therefore limits marriage, encourages the emigration of children, and leads to slow population growth (Berkner and Mendels, 1978:223). Where most people are proletarians—they have no property, they must sell their labor and that of their children—fertility is less controlled. Protoindustrialization, the expansion of manufacturing outside the industrial system (i.e., the cottage industry) apparently raised fertility because children were economic assets. They could be put to work at an early age. Furthermore, the development of the cottage industry enabled young people to marry earlier since they could support themselves on a smaller area of land than would otherwise be needed to maintain a family.

However, the demographic transition was not a move from uncontrolled to controlled fertility. In almost all societies, fertility is restrained. The key change was from control through social institutions and customs to control by private choice of individual couples (Wrigley, 1978:148). The way that European populations shifted to individual choice yields four insights that may help to predict future behavior.

First, married couples responded to economic incentives. If the costs of childrearing increased, as for the upper classes and especially for the aspiring middle classes, then fertility tended to decrease in response to the prospect of status loss (Davis, 1963). Costs also increased for peasants with impartible land holdings.

Second, fertility reduction initially resulted from using methods that required self-discipline or courage.[5] For men, the main method was withdrawal; for women, abortion. Less heroic methods were needed after the process of rubber vulcanization was invented in 1844. By

[5]Perhaps the Victorians invented the frigid lady as a means for controlling fertility. Walsh (1977:145) notes that the nineteenth century witnessed an increasing fear of "excessive" female sexuality. To our knowledge, only Cott (1979:234) has related women's frigidity to fertility control.

1880, an effective condom was available in England, but it was expensive. The cheapest condom cost as much as a pound of bread; the most expensive cost 13 times as much, at a time when food represented a much larger proportion of a family budget than it does today (computations based on Frisch, 1978:28).

Third, fertility reduction resulted from a married couple's private decisions, made within a conspiracy of silence that deprived them of the support of friends and neighbors (Kirk, 1968:83). And fourth, decisions to reduce fertility had to confront public denunciation of birth control as well as restrictive legislation and religious opposition. Today, the Roman Catholic Church is seen as the major religious opponent of "artificial" methods of birth control. The Roman Church differs from others only in being a bit slower to come around. Collective memory is short. The Anglican Communion approved the use of contraceptives only in 1922 at the Lambeth Conference, long after the United Kingdom had experienced the transition. Formal religious considerations seem to be more important to religious elites than to the masses (Berelson, 1969).

Church leaders were not the only elites to oppose contraception. It was first listed in the *U.S. Reader's Guide* in 1909 under the rubric "race suicide" (Hart, 1933:417). Most physicians opposed it as representing social and moral degeneration. In 1925, Morris Fishbein, editor of the *Journal of the American Medical Association*, stated that no safe and effective contraceptive method existed (Gordon, 1977:259; see also Himes, 1936/1970:282, 424). In sum, the transition to low fertility in the West highlights the importance of an individual couple's perception of the mix of costs and benefits of having children.

Posttransition Fertility Behavior

After the transition, fertility rates remained low. The maintenance of population growth became a major concern of French policy more than a century ago, although it was not legally implemented until the late 1930s (Spengler, 1979:311). By the 1920s, countries that had experienced the transition much later than France were also concerned about depopulation. The word itself evokes deep-seated fears. What would happen to the human race, to good old us, if young people did not want to become parents? A more practical concern is that economic growth does not typically occur in a country whose population size is decreasing (see, especially, Simon, 1977). This does not imply that economic growth and depopulation *necessarily* vary inversely. Yet, it throws the burden of proof on those who believe that economic growth can occur even when population is declining.

Fear of depopulation stimulated pronatalist policies (such as modest child or family allowances) that apparently had little effect. Because a continuous flow of immigrants supplied a disproportionate number of women of childbearing age, the United States, alone among industrial countries, instituted no such policies. It still has fewer family allowances than other countries at comparable industrial levels.

On the eve of World War II, then, United States fertility hovered around the replacement level. Women's labor-force participation (WLFP) seemed to have settled in at about 30%. Despite low fertility, it was not normative for wives to hold paid jobs. World War II brought rapid change. Nothing stimulates rapid technological innovation as much as the desire to do in foreigners who threaten the national pride or pocketbook. World War II was no exception. It immediately affected women's labor-force participation. Its indirect effects became entangled with such events as the baby boom, which we discuss shortly.

Post-1940 Women's Labor-Force Participation and Fertility

After 1940, wives formed an increasing proportion of the work force because World War II removed about 10 million young men (and a few women) from the labor force while increasing the demand for expendible goods like tanks, trucks, planes, and battleships. During the war years, women's labor-force participation shot to new highs. After the war, women left or were pushed out of the work force. But they soon began to return, and the rate of women's labor-force participation continued to rise in response to corporate expansion. Bigger bureaucracies require more paper shufflers, and paper shuffling had become defined as women's work. In addition, the baby boom increased the demand for teachers. The increased demand, however, was met by a decreased supply of traditional woman employees. Young married women were relatively scarce. Great Depression birth rates had been low. More 18- and 19-year-old women were continuing their education. A decrease in age of marriage depleted the supply of young unmarried women. Childless women were scarce because of the baby boom. The gap was therefore filled by older married women, thereby changing the life-course pattern of women's labor-force participation. Women were entering or reentering the labor force to stay (Oppenheimer, 1973).

The increase in women's labor-force participation continues. Between 1948 and 1980, the rates for women aged 16 and over soared from 33% to 51%. The rates of older women rose first, rising 10% in the 1950s owing to their work experience during World War II, the absence of young children at home, and growing opportunities in the service sector. Women under age 45 experienced a rapid increase in labor-force participation after the 1960s (United States Department of Labor, 1980). The trend is reinforced by the tendency for women whose mothers were employed to join the labor force themselves (Rosenfeld, 1978; Stevens and Boyd, 1980).

Yet, it seems to be almost a universal law that, on average, women receive between one-half to two-thirds the pay of men (Lydall, 1968:55, see also Swafford, 1978). Even Leviticus 27:3 reports that the Lord told Moses that a grown man was worth 50 shekels, whereas a woman was worth 30. United States women's wages come close to men's only in the low-wage "female" occupations (Rytina, 1981:52). Occupational segregation is an important factor (Tsuchigane and Dodge, 1974). Job tenure is another (Rytina, 1982:34). Women may avoid occupations that require considerable investment in on-the-job training and have high rates of depreciation for time out of the labor force (Polachek, 1981). The data also suggest that discrimination plays a role (Blau, forthcoming). In white-collar work, education yields lower rewards to women than to men. In blue-collar work, skill attainment yields lower rewards to women than to men. Men's skills affect their earnings. Skilled women workers, in contrast, are paid about the same wages as semi- or unskilled women workers (Form, 1982a, 1982b). The rapid rise in women's labor-force participation, coupled with the constant relationship of men's and women's wages, made a critical mass of women become aware that the ideology of equal opportunity didn't apply to them. This awareness triggered a new wave of the women's movement.

Meanwhile, in the post-war period while women's labor-force participation was rising, scholarly and popular concern about low fertility disappeared. It is important to understand why. In the past, concern with low fertility has tended to lower women's social status by emphasizing their role as mothers. As the birth rate fell in Eastern Europe in the 1950s and 1960s, for example, occupational hazards to women's health were rediscovered. Women were legislated out of many non-traditional jobs they had been holding for two decades. Information on "maternal deprivation" belatedly reached Eastern Europe. Women's natural role as guardian of the hearth was found to be her primary role under socialism, too (Scott, 1978:192).

The first reason that concern about low fertility disappeared was the population "explosion" in the less developed countries where two-thirds of the world's people live. Growth rates shot up because Western medical technology was introduced overnight, so to speak. It dramatically decreased death rates without affecting the cost–benefit ratio of childrearing that induces change in preference for number of children. Many observers think that rapid population growth in less developed countries continues to threaten world political stability.

Second, the post-war baby boom that occurred primarily in the English-speaking countries allayed concerns about low fertility. The baby boom made demographers lose confidence in their own ideas. Abandoning theoretical pretensions, they retreated into the empty safety of empiricism—but they should have stuck to their guns (Ryder, 1979:359). In retrospect, the boom was a blip in 200 years of United States fertility decline. It is important to understand why the boom occurred in order to predict whether another boom or boomlet may occur.

The baby boom resulted from the confluence of several factors that all tend to increase fertility (Easterlin, 1968; United States Bureau of the Census, 1978). The year 1940 was a watershed for economic growth. Real earnings per employee, having risen only 22% from 1920 through 1939, rose 215% from 1940 through 1959 (Spitze and Huber, 1980:320, computed from United States Bureau of the Census, 1975:279–386). In addition, these favored cohorts formed only a small proportion of the labor force because 1920s birth rates had been low and immigration had been restricted after 1922. High rates of upward mobility and rapid wage increases for young male workers led to a sharp reduction in the age of marriage (Easterlin, 1969:14). The baby boom resulted primarily from earlier marriage and earlier childbearing rather than from individual women having more children (Easterlin, 1968:107).

Easterlin (1978, 1980) predicts a new cyclical baby boom when the children born in the 1970s reach reproductive age. They will enter a more favorable labor market than did the baby boomers. The scarcity of young (15–29) to older (30–64) workers should favorably affect younger workers' wages, unemployment, and advancement opportunities. Ryder (1979:360) thinks it would be a mistake, having been betrayed by a trend theory (the demographic transition) that ignored fluctuation, to shift to a fluctuation theory that ignored trend.[6] The Easterlin theory links men's labor-market prospects to their number, on the assumption that the traditional division of labor will continue. In the future, favor-

---

[6]Microdata do not support Easterlin (Rindfuss and MacDonald, 1981). But microdata cannot test macrotheories (Udry, 1982).

able market opportunities should affect women as well as men. We shall soon discuss the future of fertility in greater detail.

A third factor that may contribute to lack of concern about declining fertility is the world energy problem that surfaced recently. It throws into relief the uneven distribution of energy resources and raises questions about optimum population size for the planet. Optimists believe that renewable sources will be put to use, making larger population size possible. Pessimists are uncertain. A fourth factor that may contribute marginally to lack of concern is the increase in teenage out-of-wedlock fertility. The United States rate tripled between 1940 and 1975 (Chilman, 1979b:1). The sharpest increase occurred between 1963 and 1970 (Chilman, 1979A:196). Rates are increasing worldwide because rates of premarital intercourse are rising, the age of fecundity is decreasing owing to better diet, and drugs have reduced the incidence of veneral disease. The availability of public assistence programs does not cause out-of-wedlock pregnancy in the United States, but it affects what is done about the pregnancy (Presser, 1974; Ross and Sawhill, 1975; Furstenberg, 1976; Moore and Caldwell, 1977; Chilman, 1979a:213). In the United States, persistent barriers continue to obstruct access to family planning and abortion services (Cutright, 1972; Zelnik and Kantner, 1975).

Part of the concern about out-of-wedlock fertility may be tinged with racism. Although the majority of black couples (with no Southern farm background) had and expected the same number of births as similar white couples (Whelpton, Campbell, and Patterson, 1966:369), black teenage out-of-wedlock birth rates are higher than white ones because the opportunity cost is lower owing to poor educational and occupational opportunities for black girls. The probability that these girls will marry the child's father is about one-fifth that of white girls because of poor labor-market opportunities for young black males (Kantner and Zelnik, 1972).

If the theory of the demographic transition is any guide, then better labor-market and educational opportunities for teenage girls would reduce the incidence of out-of-wedlock pregnancy, especially if such opportunities were coupled with more adequate contraceptive advice. In the long run, it seems likely that teenage sexual activity will be dealt with more instrumentally and less moralistically. Meanwhile, it would be a mistake to think that the singular factors responsible for a worldwide increase in teenage pregnancy apply to older women.

Fertility is now below or hovering around replacement level in the industrialized countries. By 1990, negative population growth should occur in Austria, Great Britain, West Germany, Luxembourg, Belgium,

Denmark, Czechoslovakia, Hungary, Norway, Sweden, Bulgaria, Finland, Greece, Italy, and Switzerland. By the year 2000, it should occur in France and the Netherlands and by 2020, in the United States (Westoff, 1978a:79).

Impressionistic evidence, however, indicates that many people think that, after 200 years of decline, United States fertility will level off nicely around the zero population growth rate. Yet, the view that the demographic transition will terminate in a magical balance of births and deaths at lower levels may be more aesthetic than realistic. The percentage of persons not marrying has increased, cohabiting is increasing, divorce is increasing, and the remarriage rate after divorce is declining (Westoff, 1978a:80). The middle-aged are marrying less and cohabiting more (Westoff, 1978b:54). These facts indicate that the industrialized countries are in a new game. We first explain why we expect fertility to decline. Then we explain why, unlike its effects in the past, declining fertility may result in public policies that improve rather than harm women's social status.

We argue that the following factors make the United States structurally antinatalist: Basically, the costs of childrearing are increasing and the rewards are decreasing. In addition, it is psychologically less costly to avoid pregnancy than it used to be. The link between the sex drive and an unwanted pregnancy is nearly severed. Pregnancy will increasingly result from rational decision making. Consequently, the cost–benefit factors should affect the number of children that men and women decide to have.

First, the direct cost of rearing a child continues to rise. At 1980 price levels, rearing a child to age 18 was estimated to cost between $48,000 and $73,000. Sending the child through college would add another $10,000 to $50,000 (Hall, 1981). Espenshade's (1980) estimate is similar. Combining the direct cost and the opportunity cost of the mother's time, it would take $100,000 to $140,000 to rear a child and send it to a state university.

In part, the cost rises because of the continual increase in educational attainment needed to avoid downward social mobility together with a rise in the demand for quality children (Becker, 1981:93–134). Whether or not different childrearing methods affect the child's human capital (Scarr and Weinberg, 1978:690), higher-status families receive more of the mother's time (Leibowitz, 1975; Hill and Stafford, 1980). For example, women professionals married to professional husbands are more likely to breastfeed than are other women (Hirschman and Butler, 1981:40).

Some of the costs of rearing children are borne by the taxpayers.

Others are borne by the parents, including the opportunity cost of the mother's time (DeTray, 1973). A substantial literature documents the relatively low level of support to families rearing children in the United States compared to other developed countries (Bronfenbrenner, 1979; Kamerman and Kahn, 1979; Moore and Hofferth, 1979; Presser and Baldwin, 1980). Picking up more of the bill would be expensive for the taxpayers, but that is just the point. It is expensive for parents to supply the next generation at marginal cost to taxpayers.

Second, the indirect cost of childrearing has risen as a result of women's rising education levels that, in turn, increase the opportunity cost of the mother's remaining home (Mincer and Polachek, 1974:107; Spitze, 1979; Ward and Butz, 1978). Economists typically value child care as the wife's opportunity cost, assuming it to be proportionate to the full-time earnings rates of employed women (Easterlin, 1978:65). The two-earner family's current popularity indicates that many couples seemingly grasp the principle: Forty-three percent of children under 6 now have a mother in the labor force (United States Bureau of the Census, 1982:1). The advantage of being married to a full-time market worker seems compelling for husbands.[7] The added income costs most husbands little time in added housework. For example, the average husband's daily time spent in food preparation increased from 6 minutes a day if his wife is not employed to 12 minutes if she is employed full-time year round (Walker and Woods, 1976:157).

Third, a rising divorce rate (Glick, 1979:5)—in North America and Europe it doubled from the mid-1960s to the mid-1970s (Michael, 1977)—increases the cost of rearing children in complex ways. The prospect of divorce lowers fertility (Becker, 1981:250). The experience of divorce also lowers fertility (Cohen and Sweet, 1974). Mothers usually have custody of children because fathers do not typically want it (Weitzman, 1981:112). Yet, rates of child support payments are low (Bergmann, 1978; United States Bureau of the Census, 1979:5). Hence divorced mothers tend to be aware of childrearing costs. Divorce also makes parents aware of the normative and legal problems of child custody and of rearing children with stepparents (Cherlin, 1978; Weiss, 1979; Ambert, 1980).

Fourth, the psychological costs of childrearing are rising in a number of ways. One reason is that so many people have been reared in small families that many parents have never observed daily childrearing practices. Even the lore acquired by persons reared in large families

---

[7]In France, only the least educated husbands oppose wives' employment (Sullerot, 1973:225).

diminishes in value because of the speed of social change. Each generation of parents confronts new conditions.

The attrition of commonsense knowledge about childrearing spawned the rise of a class of experts, psychologists, home economists, and physicians as well as popular journalists (Ehrenreich and English, 1979). Learning skills by reading books or articles requires an investment in parental time. Furthermore, there are no guidelines for producing adult competency. Instead, adults who "succeed" in American society show a complex of characteristics as children that childrearing experts would evaluate as poor to bad (Rossi, 1968). Moreover, mothers do not seem to profit much from the experience of rearing their first children. The larger the family, the more difficulty the mother reports in childrearing (Rossi, 1980:25).

Perhaps the heaviest psychic cost stems from the belief that parents are responsible for the way the child turns out. Most parents graciously accept credit for their offspring's medical degree. They are less eager to tell their friends that one child dropped out of high school and another makes a living dealing in drugs. When things go wrong, middle-class parents may pay high fees to therapists and lawyers, but the highest cost may be to their own self-esteem. After investing so much for so long, it is hard for parents to accept the fact that they have so little control over the outcome. If the children are to amount to anything, they must learn to get along with their peers. But peer groups may teach teenagers how to do things the parents never even thought of. Just when the parents need to decrease their control in order that the children may learn to act independently, the child escalates its demand for clothes, sports and music equipment and, for some, college tuition and living expenses. Parents often feel they pay while the children call the tune. One reason for the declining fertility of the current crop of young adults may be that they know what a pain in the neck they were to their own parents in the 1960s and they don't want anyone to do that to them (Griliches, 1974).

Psychological costs are reflected in survey data (see Chapter 6). Childless couples report fewer psychiatric symptoms than do parents of one or two children who, in turn, report fewer than parents of three or more (Gove and Geerken, 1977). The happiest United States couples are those over age 30 who have no children (Campbell, Converse, and Rodgers, 1976:30). Conversely, the low psychological cost of having no children is documented by Veevers's (1979) exhaustive literature review.

Fifth, the economic rewards of childrearing are declining. In preindustrial societies, children worked. Now the high rate of women's labor-force participation and the low rate of children's economic activity depresses fertility in 50 countries (Kasarda, 1971). In addition, children once represented security against the day that the parents were too old or too ill to work, however much the ideal may have deviated from the real. Now the ideal has disappeared. Financial security for the elderly is a function of government or corporate bureaucracies. Such retirement systems enjoy widespread support. No one wants to be dependent on children in old age. The rapid increase in recent decades in the percentage of elderly men and women living apart from their children, caused in part by the growth in Social Security payments (Michael, Fuchs, and Scott, 1980), manifests the weakened ties between children and older parents (Becker, 1981:253).

Last, it is harder now to reap the psychological rewards of childrearing than it used to be. Industrial societies have highly mobile labor forces. Grown children often live far from their parents. The more educated the children, the more likely they are to move in search of good jobs. The telephone can transmit communications of love effectively, but it cannot do the daily tasks that make life agreeable, bearable, or even possible for old men and women.

To the extent that the conditions we describe here continue to prevail, we would predict a continued decline of fertility, down below the zero population growth rate, on toward zero. In contrast, economist Gary Becker (1981:255) concludes his treatise on the family with the prediction that if economic development continues to slow down, and if the expansion of the welfare state moderates, then there may be less steep declines in fertility and less rapid increases in divorce, labor-force participation rates of married women, illigitimacy, and female-headed households. Becker thinks that a sufficient slowing of the pace of development could eventually raise fertility and also reverse trends in other aspects of family behavior. Although we agree that a decrease in Aid to Families with Dependent Children (AFDC) grants would contribute to a lower illegitimacy rate (more women would terminate the pregnancy or marry) and to a lower rate of formation of female-headed households, we see no reason to expect decreases in rates of divorce or of married women's labor-force participation. It therefore seems unlikely to us that the downward trend in fertility would reverse itself.

How would a continued downward trend in fertility affect women's status? The most important long-run effect may be to increase the perception that parenting couples are disadvantaged compared to non-parenting ones. Although the women's movement has often been perceived as setting women and men in a zero-sum contest for jobs and incomes, a more important zero-sum game may be that of parents and nonparents. A society that wants to maintain its population will probably need to confront the problem of equalizing the economic and social burdens of parents and nonparents. This will be expensive. Direct subsidies to induce women to remain at home will be incredibly costly because of the high opportunity cost of the mother's foregone wages in a society with high secondary school completion rates. In the long run, the most efficient way of equalizing economic advantages for parents is to ensure that mothers can be employed as easily and conveniently as nonmothers. This implies a vast network of extrafamilial support. A nation will have to be quite worried about reproducing itself before it will define child care and child support as a collective obligation.

A MACROPERSPECTIVE

We now outline the macro- and microperspectives that undergird this research. The major variables may not have quite the same effects at both levels. The engines of change differ (Udry, 1982). We first present a macroperspective, then a microapproach suited to individual-level cross-sectional data. The macroperspective tries to make sense of the way people actually responded to changed conditions over time. Taking history into account tends to reduce the ethnocentrism of time and place that often afflicts microtheories.

In principle, a macroperspective on sex stratification should show how environmental constraints on human organization, the type of subsistence technology, and the need for generational replacement tend to determine who produces, who consumes, and who controls distribution beyond the family. In practice, however, we exclude the natural environment. Average rainfall, temperature, and soil fertility limit the range of solutions to meshing subsistence work and reproduction. Yet the environment changes so slowly that it is more a constant than a variable in an analysis that covers a brief period. We also exclude technological *change*, taking extant technology as a given. Technological change occurs so fast that one cannot readily predict outcomes. The rapid or slow depletion of oil reserves, for example, may stimulate the development of energy technologies that, in turn, make new living patterns possible—to say nothing of the fact that extant technology can now provide a final solution to all human problems.

Our truncated macroapproach suffices for the purpose at hand. It is based on the analysis of how people behaved during industrialization. Contrary to fact, we assume monocausal effects for the sake of brevity. The main variables are mortality, education, fertility, and women's labor-force participation. Decreasing mortality, coupled with increasing levels of education, early in industrialization led, over time, to decreased fertility. As industrialization and urbanization advanced, men in large numbers became hired workers. Women became housewives, producing or buying household goods; facilitating consumption, in economic terms (Ferber, 1982). Although young, married, and poor women worked for pay from the outset, massive increases in women's labor-force participation occur only in countries that have experienced the transition to low fertility. In such countries, a high demand for women workers triggers a rapid rise in women's labor-force participation. Such a labor shortage in "female occupations" occurred in the United States after World War II. In turn, increased rates of women's labor-force participation are associated with a lower proportion of persons ever marrying, a later age at first marriage, a higher probability that the marriage will end in divorce, and lower fertility (Westoff, 1978a; Ryder, 1979; Schoen, Urton, Woodrow, and Baj, 1982). These trends tend to increase women's labor-force participation still further.

A rapid rise in women's labor-force participation tends to be accompanied by an increased consciousness of unfairness. Since the proportion of the life course that women are employed rises with their education (Polachek, 1975b:97), employed women tend to be more sensitized to political issues. In countries where labor and radical movements are weak, as in the United States, this sense of unfairness tends to stimulate the emergence of a new women's movement addressed to issues of labor-market equity. In countries dominated by strong socialist or leftist parties, a sense of grievance specific to women is defused because the most basic inequities are thought to arise from capitalist exploitation.[8]

The current women's movement, composed of many strands, is unlikely to disappear because the trends that spawned it—decreased mortality, higher educational attainment, lower fertility, and increased women's labor-force participation—seem unlikely to be reversed (see Shaw and Statham, 1982:62). Infant mortality is so low in industrialized countries that a further decrease could have only a marginal effect. No one has predicted a decrease in women's educational attainment, a sustained fertility increase, or a decline in women's labor-force participation. Indeed, most observers expect women's labor-force participation rates to continue to rise. Younger cohorts of women should

---

[8]No one has systematically explored why the current women's movement is only now beginning to emerge in Western Europe (see Bradshaw, 1981) and why it is nearly invisible in communist countries.

experience essentially continuous lifetime employment (Land and Pampel, 1980). Moreover, economists have been too conservative and therefore inaccurate, in their past predictions of women's labor-force participation. The earlier movement of women into the labor force was greatly underestimated in nearly every economic forecast, even as late as 1965, when the upward trend was clear (Freeman, 1979:65).

In sum, the macrocausal arrows go from lower mortality and higher level of education to decreased fertility to increased women's labor-force participation. Together these may set the stage for an increasingly equal division of household labor, a topic we discuss in the last chapter. These macrofactors, as Ryder (1981) notes, are in effect collective system properties that can be explained only in relation to other properties of the same system. They constitute the conditions implicitly accepted by, or imposed on, individuals. One cannot calculate individual costs and benefits without knowing about them. They may well operate below the level of consciousness, but they may still constrain thought and behavior (Riley, 1976:295).

A MICROPERSPECTIVE

Our microperspective includes the same variables as the macro one. But the strength of micro effects should depend on the macro order of change over time. We hypothesize that, in a study of traditional versus nontraditional behaviors and attitudes, the socioeconomic variables that should have the strongest effects are those whose aggregate rates most recently changed. We argue this point by using an abstract example, again assuming monocausal effects for the sake of brevity.

At the micro level, suppose that variable A increased at historical $time_1$, causing, in turn, an increase in variable B at $time_2$ some years later. These changes occur over a century or more. Cohorts born into the society at $time_3$, however, confront levels of A and B that have existed for some time and that have become part of a taken for granted social structure. Hence a given individual's behavior and attitudes are shaped by the socioeconomic structure and climate of opinion that resulted from earlier changes in the levels of variables A and B. The further back in time a given variable changed, the more the effects of that variable should have become part of the climate of opinion of a given society. Therefore, even if variables A and B continue to have effects, those of later-changing variable C should best differentiate behavior and attitudes at $time_3$. If this reasoning is correct, then the most important microvariable in this study should be individual women's labor-force participation. Of all variables relevant to sex stratification, its rates are the ones that have most recently changed.

In contrast, a well-known microeconomic theory stresses the importance of a different variable. The New Home Economists expect husbands' and wives' relative productivity in household and market to explain the sexual division of labor or, in sociological terms, sex stratification. This theory tends to lay most emphasis on the female–male wage ratio. Unlike the rapidly rising rate of women's labor-force participation, however, the female–male wage ratio has been remarkably resistant to change. We therefore argue that it should be less effective than women's labor-force participation in predicting traditional versus nontraditional sex-role behavior or attitudes. We briefly outline this economic theory because it will throw the main features of our approach into relief.

The New Home Economics, an extension of the human capital approach to the household (Blaug, 1976:829), derives from the work of Gary Becker and his associates at the University of Chicago. One cannot overestimate the importance of Becker's empirical point of departure, the observation that productive activities occur in households. Neoclassic and Marxist economists treated the household as a kind of black box. In the neoclassic version, market goods came in one side. Utility (satisfaction) came out the other (Berk, 1980:116, 128). A major weakness of the traditional neoclassic model is the inability of market or monetary price and income variables to explain a significant fraction of the variation in consumption (Keeley, 1975:462).

The New Home Economics theory is explicated in articles authored by Becker or by Becker and a colleague and collected in Becker (1976), *The Economic Approach to Human Behavior*, and in Becker (1981), *A Treatise on the Family*. In both books the arguments concerning topics relevant to this research are consistent except for the theory of fertility. The following discussion will show how Becker changed his approach to that topic. We now briefly describe Becker's theory of consumer behavior, of marriage (including the household division of labor and divorce), and fertility (including quality versus quantity of children). We then criticize Becker's approach from our own perspective, thereby deriving the main hypothesis of this study.

The received neoclassic theory of consumer behavior holds that the household tries to maximize utility, which it obtains directly from the services of goods purchased in the market. Therefore, price changes lead to changes in the quantity demanded. In turn, to whatever extent income and prices do not explain behavior, the explanation must rest with taste variations. But this is disturbing because no well-developed theory of tastes exists (Michael and Becker, 1976:131–133). By incorporating production concepts into the theory of consumption, the household production function approach implies that households respond to changes in the prices and productivities of factors, to changes in the relative shadow prices of commodities, and to changes in their full real income as they try to minimize their production costs and maximize their utilities (Michael and Becker, 1976:139). In ordinary language, if households rationally try to increase their satisfactions, then the division of market and household work by sex makes economic sense. Being married and having children oppositely affects husband and wife wage rates (Polachek, 1975a).

The main purpose of marriage is the production and rearing of own children (Becker, 1981:93). Being married yields economic gain because husbands and wives play complementary roles. Becker assumes that (a) each person seeks a mate who maximizes his or her well-being, with well-being measured by the consumption of household-produced commodities; and (b) the "marriage market" is in equilibrium in the sense that no one could change mates and be better off. The gain from marriage positively relates to incomes, the relative difference in their wage rates, and the level of nonmarket productivity-augmenting variables such as education or beauty. Each spouse cooperatively allocates time between the market and nonmarket sectors in appropriate proportions so as to serve total household satisfactions. Becker's analysis therefore predicts that women would be weakly attached to the labor force. During any given year, he says, most wives do not participate, and a significant number never participate throughout married life (Becker, 1976:220).[9] Assuming that one can become increasingly efficient at housework, Becker also predicts that households operate most efficiently if only one person specializes in market and household work. If both do, then they could become more efficient by switching their time inputs so that at least one can invest solely in market or household capital (Becker, 1976:205–250; Becker, Landes, and Michael, 1977; Becker, 1981:14–37, 219–236).

Becker put fertility decision making into an economic framework for two reasons. First, the 1941 Indianapolis fertility survey (Whelpton, 1943–1958) reported that, although no single variable explained more than a small fraction of the variation, economic variables worked better than others. Second, Becker wanted to extend Malthus's argument that increased income led to larger family size because it decreased child mortality (better nutrition) and because it induced people to marry

[9]Becker (1981) is now aware of the increase in married women's labor-force participation, but he does not formally integrate this knowledge in his theory.

earlier and abstain less. Becker felt that he generalized Malthus by relating quantity to quality of children (Becker, 1976:171, 174). Becker's theory of fertility has been changed somewhat, presumably because the prediction that increased income led to larger family size received poor empirical support. Becker's 1976 fertility chapter appeared first in 1960, before United States fertility began to fall. Furthermore, the proposition that income positively affects fertility was attractive because, as we explain soon, the desire for children is the key assumption of the New Home Economics.

Becker assumes that, for most parents, children are a source of psychic income and are therefore akin to consumer durables. The shape of the indifference curve is determined by tastes. As is true for other consumer durables, the quantity income elasticity is small compared with the quality elasticity. That is, an increase in income should increase both quantity and quality of children, but it will increase quality more than quantity (Becker, 1976:172–174). In ordinary language, wanting a baby is akin to wanting a car:[10] Both give satisfaction. As income rises, the desire to buy a more costly unit rises faster than the desire to buy more units. Rich people typically own a few Cadillacs in preference to many Chevrolets. They send a few children to private schools rather than sending many children to public schools.

Fertility should therefore be explicable by the relation of the cost of children to parental income (Becker, 1976:193). The net cost equals the present value of expected outlay plus the imputed value of the parents' services minus the present value of the expected money return and the imputed value of the children's services. In the nineteenth century, children may have been a net producer's good, providing rather than using income, but the cost of children has increased due to their decreasing contribution to family farms and businesses and due to the increased value of married women's time. It has decreased due to the availability of AFDC (Becker, 1981:96–98). For most families, the net expenditure on children has been very large. (Becker, 1976:175). The price of children is higher for the rich than for the poor because the rich choose to raise more expensive children as they similarly choose to buy more expensive cars (Becker, 1976:197).

Although crude cross-sectional data show a negative relationship of fertility to income, the relation is positive if contraceptive knowledge is held constant (Becker, 1976:192). The decline in child mortality and the increase in contraceptive knowledge have been important causes of the fertility decline. With the weakening of these forces, much of the

---

[10]Folk wisdom differentiates babies and cars. No one ever accused a rich couple of being selfish because they did not want to buy two or three Cadillacs.

steam behind the secular decline in birth rates would be removed. Therefore, positive forces like income growth would be opposed by much weaker negative forces. It is therefore not surprising, Becker (1976:192) concluded, that fertility had ceased to decline and had even risen in some countries. The negative correlation between the secular changes in fertility and income is not strong evidence against the hypothesis that an increase in income would cause an increase in fertility—tastes, costs, and knowledge remaining constant (Becker, 1976:190).

Today it is clear that the fertility theory presented in Becker (1976) has had difficulty accommodating the observed association between long-term economic growth and fewer births (Schoen et al., 1982). Even a sympathetic critic noted its apparent inability to explain major changes in United States fertility in the past 35 years. Real income rose throughout that period. Yet, it is difficult to show that any variables commonly regarded as proxies for the price of children fell during the 1940s and 1950s and rose during the 1960s and 1970s (Keeley, 1975:466).

Becker's theory of fertility now predicts an inverse relation between income and fertility in developed countries. A long-term rise in income is combined with a decrease in fertility because of the quality–quantity interaction (Becker, 1981:93–112). The price of children has increased due to changes in their economic contribution to the family, the value of the wife's time, and the increased cost of rearing children in line with one's own increased standard of living. In addition, industrialization increases the rate of return to investment in children's education. That makes the inverse relation between income and number of children in developed countries consistent with a positive relation in underdeveloped countries.

Becker's change in the fertility theory is akin to a change in the popular vote from 51% to 49%, a change from a small positive effect to a negative effect. Nonetheless, it is important because it makes fertility problematic. It raises the question, How far will fertility fall? At the end of his 1981 book, Becker (1981:245–256) speculates on the future of the family. We therefore report his speculation and his conclusion.

Since 1950, Becker (1981:245) says, the United States family changed more rapidly than during any equivalent period in its history. The major cause of the change is the growth in women's earning power. It raises the rate of married women's labor-force participation by raising the foregone value of time spent at nonmarket activities. It also raises the relative cost of children and thereby reduces the demand for them. The gain from marriage is reduced by a rise in earnings and in labor-force participation of women and by a fertility decline because a sexual division of labor is less advantageous. And divorce is more attractive when the gain from marriage falls. The expectation of greater labor-force participation at older ages encourages women to invest more in market-oriented human capital, which further increases their earning power and their labor-force participation and further reduces fertility. Hence the increase in labor-force participation and decline in fertility eventually accelerated, even when the growth in female earnings power did not. Moreover, these two factors accelerated the increase in the divorce rates because the decline in the gain from marriage also accelerates. Furthermore, a growth in the divorce rate itself eventually encourages additional divorces because persons are stigmatized less.

Becker concludes that, if economic development continues to slow down and if the expansion of the welfare state moderates, then he would predict much less steep fertility declines and a less rapid increase in rates of divorce, married women's labor-force participation, illegitimacy, and formation of female-headed households. "Indeed, a sufficient slowing of the pace of development could eventually raise fertility and also reverse the trends in other aspects of family behavior [Becker, 1981:255]." Thus, the change from 51% to 49% appears to have produced a theoretical flip-flop. Fertility will begin to rise only if economic development slows down enough.

Although the New Home Economics has been extensively criticized (see Leibenstein, 1974; Ferber and Birnbaum, 1977; Berk, 1980), we focus only on its main weakness from our own perspective: the central assumption that for most people, children are valued goods. To the extent that this assumption is inaccurate, the edifice wobbles, as we shall show. It makes more sense to assume, instead, that children are relatively valued goods, depending on the costs and benefits of rearing them at a given time. This assumption would not necessarily make the theory less precise because costs and benefits, unlike utilities, can be measured rather well. However, the assumption that children are valued goods cannot lightly be disposed of. It is the keystone of the New Home Economics for three reasons. First, if children are not wanted by most parents, then the economic advantage of a complementary-role marriage disappears. Complementary roles maximize household utility only because the presence of children implies the presence of a caretaker. Second, if complementary households and market roles for spouses do not maximize efficiency, then there is no obvious reason why the theory should consider household utility as a unit. Instead, it would seem more logical to consider individual utilities. Finally, in the absence of children, there is no obvious reason why either the couple or the individual wives would benefit more from a wife's household than from her market work.

Yet, the New Home Economists are on the right track. People often do act rationally so as to maximize their satisfactions. A new theory seems to be in order, however. Perhaps nearly everyone does want a child. But the child may be wanted less than some other goods. Theorists should relate the desire for children to their current costs and benefits, which can be measured. The problem with Becker's theory is not that it is too economic. It is not economic enough. As Tilly (1978) remarked, "We may admire the humanity of the economists who emphasize the pleasure children provide. In addition to pleasure, we need room for the incentives of pensions, patrimony, and pecuniary return [p. 347]."

In sum, the assumption that most people want children makes the female–male wage ratio the critical variable that affects household decisions. If households include children, someone must care for them. It is economically rational for the spouse who commands lower market wages to work at home.[11] The higher the female–male wage ratio, the less likely is a couple to marry, remain married, have children, the wife to remain at home (Becker, 1981:248).[12]

In contrast, we predict that women's labor-force participation will be the major variable explaining attitudes and behaviors relevant to sex stratification. This prediction is not consistent with Becker's theory. However, it is consistent with Becker's analysis of recent trends. As we have just pointed out, Becker (1981:245) claims that the rise in women's earning is the major engine of change in trends affecting the family. Women's earnings rose after 1950, but that is not the point.[13] Men's earnings rose also. Yet, the aggregate female/male wage ratio remained essentially the same.

Unlike the unchanging wage ratio, women's labor-force participation rates have increased dramatically since 1950. Whether a woman works for pay may be more important than how much she earns. The spread of

---

[11]However, Becker (1981:24) says that specialized investments in children are made prior to full knowledge of their biological orientation, hence some of them will not pay off. A small fraction of girls, he says, may be "biologically oriented" to market rather than to household activities and a small fraction of boys may be "biologically oriented" to housework.

[12]Becker's theory does not predict how equality of husband–wife wages would affect household organization.

[13]Becker's evidence is flawed. He cites data from Current Population Reports. But women's income includes AFDC grants, which rose dramatically during this period and which would oppositely affect fertility. Nonetheless, Becker correctly claims that women's earnings rose.

women's earnings is narrower than that of men's. It is the fact of doing market work that makes the difference, even if it is for relatively low pay, because it makes women economically independent of their husbands. This implies many consequences, which are what this book is about.

CHAPTER TWO

Data and Methods

In this chapter we shall discuss the data and methods that are the basis of all of the following empirical chapters: the sampling and data collection procedures used for the survey and an overview of the demographic characteristics of the sample and of the subsample of married couples. Variable codings and other procedures unique to a given chapter will be described within individual chapters in order to make such details easier for readers to follow. Hence the empirical chapters in this book will be, for the most part, self-contained.

This research is based on a telephone survey conducted by the Survey Research Laboratory of the University of Illinois in November and December 1978 on a national probability sample of households. Telephone interviews have become increasingly acceptable in recent years as a lower-cost substitute for personal interviews. Comparisons have shown the two methods to yield data of equal quality, even when the questions concern complex attitudes, detailed knowledge, or personal information (Rogers, 1976).

Random digit dialing procedures were used to ensure the inclusion of unlisted numbers (Sudman, 1973; Waksberg, 1978). This sampling procedure works as follows: Primary sampling units are drawn from a list of all telephone area codes and prefixes. All possible two-digit numbers are added to the selected primary sampling units, then random two-digit numbers are chosen to add to these. If the first number called is not residential, a new primary sampling unit is chosen. If the first number called is residential, other numbers from that primary sampling unit are called. The technique is efficient because it avoids calling a large quantity of nonresidential telephone numbers. In all, this study used 189 primary sampling units. Numbers were called five times if there was no answer the first time. Once a household was found to be eligible, up to 10 attempts were made to make contact with a respondent.

Interviews were conducted by 15 professional interviewers employed by the Survey Research Laboratory. All interviewers were women. The Survey Research Laboratory feels that the quality of a survey depends upon the interviewer's ability and not on the interviewer's characteristics. Carefully trained and experienced interviewers are less likely to misperceive and miscode respondents' answers or to suggest an answer by verbal or nonverbal method (Sudman and Bradburn, 1975:139).

When a call was answered, the interviewer confirmed the telephone number and asked to speak to the head of the household. This term, although recently abandoned by the United States Bureau of the Census, is still used by the Survey Research Laboratory for telephone interviews because it allows interviewers to speak with male adults if they are present without insulting female household heads. Since men are less likely to be home than women are, this procedure ensures an approximately equal initial distribution of men and women respondents.

The interviewer would identify herself and state, "We're calling all over the United States to find out what people think about working, family life, and other issues facing the United States today." When the interviewer made contact with the household head or spouse, she used a screening question to check for the respondent's age. Only people between the ages of 18 and 65, or their spouses, were interviewed, since we were particularly interested in labor market-related experiences. Seventeen male spouses were aged 66–75.

Following a suggestion by Seymour Sudman, Head of the Sampling Section at the Survey Research Laboratory, we decided to interview both members of married couples whenever possible. In addition to the obvious desirability of having data for a national sample of married couples, two other reasons made this procedure seem attractive. First, including men and women married to one another would highlight sex differences in attitudes since this procedure, in effect, controlled for many background variables, such as family income. Second, it would shorten the interviews since information for spouses of married respondents would already have been recorded.

Interviews averaged 35 minutes, depending mainly upon the applicability of several sets of questions to a given respondent. A total of 2002 persons were interviewed. Of these, 391 were single (divorced, widowed, separated, or never married), 913 were married and first to be interviewed in the household, and 698 were spouses of interviewed respondents.

The overall completion rate was 85.9%. A breakdown by marital status and reason for failure to obtain an interview (see Table 2.1) shows that the refusal rate was low for the initial married respondents (4.2%) and for single respondents (2.4%) but it was much higher for the initial respondent's spouses (20.1%) which will be discussed later. Rates of noncontact and unavailability, negligible for initial married respondents and single respondents, were also higher for initial respondent's spouse, almost 4% for each category.

The marginals by sex for several demographic variables, both for the total sample and for the couples subsample, show that more than nine-tenths of the men and nearly three-fifths of the women were employed

Table 2.1
FINAL CONTROL REPORT

Result of interviewer contact	Initial married respondent		Initial respondent's spouse		Single respondents	
	N	%	N	%	N	%
Eligible	959	99.3				
Interviewed	913	94.5	698	71.7	391	95.4
Refused interview	41	4.2	196	20.1	10	2.4
Noncontact	2	.2	37	3.8	2	.5
Unavailable	3	.3	37	3.8	0	0
Other eligible	0	0	1[b]	.1	0	0
Ineligible	5	.5	2	.2	2	.5
Eligibility unknown	2	.2	2	.2	5	1.2
TOTAL	966[a]	100.0	973[a]	100.0	410	100.0

[a] The numbers in the first and second columns are not equal because several married women respondents were mistakenly designated as initial respondent's spouse instead of as initial respondent.

[b] By the time the second contact was made in this household, the couple had separated.

Table 2.2

DISTRIBUTION OF TOTAL SAMPLE AND COUPLES SUBSAMPLE ON DEMOGRAPHIC VARIABLES BY SEX (IN PERCENTAGES)

Demographic variables	Individuals		Couples	
	Men	Women	Men	Women
Current employment status				
Full or part time	90	59	92	56
Retired or unemployed	8	13	7	9
Not employed, not looking	2	29	1	35
Number children ever born				
0	23	22	16	17
1	18	17	20	20
2	25	25	27	27
3	16	16	19	16
4+	18	19	19	20
Age				
18-29	19	27	21	32
30-39	32	26	33	28
40-49	21	20	20	20
50+	28	27	26	20
Religion				
Protestant	59	62	62	64
Catholic	20	23	20	22
Jewish	4	4	3	4
Other	1	1	1	2
None	16	9	13	8
Race				
White	90	89	92	91
Black	6	8	6	6
Other	4	3	2	3
Education				
Under 12 years	17	17	17	15
12 years	36	49	37	49
13-15 years	21	18	21	18
16+	26	16	25	18
Family income				
Under $10,000	16	28	12	16
$10,000-14,999	24	23	24	21
$15,000-19,999	20	20	21	24
$20,000-24,999	16	13	18	16
$25,000-29,999	10	7	11	9
$30,000+	13	10	15	14
N	910	1092	682	682

full- or part-time (see Table 2.2). About a tenth of the women and less than a tenth of the men were retired or unemployed. Almost none of the men but about a third of the women were out of the labor force (not employed and not looking for work). Reports on the number of children ever born, as would be expected, varied little by sex. More than a fifth of the individuals and less than a fifth of the married couples reported having had no children. About a fifth of the respondents reported having had one child; about a quarter reported having had two; less than a fifth reported three; and less than a fifth reported having four or more. About three-fifths of the respondents were Protestant; about a fifth were Roman Catholic; about a tenth reported having no religion; 4% were Jewish; and 1% reported being "other." About nine-tenths of the sample reported being white; about 7% were black; and 3% were "other".

Because this study is a random sample of households rather than of individuals and because the data analysis undertaken here treats the data at times as a sample of individuals and at times as a sample of married couples, we need to determine what biases, if any, either of these treatments would imply. As a sample of individuals, one possible bias relates to adults living in households with persons other than their spouses. In the case of one adult or married-couple households, the interviewer attempted to interview all adults. However, persons living with relatives or as unmarried couples would then be underrepresented to an unknown extent. A second bias would stem from nonresponse. The refusal plus the noncontact rates for the initial married and nonmarried respondents were very low, as we noted earlier, and those for spouses were much higher (see Table 2.1). The average rate of nonresponse for married persons was therefore around 14%. We shall argue that the married nonrespondents did not differ from the respondents in discernible ways, but of course this rate of nonresponse implies that married persons were slightly underrepresented in the individuals sample. Finally, men are known to be slightly more likely to refuse survey interviews. The sample of individuals is 54.5% women, slightly higher than the percentage of United States residents who are women (52%).

As a sample of married couples, several sources of bias might arise: couples living in separate households but with intact marriages; failure to make contact with a spouse because the first person called refused to be interviewed or could not be located; and the refusal or noncontact of spouses of interviewed married persons. We assume that persons with intact marriages living in separate households are rare enough not to bias a probability sample of this type. Presumably if they occurred, they would fall into the "unavailable" category of spouses (see Table 2.1); they would therefore comprise, at most, 3.8% of spouses. Refusals by or noncontact of the first person in the household to be called were, again, not common enough to cause much bias. Such persons comprised 4.7% of the original respondents contacted. Refusals by or noncontacts with spouses of persons who were already interviewed were, however, high enough to be a potential problem (20.1% and 7.6% respectively). In order to determine whether these rates bias the sample of married couples, we compare the married respondents in the sample of individuals to the married respondents in the sample of couples by sex (see Table 2.3). Any major differences between respondents and nonrespondents should appear in this comparison. (Minor differences might appear if nonrespondents were separated and compared to respondents. Unfortunately, due to the way the two files were constructed, we cannot perform that type of analysis.) We see that there are no substantial differences between the two groups, and, in fact, when t tests are computed, no significant differences appear. Thus, we conclude that the nonrespondent spouses do not differ from the responding ones on the demographic variables examined here.

The questionnaire (see Appendix) included questions on a variety of issues, although the major focus was on sex-role attitudes, women's labor market activity, and household functioning. Since this variety is represented in the chapters of this book, we shall not try to report further frequency distributions, variable coding, or specific statistical methods of analysis in this chapter.

Analyses are conducted with either the individual or the couple as the unit of analysis. For analysis, the maximum sample sizes are 910 men and 1,092 women (as individuals), and 682 couples. The actual

Table 2.3
COMPARISON OF COUPLES AND MARRIED INDIVIDUALS (MEANS)
(STANDARD DEVIATIONS IN PARENTHESES)

Demographic characteristics	Couples		Married individuals	
	Husbands	Wives	Men	Women
Percent employed full- or part-time	91.8	55.6	91.3	53.5
Number of children	2.3 (1.8)	2.2 (1.7)	2.2 (1.8)	2.3 (1.7)
Years of education	13.1 (2.9)	12.7 (2.3)	13.0 (2.9)	12.6 (2.3)
Age	40.4 (12.3)	37.7 (11.7)	40.8 (12.4)	38.8 (12.1)
Percent black	5.6	5.7	5.7	6.1
Percent Protestant	61.6	63.9	61.6	62.8
Family income categories	4.3 (1.6)	4.2 (1.7)	4.3 (1.7)	4.1 (1.7)
N	682	682	770	841

numbers vary with each analysis due to deletion of cases with missing data.

In all but one of the analyses (Chapter 5), multiple regression is the primary method used. This is appropriate, given the level of measurement of variables, and its interpretation is widely understood. We generally report both unstandardized and standardized coefficients to permit both between- and within-equation comparisons.

CHAPTER THREE

Husband–Wife Reporting Consistency

The purpose of this chapter is to investigate the extent, sources, and consequences of inconsistent reports by spouses and to determine the necessity of dual reports about household functioning. We are interested in reports of presumably objective information, rather than attitudinal agreement (e.g., see van Es and Singi, 1972). Although attitudinal agreement is of substantive interest, the agreement about objective information has major methodological and substantive consequences for family research.

We focused on two areas: reports of household decision making and of the division of household labor. In each of these areas, major works have been based on reports of one family member, generally the wife, since she is most accessible to interviewers. For example, the classic study on family decision making by Blood and Wolfe (1960) and that on household labor by Walker and Woods (1976) both relied on wives' data. Such statistics rely on the assumption that wives' reports of family functioning are accurate.

Reliance on one family member's report has been justified on grounds of economy and sample size (Scanzoni, 1965), convenience (Blood and Wolfe, 1960), and her superior knowledge of household behavior (Walker and Woods, 1976). Yet a large number of small-scale studies, generally based on convenience samples, have reported discrepancies between husband–wife reports of up to 48% on household tasks and up to 60% on decision-making items (see Douglas and Wind, 1978; Booth and Welch, 1978; and McDonald, 1980, for reviews of this research). Some researchers suggest that this discrepancy implies major problems since it may reflect systematically distorted perceptions, whereas others suggest that the error is random and no major problem exists (Granbois and Willett, 1970; Douglas and Wind, 1978). A third group proposes that the discrepancy is not a methodological issue at all, but rather a substantive one, since it results from the differentially perceived realities experienced by the two spouses (Safilios-Roth-schild, 1969; Rollins and Bahr, 1976). Finally, none of these investigators has proposed a solution to husband–wife reporting discrepancies. Sarah Berk and Anthony Shih (1980) and others have concluded, after revealing high levels of discrepancy, that it is important to measure both spouses' perceptions, but they proposed no method for handling the dual data.

In this chapter, we present evidence as to the sources of discrepant reporting and the substantive consequences of using a single household informant and briefly describe previous studies that have attempted to deal with this issue. Although numerous studies have reported levels of consistency for a variety of other types of items (e.g., van Es and Singi, 1972; Jaco and Shepard, 1975; Booth and Welch, 1978; Ballweg, 1969; Mason, 1974; Coombs and Fernandez, 1978), we will limit our discussion to research on decision making and household labor.

THEORETICAL APPROACHES TO CONSISTENCY

Spousal inconsistency may arise from several sources. First, as mentioned earlier, it may reflect husbands' and wives' differential experience of reality (Safilios-Rothschild, 1970; Larson, 1974). From this perspective, there would be no objective correct response to a given question about family functioning; rather, there would be as many responses as family members, or observers. Although this may be true of characteristics like marital happiness, and, to a limited extent, decision-making processes, it would be hard to argue that "who washes the dishes" is merely subjective reality.

Second, discrepancies may arise from vagueness in question wording. A phrase such as "most of the time" or "usually" in response to the "dishes" question could easily be interpreted in many ways. If a couple divides dishwashing 60–40 one might view this approximately equal, whereas another might view it as wife (or husband) dominated.

Third, and theoretically more interesting, couple characteristics could influence consistency. Consistent perceptions could vary with structural characteristics in part because they would influence effectiveness of communication (Booth and Welch, 1978; Jaco and Shepard, 1975). Some scholars argue that more communication would lead to higher agreement levels. Safilios-Rothschild (1969) suggests the opposite, at least in the area of decision-making reports: The more couples discuss an issue, the more blurred the role of each in the decision-making process may become, thus leading to a higher disagreement on decision-making items. Relevant structural characteristics might include length of marriage, age, education, income, wife's employment, race, and heterogeneity of background. Quality of the relationship could also influence consistency (Safilios-Rothschild, 1969) since a certain minimal level of agreement is necessary for a relationship to survive (Booth and Welch, 1978).

Finally, a couple's sex-role ideology might influence consistency of reporting, particularly in the areas of decision making and housework sharing. A couple making an effort to share these responsibilities probably discusses and reevaluates inputs more often and thus should have more consistent perceptions.

If discrepancies are caused by characteristics of the couple or the relationship, one would expect generally similar overall levels of agreement across items for a given couple, but varying levels across couples. On the other hand, if agreement varies across items, it would more likely be a product of vague wordings or degree of objectivity of each activity (Jaco and Shepard, 1975). The latter could also reflect differentially strong norms regarding sex-stereotyping of tasks or decision making (Douglas and Wind, 1978), although such norms could vary across couples as well (Safilios-Rothschild, 1969).

EMPIRICAL STUDIES OF CONSISTENCY

At the aggregate level, husbands' and wives' reports of family decision making and household labor are very similar; that is, similar percentages of husbands and wives report a given authority or task distribution (Wilkening and Morrison, 1963; Centers et al., 1971). This aggregate-level agreement has been suggested as evidence that the error reflected by the disagreement is random (Granbois and Willett, 1970). However, unless one is interested only in reporting aggregate raw data, similar means are not sufficient to justify using only one respondent (Wilkening and Morrison, 1963). One would need also to show that discrepancies are unrelated to other variables and that the choice of respondent would not influence substantive conclusions.

With very few exceptions researchers who investigate levels of inconsistency in responses have found these levels high enough to present potential problems. Exceptions include two studies that did not actually report levels of agreement but simply reported them to be high (Buric and Zecevic, 1967; Ericksen et al., 1979), Heer's (1962) report of 84% agreement on who usually wins disagreements, and Blood and Hamblin's (1958) report of 86% agreement on whose suggestions are adopted (both 3-category items).

In studies using 5-category items regarding who makes specific decisions or who does specific household tasks (generally coded wife always; wife usually; both equally; husband usually; husband always), levels of agreement vary widely, from 40% to 95%. Agreement appears to be higher for tasks than for decisions, probably reflecting their more objective character (see Granbois and Willett, 1970; Douglas and Wind, 1978). Agreement also is highest for the most frequently performed tasks or decisions and for sex-stereotyped tasks (Douglas and Wind, 1978; S. Berk and Shih, 1980). However, levels of agreement differ greatly across studies for the same task, even when the same response categories are used (e.g., compare Granbois and Willett, 1970, Table 2, to Douglas and Wind, 1978, Table 2). Such differences may be a product of the composition of small convenience samples used.

Attempts to relate consistency to other characteristics have met with little success. Safilios-Rothschild (1969) determined that spouses' perceptions differ significantly *within* groups defined by several structural characteristics (e.g., by education), with the exception of low-education-wife couples and low-education-husband couples. She did *not* measure differences in consistency levels *between* these groups, however. Vicky Cromwell and Ronald Cromwell (1978) determined that black couples had higher levels of disagreement than white or Chicano couples on who made decisions. Scanzoni (165), Sarah Berk and Anthony Shih (1980), Granbois and Willett (1970), and Booth and Welch (1978) all attempted to relate couple consistency to a variety of couple characteristics, using samples ranging from 31 clergymen and their wives (Scanzoni) to a national probability sample of 350 couples (S. Berk and Shih). None was successful.

Measuring decision-making reporting discrepancies between husbands and wives, Granbois and Willett (1970) found a positive correlation between discrepancy and mean rating, implying regression toward the mean. This implies random error, although the researchers did not discuss implications for how more accurate measurement can be made in future studies.

None of the studies on consistency has attempted to determine substantive consequences of alternative methods of data collection. In fact, as Burr et al. (1977) point out, researchers in this area have yet to adopt techniques allowing the analysis of both spouses' responses if they are available, tending to focus instead on the discrepancy exclusively (e.g., Turk and Bell, 1972). The advisability of dual reports would be of key interest to researchers who are ultimately interested in, for example, determining how family characteristics relate to the division of household labor or what the consequences of that division are for women's occupational achievement. The crucial question is how we can obtain the most precise measure of the objective situation regarding family decision making and the division of household labor and how our conclusions would vary if we used data from only one respondent.

MEASURING DECISION MAKING AND HOUSEHOLD LABOR

For this chapter we use the couple as the unit of analysis. For each couple, therefore, we have two variables for every one on the original questionnaire, representing husbands' and wives' responses to that item.

In past research, measures of decision making have included single-item measures with attendant problems of reliability (e.g. see Heer, 1963; Scanzoni, 1970:148; Bahr, 1974:171) and series of questions regarding who makes various decisions for the family. When combined into a scale, the variety of these items can be a problem in itself, since decisions vary in importance to the family and frequency with which they are made (Safilios-Rothschild, 1969, 1970; Heer, 1963; R. Cromwell and Wieting, 1975). For example, Blood and Wolfe's (1960) decision-making scale gave equal weight to what doctor the family should use (a relatively trivial, infrequent decision) and what job the husband should take (an infrequent decision vitally affecting every aspect of the family's lifestyle). Other decisions may be highly frequent but also highly trivial, of the type that are relegated. One attempt to deal with this problem used a weighting scheme based on the perceived importance of each decision (Price-Bonham, 1976). It met with difficulty since the criterion of validity was correlation of the scale with resources of each spouse, thus assuming a relation between individual resources and power.

A possible solution to these problems is to limit study to infrequent decisions about which people have strong feelings that vitally affect family welfare, and that a powerful spouse would be unlikely to relegate. In this research we used such a measure of decision making. Respondents were asked who decides:

1. Where to go on vacation
2. What job the husband should take
3. What house or apartment to live in
4. Whether the wife should have a job
5. Whether to move if the husband gets a job offer in another city

Answer categories were: wife always; wife usually; both equally; husband usually; husband always. Responses of "other" and "nonapplicable" were also recorded.

The measurement of household labor also presents problems. Time-budget studies probably give the clearest picture of hours spent by each family member on each household task (Walker and Woods, 1976; Meissner et al., 1975; J. Morgan et al., 1966; Farkas, 1976) but are costly to collect and cannot be included in a survey that has other major focuses. A minor problem is that several household tasks may be performed simultaneously, making it difficult for the respondent to divide them on the schedule (Hedges and Barnett, 1972).

Survey questions on housework typically ask how each of various household tasks is divided, with a series of response categories (Blood and Wolfe, 1960; R. Stafford et al., 1977) or a simple yes–no as to whether the husband ever helps (Presser, 1977). The number of tasks included varies greatly—Blood and Wolfe (1960) use 8; Sarah Berk and Anthony Shih (1980), 60. Attempts to approximate the precision attained in time-budget studies by weighting responses according to frequency of task performance (R. Stafford et al., 1977) meet with obstacles connected with the variety of tasks included, variation in households, and imprecision inherent in multiplying two ordinal scales together.

For this study household labor was measured by asking:

1. Who prepares regular meals for the household
2. Who shops for food for the household
3. Who takes care of the children or old people in the household
4. Who does the daily housework
5. Who cleans up after meals

Answer categories were: wife always; wife usually; both equally; husband usually; husband always. These daily, repetitive household tasks are those requiring the most time on a daily basis and took 72% of total time spent in housework by the families studied by Walker and Woods (1976).

Table 3.1

CODING OF INDEPENDENT VARIABLES USED IN CHAPTER 3 ANALYSES

Variable	Coding
Wife employment	1=yes, 0=no
Family (also husband or wife) income	in categories, from 1=under $5,000 to 7=over $30,000
Race	1=black, 0=other
Wife's (husband's) education	coded in years
Age difference	in years, husband minus wife
Education difference	in years, husband minus wife
Religion difference	coded 1 if husband and wife in different major religious groups, 0 if same
Marital duration	in years
Thought of divorce (husband or wife)	"Has the thought of divorce ever crossed your mind?" 1=yes, 0=no
Sex-role attitudes	sum of responses to 8 items (see Appendix I, Q26, f,g,h, i,j,l,n,o). High values indicate more liberal responses.
Housework equity	response to "If a husband and wife both work full time, do you think the wife should be responsible for the daily housework, that the husband should help her, or that the husband and wife should share daily housework equally?" Coded 1=both equally, 0=other.

Both the decision making and the housework items are analyzed, first separately, and then combined into indices reflecting relative contribution of husband and wife for nonmissing, applicable items. Higher values reflect greater participation by husbands.

Our strategy here is, first, to compare husband–wife responses at the aggregate level. We then examine presence, degree, and direction of inconsistency for items and groups of items, and we analyze their relation to couple characteristics. Coding of independent variables used in this chapter can be found in Table 3.1. Consistency variables are measured as the difference between husband's and wife's response on each item, examined as a dichotomy (agree–disagree), as an absolute value (level of inconsistency), and as a difference (direction of consistency).

FINDINGS

As in previous studies, we found that overall aggregate response patterns are similar for husbands and wives (see Table 3.2, columns 1 and 2). For decision items, responses are nearly identical at the aggregate level, and differences are not statistically significant. For housework items, however, there is a consistent tendency for one or both spouses to overestimate their own contribution, and this difference is statistically significant for all items. Since we have no objective measure of the household situation, we have no way of knowing whether it is the husband, the wife, or both who everestimate their own share of the work in a given case. We do know that, generally, more couples disagree in the direction of overestimating one's own rather than one's spouse's contribution.

The general degree of aggregate similarity, especially for decision-making items, masks much disagreement among individual couples (see Table 3.3). Reliability measures are moderate but could hardly be described as high. The percentage of couples choosing the same category ranges from 47% to 62% for housework items and from 41% to 80%

Table 3.2

HUSBANDS' AND WIVES' MEAN RESPONSES FOR HOUSEWORK AND DECISION-MAKING ITEMS

	Husbands	Wives	Mean Difference	t-value
Housework				
Meals	1.64	1.49	.15	5.06*
Shop	1.92	1.76	.16	4.24*
Kids/old people	2.15	1.91	.24	5.26*
Housework	1.79	1.58	.21	6.49*
Clean up	2.10	1.83	.27	7.07*
Mean	1.92	1.67	.25	11.16*
Decisions				
Vacation	3.02	3.04	-.02	-.72
Husband job	4.53	4.54	-.01	-.29
House	3.01	3.00	.01	.14
Wife job	2.36	2.31	.05	.93
Move	3.43	3.37	.06	1.26
Mean	3.24	3.24	.00	-.21

Note: Coded from 1-wife always to 5-husband always.

*p < .001

Table 3.3

HUSBANDS AND WIVES CHOOSING SAME CATEGORY RESPONSE AND CHOOSING CATEGORIES NO MORE THAN ONE APART FOR HOUSEWORK AND DECISION MAKING (IN ROUNDED PERCENTAGES)

	Same Category	0-1	Mean Categories Apart	r(husband and wife)
Housework				
Meals	62%	93%	.43	.63
Shop	59	86	.56	.59
Kids/old people	47	78	.64	.55
Housework	57	86	.52	.58
Clean up	50	76	.68	.49
Mean for nonmissing items	58	84	.79	.65
Decisions				
Vacation	80	91	.27	.76
Husband job	59	82	.59	.54
House	72	95	.43	.69
Wife job	41	64	1.02	.40
Move	65	75	.60	.57
Mean for nonmissing items	60	81	.67	.27

on decision making. On average, about three-fifths of couples respond similarly to a given item of either type; the greater aggregate similarity for decision making than for housework does not imply greater consensus at the individual level.

When we expand the definition of consensus to responses that are at most one category apart, the vast majority of couples agree on almost all items. Average disagreement appears to be two-thirds to four-fifths of a point per item, although for one item (who decides whether wife should have a job), it is as high as one point. However, this level of disagreement appears substantial when one considers the difference implied by an equal contribution versus one spouse "usually" performing a task (which are one point apart).

Given the substantial level of disagreement here, one is next tempted to ask, who is disagreeing? Do the same couples tend to disagree on a number of items, or is the tendency to report inconsistency spread across couples fairly broadly? One way of tackling this question is to construct measures of consistency and to look at their intercorrelations across items. For Table 3.4, we have constructed three measures of consistency for each of the two sets of items. The first consistency measure is simply a dichotomy and measures whether or not (0 if no, 1 if yes) a couple gave the same respone for a given item. The "level of

Table 3.4

INTERCORRELATIONS AMONG CONSISTENCY MEASURES

	Number of Correlations Significant at .01 Level	Mean Correlation
Husband-Wife Consistency		
Decisions	5/10	.069
Housework	9/10	.158
Decisions w/housework	0/25	-.017
Husband-Wife Level of Inconsistency		
Decisions	5/10	.074
Housework	7/10	.159
Decisions w/housework	0/25	.001
Husband-Wife Difference		
Decisions	5/10	.083
Housework	9/10	.223
Decisions w/housework	0/25	-.007

inconsistency" measure is the number of categories apart a given couple's responses were. The difference measure is the husband's response minus the wife's; if positive it indicates overestimation of own contribution to housework or decision making by one or both spouses; if negative, underestimation.

If intercorrelations among these consistency items are high, it should imply that the same couples tend to reply consistently across items, and one would then search for the characteristics of those couples. If they are low, it could imply a random error effect. In Table 3.4 we see that correlations are relatively low, although positive, for decision-making consistency items and slightly higher for housework items. In other words, couples who exhibit consensus on one item in a set tend slightly to answer consistently on another, particularly for housework items. This tendency makes sense in light of the earlier finding that aggregate responses are more similar for decision making than for housework items. Disagreement about who makes decisions appears to cancel itself out and to be distributed somewhat evenly across couples.

We also see in Table 3.4 that consistency measures *between* decision making and housework items are totally unrelated. A couple that reports consistently on one type of item is no more or less likely to do so on the other set of items. This implies that whatever tendency there is for a couple to exhibit consistent consensus is highly restricted to a specific subject matter. This statement is consistent with Booth and

Welch's (1978) general conclusion: Their canonical correlation failed to isolate a general consensus factor from a series of agreement items.

Given that there is a slight tendency for couples to exhibit consistency across consistency measures within a set of items on a given topic (again, this is true for housework more than for decision making), we next turn our attention to determining whether couples who tend to exhibit more or less consistency can be characterized in any particular way. We suggested earlier several hypotheses regarding couple characteristics that might lead to greater or lesser consensus. These hypotheses involved structural characteristics (education, age, and spouse differences in both; income, religious differences, wife's employment status, and race) thought to affect, potentially, the level of communication between spouses. Degree of discord in the marriage, indicated here by thoughts of divorce by either spouse, also might indicate degree of communication. Finally, notions about sex-role equality might lead both spouses to be more or less cognizant of the degree of equality in behaviors reported here.

In Table 3.5 we report bivariate relations between measures of agreement for decision making and housework items and the couple characteristics just listed. The agreement measures are summary measures across each set of five items, for amount of inconsistency (number of categories in disagreement) and difference scores (sum of all differences). We omit the dichotomous agreement items described earlier since they appear in Table 3.4 to behave in a highly similar fashion to the level of inconsistency measures.

We find, in Table 3.5, that the degree of inconsistency in reporting about decision making is significantly higher for couples in which either spouse has lower education, is older, where age differences are greater, the husband's educational advantage is smaller, either spouse is less liberal on sex-role matters, and for black couples. Consistency level for housework items related to only some of these characteristics: education, age, and education difference.

It seems reasonable that this pattern of variables would lead to higher levels of inconsistency, since one would expect couples who are young, educated, have a higher income, and are more liberal and communicate more often and more effectively, particularly about topics relating to egalitarian household management. Such couples might tend to have more leisure for communication and to be more articulate. The difference scores, however, relate to almost no couple characteristics. Only age relates to the decision-making difference score and only wife's employment to that for housework. In other words, to some degree, couples who report inconsistently can be characterized, but the

Table 3.5
BIVARIATE RELATIONS BETWEEN CONSISTENCY MEASURES AND COUPLE CHARACTERISTICS

	Decisions		Housework	
	Consistency Level	Difference Score	Consistency Level	Difference Score
Wife education	lower education*a		lower education*a	
Husband education	lower education		lower education*	
Wife age	older*	younger*b	older*	
Husband age	older*	younger*	older*	
Age difference				
Educational difference	husband minus wife smaller*		husband minus wife smaller	
Absolute value age difference	greater age difference			
Absolute value education difference				
Family income	less income*			
Religious difference				
Wife employment status				wife employed*b
Race	black*			
Wife divorce thought				
Husband divorce thought				
Husband sex-role attitude	husband less liberal*			
Wife sex-role attitude	wife less liberal			
Wife housework equity				
Husband housework equity				

* p < .05 T-tests used when independent variable is a dichotomy, Pearson correlations where independent variable is continuous.

a Indicates characteristic which increases in inconsistency.

b Indicates characteristic which increases net overestimation by one or both spouses of own contribution.

tendency to report inconsistently in one direction or the other is much less systematic.

In an attempt to determine how well, as a whole, these characteristics explain degree of consistency for these two sets of items, we regress the consistency measures on all couple characteristics that relate significantly to any of the four measures. For three characteristics, we are constrained to enter only one variable in the equation at a time due to multicollinearity (i.e., age, education, sex-role attitudes). Controlling for other factors, only education and age relate significantly to consistency level for both decision making and housework items, and age appears to be a somewhat stronger predictor (see Table 3.6). The bivariate effects of other factors disappear and are apparently due to their relations with these two variables. We find greater inconsistency among couples with less highly educated husbands and with older wives.

The choice of husband's over wife's education, and wife's rather than husband's age and sex-role attitudes for these equations was somewhat arbitrary. These characteristics correlate .60, .93, and .47, respectively, in this data set. Both members of each pair behave similarly when substituted for each other in the equations. For similar reasons we omitted the education and age difference variables. In equations (not presented here) in which they are included instead of the respective

Table 3.6
REGRESSION OF CONSISTENCY MEASURES ON COUPLE CHARACTERISTICS
(STANDARDIZED COEFFICIENTS IN PARENTHESES)

| | Decisions | | Housework | |
	Inconsistency Level	Difference	Inconsistency Level	Difference
Husband education	-024(-.121)*	.003(.011)	-018(-.100)*	.001(.003)
Wife age	.010(.212)*	-.004(-.067)	.008(.186)*	-.001(-.011)
Family income	-.010(-.029)	.025(.059)	-.006(-.019)	-.014(-.035)
Wife race	.147(.060)	-.117(-.039)	-.040(-.018)	.025(.008)
Wife employment status	.018(.015)	-.051(-.036)	.059(.055)	.128(.092)*
Wife sex-role attitude	-.003(-.019)	.002(.010)	.009(.067)	.010(-.060)
a	.799	.069	.428	.443
R^2	.08	.01	.05	.01

*$p < .05$

spouse characteristics from which they are computed, we find that lesser education difference (husband minus wife) and greater age difference (absolute value of the difference) are significantly associated with more inconsistency. Not surprisingly, again we find that with one exception, the dependent variables representing actual differences between husband and wife responses are not explained by the variables measured here. The effect of wife's employment status on housework difference found in the bivariate tables, does remain.

Since the only substantial effects here appear to be due to age and education, it would seem worthwhile at this point to further specify these relationships by determining whether they are linear. In Table 3.7 we present the mean categories of inconsistency (difference scores are not included since they do not relate to age or education) within categories of husband's and wife's age and education. The relations are generally monotonic and somewhat linear. Consistency level increases with education.

The effect of age on decision-making consistency is fairly straightforward. For housework, however, the effects are neither linear nor monotonic; one can state with certainty only that couples over 40 are less consistent than those below. It is possible that other categorizations of age would provide more clear-cut results.

To summarize, we have found that the level of consistency in husband–wife reporting of factual data about household functioning varies

Table 3.7
MEAN CATEGORIES OF INCONSISTENCY WITHIN AGE AND EDUCATION LEVELS

	Housework		Decision-making	
	Husband's Education	Wife's Education	Husband's Education	Wife's Education
Education Categories				
Under 12 years	.78	.71	.96	.93
12 years	.70	.70	.83	.79
13–15 years	.67	.68	.82	.81
16–18 years	.58	.56	.63	.67
	Husband's Age	Wife's Age	Husband's Age	Wife's Age
Age Categories				
18–29	.59	.60	.65	.64
30–40	.59	.56	.62	.78
41–50	.67	.86	.80	.84
51+	.87	.81	1.02	1.04

across specific subject matter. At the aggregate level, reports about decision making are more in agreement than are reports about housework.
Spouses overestimate slightly their own relative to their spouse's contribution to housework. There is a slight tendency, somewhat more
pronounced for housework than decision-making items, for couples
who report similarly on one item on a topic to do so on other items of
that category. This tendency does not, however, extend *across* items in
different categories, that is, between housework and decision making.
There appears to be no overall couple characteristic of "consensus" or
"reporting consistency."

It does appear, however, that more highly educated and younger
couples tend to report more consistently than others. This applies only
to *degree* of consistency in reporting rather than *direction* of disagreement. Thus, although disagreement does not derive from random error,
since it is greater for certain types of couples, there is little evidence
that couples with certain sociodemographic characteristics disagree in
a systematic direction. The only characteristic that relates to direction
of disagreement for either topic is wife's employment status; members
of couples with employed wives are more likely than others to overestimate their own individual contribution to housework. Perhaps this is
because there is a norm indicating that husbands should contribute
more in those cases. It was felt by 80% of our respondents that housework should be divided equally when both spouses work full-time.
Since time-budget data show that this does not in fact occur (Walker
and Woods, 1976), there may be a tendency for husbands to overestimate their own contribution in such households and for wives to be
aware of the true state of affairs.

What does all this imply about how these behaviors should be measured? First, it may mean that separate parallel reports are more useful
for some topics than for others. For decision making, we would derive
the same conclusions about aggregate participation by interviewing
husbands or wives. Reliance on reports by one spouse would produce
less accurate data, particularly for older couples and those with less
education, but inaccuracies would not be systematic. For housework,
reliance on one member's report would result in overestimation of that
member's contribution on average, and this would be especially true
for wife-employed couples.

Dual reports may therefore be useful for measuring housework, but
unnecessary for decision making. They might serve to reduce error,
particularly among less educated and older couples, but only at great
expense. Random inclusion of husbands or wives might be a useful
way to deal with slight overreporting of own contribution to household

labor, although when absolute levels of contribution are of interest, time-budget data would be preferable to survey data. When the research goal is to relate relative contributions to demographic characteristics of couples, strong relationships will appear no matter who is the informant, and weak relationships are probably not worth the large additional expense involved in detecting them. This conclusion is consistent with the analysis of husbands' and wives' perceptions of housework in the next chapter.

CHAPTER FOUR

The Division of Household Labor

In agricultural societies, men's and women's work was organized around the household. After industrialization, household production became women's work (Reid, 1934:71). It has been suggested that since taking care of a family, like having a baby, apparently came naturally to women, it received little analytical attention (Moffat, 1976:90); sociologists preferred to study the attitudes, values, and daily activities of autoworkers, skid-row bums, medical students, and soldiers. Not a single entry in the 1968 International Encyclopedia of the Social Sciences refers to housework. Even in the 1970s neither the Marxists nor the New Home Economists ever closely looked inside households to find out how production is organized on a daily basis (R. Berk, 1980:137).

Technological development dramatically changed the methods of doing housework, but the basic tasks remain much the same. Care of young children, preparing and cleaning up after meals, doing laundry, shopping, and cleaning still require the most time, as they did a century ago. Laundry no longer involves carrying water, boiling, rubbing, bluing, rinsing, wringing, and hanging (Strasser, 1980), but housewives spend as much time at it because the standards have risen. Today a United States housewife spends as much time on housework as her counterpart did 50 years ago (Vanek, 1974)—an average of 52 hours a week for full-time housewives (Walker and Woods, 1976).

In contrast, employed wives average only 26 hours a week on housework. Yet their total time spent on household maintenance and financial support greatly outweighs that of their husbands, who typically spend little more time on housework than do husbands of unemployed women—about 11 hours for each (Walker and Woods, 1976:45, 50; Robinson, 1977; Gauger and Walker, 1980; Strober and Weinberg, 1980). Many researchers have suggested that employed women therefore have much less time than their husbands for sleep or leisure (Szalai, 1972; Meissner et al., 1975; Robinson, 1977; Pleck, 1977; Newland, 1980; Nickols and Fox, 1980) and that their household duties impede occupational success by cutting into time needed for the overtime work that professionals normally do in evenings or on weekends, by creating negative expectations in employers, by preventing the wives themselves from wanting more responsibilities or even full-time jobs, and, finally, by adding mental and physical stress (Gove and Tudor, 1973; Gove and Geerken, 1977; Rosenfield, 1980).

In the last decade the division of household labor, defined as unfair by feminists, has been seeping into public consciousness as an issue. Opinion polls now include questions about a proper division in a two-earner family. The public supports the notion that the division ought to be equal in such families (Scanzoni, 1978; Huber and Spitze, 1981), but this ideal is unrealized, and attitudes are apparently more egalitarian than behavior (Araji, 1977). Yet pressures to change the division of household labor will undoubtedly persist, since women's labor market equality largely hinges on the distribution of housework between spouses.

Using national probability survey data of 682 couples married to one another (N = 1364), the purpose of this chapter is to explain between-couple variation in the division of household labor in order to suggest how change may occur. We are limited, as past researchers have been, by having to use data collected at one point in time, although we are interested in change over a span of time. We are also limited by having to use household-level data. All couples operate in a context of male dominance, hence weighing the resources of individual members of couples gives an incomplete picture (D. Gillespie, 1971). Nevertheless, we feel that examining individual variations may fruitfully add to knowledge about future change.

THEORETICAL PERSPECTIVES

In this section we shall discuss what we expect to find and why we expect to find it in the context of earlier work on the determinants of the division of household labor (DOHL). We shall present and evaluate four hypotheses to be tested with our data. The four hypotheses are derived from several theoretical perspectives.

Time Availability

The hypothesis that available time determines the division of household labor stems from a theory developed by the New Home Economists. The theory suggests that decisions about the allocation of a husband's and wife's time to work in the marketplace and in the home result from men's and women's relative productivity in each sphere (Becker, 1976, 1981:14–37). The advantage of the theory is that it explains the division of household labor on rational grounds, thus demystifying it. However, the theory has some problems. The New Home Economists have never clarified whether decisions about housework and market work are made sequentially or concurrently, hence it would be difficult to confirm the theory in the absence of information on the actual decision-making process. It is just as plausible to suppose that women's prior assignment to housework makes them less able to compete with men in wage work as it is to conclude that women do housework because their wages are lower than men's. A worse problem is that, although wage rates straightforwardly measure market productivity, there is no way to measure household productivity. The New Home Economists simply assume that women's socialization makes them more productive than men in the home, as Ferber and Birnbaum (1977) point out. Hence, whatever its merits, the theory that differential economic productivity causes the household division of labor is not testable.

However, one can apply the reasoning of the New Home Economists and test whether the number of hours of wage work performed by husbands and wives affects the division of household labor. If the decisions about the household labor are made rationally, as the New Home Economists suggest, then the more hours of wage work that husbands perform relative to wives, the smaller will be the husband's share of housework.

However, data from time-budget studies and from surveys about the division of household labor do not clearly support the expectation that it is a rational function of each spouse's available time. Time-budget studies, the most precise way to measure household labor (F. Stafford and Duncan, 1979), have shown that employed women do fewer weekly hours of housework than do nonemployed women, but the husbands of both employed and nonemployed women do equally small amounts of housework (Meissner et al., 1975; Walker and Woods, 1976; Gauger and Walker, 1980). Analyses of survey data on relative spouse contributions reveal that the wife's employment increases the husband's share (Blood, 1963; Hoffman, 1963; Powell, 1963; Silverman and Hill, 1967; Bahr, 1974), unless other kin are able to do the work (Szinovacz, 1977). Apparently the husband's contribution increases simply because the wife's necessarily decreases (Pleck, 1977)—that is, only the husband's relative time, not his absolute time, spent in housework increases. Although a few recent studies have suggested small increases in husband's hours of housework associated with wives' employment (Presser, 1977; Pleck, 1977), these differences are not striking. Other studies have indicated little or no change (Moore and Sawhill, 1976; Walker, 1979; Gauger and Walker, 1980). We therefore expect a small increment in husbands' relative contribution to the division of household labor with wives' increased hours of market work but little or no change with decreases in husbands' market work. This expectation implies that, unlike the New Home Economists, we doubt that the division of household labor results mainly from a rational decision-making process.

Relative Power

The reason we doubt that the division of household labor can be explained on the basis of rational decision making is that women seem to be in a disadvantaged power position in the family (D. Gillespie, 1971). Their relative lack of power stems from their disadvantaged labor market status, from their disadvantaged status in the remarriage market as they age, and from their role in rearing children. Even if a women is working for pay, she is likely to earn less than her husband does and to be less able to support herself and her children (or to find a spouse substitute) were the marriage to dissolve. If this is true in the aggregate, leading to the generally uneven distribution of housework in two-earner families, perhaps intercouple variation in relative resources (such as wages and alternatives to the marriage) would relate to the division of household labor. Housework, generally not highly valued or rewarded (Oakley, 1974; Berheide et al., 1976; Ferree, 1980), may perhaps be described as routine domestic service work performed by a less powerful for a more powerful person.

The relative power or resources hypothesis has been tested in a number of ways. First, relative power may be a product of relative resources derived from or related to market position: education, earnings, or occupational status. Some studies have compared the effect of the relative availability of resources between spouses as required by the hypothesis. Others have tested the effects of absolute levels of such resources. Results for these tests have been mixed. More sharing of housework occurs at higher levels of the wife/husband earnings ratio (Scanzoni, 1978) but not at higher levels of the wife/husband education ratio (Farkas, 1976). When testing the effect of absolute levels of earnings and education, high earnings, educational level, and occupational status have been reported to lead to both lower (R. Clark et al., 1978) and higher male contribution to the division of household labor (Farkas, 1976; R. Berk and Berk, 1978). For wives, having managerial jobs is related to lower levels of responsibility for housework (R. Berk and Berk, 1978), but high earnings decrease only the time spent in cooking (F. Stafford and Duncan, 1979). Finally, more sharing of housework occurs among blacks (Farkas, 1976; F. Stafford and Duncan, 1979), which may reflect more equal levels of spouse resources.

A second way to conceptualize power is in terms of commitment to the marriage. According to the principle of least interest (Thibaut and Kelly, 1959), the person with the least interest in maintaining a relationship has the most power in it. Testing this effect empirically, R. Stafford et al. (1977) found that both men's and women's contribution to housework related directly to their commitment to the marital or cohabiting relationship.

A third way to measure relative power would be simply to ask couples to report who makes major household decisions (Ericksen et al., 1979). Although suffering from a number of conceptual or measurement problems (Safilios-Rothschild, 1969), such a measure would avoid the assumptions implicit in measuring power through relative resources.

Thus we expect to find a moderate to strong relationship between spouses' relative resources or power and their contribution to the division of household labor. Given the external environment in which they operate, equal resources may not yield equal time inputs, but the differences among couples should become apparent.

Sex-Role Attitudes

Popular conceptions of changing family organization often appear to stem from vague notions of changing values. Although it seems reasonable that less traditional attitudes might lead to a less traditional division of household labor, the reverse is also possible: Changed behaviors may induce changed attitudes. Problems of causal ordering plague attempts to test attitude–behavior relations such as this.

A second problem involves the identity of the reporting respondent.

Often wives tend to report for the household, so that only their attitudes are measured. The issue of which spouse's attitudes should be more influential has not been addressed in past research. We suggest that the husband's attitudes may be more influential than the wife's. Since the weight of tradition favors assigning the wife a disproportionate share of housework, she would probably welcome help no matter what her attitudes were. However, the husband would probably offer to help only if he favored more egalitarian roles.

Given problems of interpretation due to concurrent measurement of behavior and attitudes, evidence tends to favor a relation between sex-role attitudes and the division of household labor (R. Stafford et al., 1977; R. Clark et al., 1978; Scanzoni, 1978). However, Hiller (1980) reports that wives' attitudes (but not husbands') affect help with child care and neither wives' nor husbands' attitudes affect division of household labor. Although we expect a moderate relation between attitudes and the division of household labor, we would also expect, as previously stated, that husbands' attitudes will be more influential than wives' attitudes. We would also exercise due caution in interpreting the causal ordering. A further possibility here is that neither relatively high-wife resources nor nontraditional attitudes suffice alone to cause a break with custom. We shall also investigate the possibility of an interaction between the two, on the assumption that nontraditional sex-role attitudes would affect the division of household labor only if the wife had a relatively high share of resources to back her up.

Taste for Housework

Economists have suggested that women perform market work inversely to their "taste for housework" (Cain, 1966). Such a taste explained the labor force participation rates of young, childless college graduates during the mid-1960s (Spitze and Spaeth, 1978). Such a taste might also affect the division of household labor, either directly or through its effect on hours of market work; married women might actually confront the choice of whether to have one job or two jobs (Ferber and Birnbaum, 1980). Wives with a taste for housework might be, in fact, expressing a taste for doing *only* housework rather than housework plus market work.

This study tests the effect of husbands' and wives' taste for housework on the division of household labor. If, following the reasoning of the economists, a taste for housework is related to doing more or less of it, then we would expect men with such a taste to assume more responsibility for it than would men with no taste for it. However, we are not convinced that the economists are right. Furthermore, we know of no earlier study that tested the effect of either spouse's preference for housework on household labor. If wives are capable of preferring housework or market work, husbands should also be capable of making such a preference. We are inclined, however, to expect that husbands' preferences for housework will have little, if any, effect on the division of household labor, and wives' preferences to have some effect.

Summarizing our hypotheses, we expect the division of household labor to be affected somewhat by the availability of time, especially the wife's time. We expect strong effects of relative power, as measured by market-related resources, marital commitment, and decision making. We expect weak effects for sex-role attitudes and taste for housework, particularly for the husband's taste.

DATA AND METHODS

Data for this chapter come from a subsample (N = 1364) of husbands and wives married to one another, part of a national probability sample of United States households (N = 2002). The unit of analysis is the married couple.

Coding of variables is described in Table 4.1. We measured the constructs for each hypothesis as follows: The available-time hypothesis is tested using spouses' employment status (we have no data on number of hours worked) measured as a 0–1 dichotomy with part-time employment coded as .5. Means are .91 for husbands and .49 for wives.

Relative interpersonal power is measured three ways: first, by using earnings and education ratios of husbands and wives. Another market variable, occupational status, is not included since it would be missing for wives not currently employed. Second, we use spouses' perceptions of decision making. The summated scale includes five major and infrequent decisions. Third, we tap frequency of thoughts of divorce for each spouse. According to the principle of least interest, the person who gains least by maintaining a relationship or gains most by dissolving it thereby controls it more effectively (Thibaut and Kelly, 1959). Our operationalization assumes that a person considering divorce feels that she or he has potentially more to gain by marital dissolution (For a different analysis of thought of divorce, see Chapter 5.).

We measure sex-role ideologies by husbands' and wives' summated responses to a series of question about women's and men's work and family roles (see Appendix I, items 26f, g, h, i, j, l, n, o).

Table 4.1
CODING OF VARIABLES USED IN CHAPTER 4 ANALYSES

Variable	Coding
Employment status of wife, husband (EMPSTAT)	1=employed full-time, .5=part-time, 0-not employed
Earnings ratio of wife and husband (EARNRATIO)	Ratio of wife's to husband's 1977 earnings, coded in categories from 1=under $5,000 to 7=over $30,000 and recoded to midpoint
Mean earnings (EARNMEAN)	Husband and wife's combined mean earnings, coded as above
Education ratio (EDRATIO)	Ratio of wife's to husband's education, in years
Education mean (EDMEAN)	Husband and wife's combined mean education, in years
Husband's and wife's thought of divorce (DIVTHOUGHT)	"During the past year, would you say that you have thought about getting a divorce . . . .," coded 0=never (in response to filter question), 1=hardly ever, 2=once in awhile, 3=sometimes, 4=often
Decision-making (DECISION)	Husband and wife's combined mean sum of 5 items: who decides about vacations, husband's job, dwelling, wife's jobs, moving, coded 1=wife always, 2=wife usually, 3=both equally, 4=husband usually, 5=husband always (range 5-25)
Sex-role attitudes of husband, wife (SRATT)	Sum of responses to items (26f, g, h, i, j, l, n, o in Appendix I) regarding women's work and family roles, recoded so that 1=traditional, 5=nontraditional
Taste for housework of husband, wife (HWTASTE)	"In general, would you rather do the kind of work that people do on jobs or the kind of work that is done around the house," coded 0=job, .5=both or neither, 1=house
Wife's race	1=black, 0=other
Husband's age	Age coded in years
Division of household labor (DOHL)	Husband's mean contribution to 5 tasks: preparing meals, shopping, caring for children or old people, doing daily housework, cleaning up after meals, coded 1=wife always, 2=wife usually, 3=both equally, 4=husband usually, 5=husband always with a range of 1-5, adjusted to exclude jobs performed by someone other than husband or wife

Taste for housework is measured by asking each spouse whether he or she generally prefers work or home activities or both or neither. Controls are included for wife's race and husband's age. Either spouse's age or race could have been included; they correlate very highly. We also control for mean levels of education and earnings since this may relate to their relative levels.

Finally, measuring housework presents problems. We ask who does each of five daily household tasks, adjusted for tasks not performed in a given household, on a scale of 1–5. The high score indicates more work performed by the husband: meal preparation, food shopping, care of children and old people, daily housework, and after-meal cleanup. Although the most precise household labor data derive, as noted before, from time-budget studies, most research is based on surveys reporting spouses' relative contributions to household tasks because time-budget data are so costly to collect. Also, when research focuses on the relative rather than on the absolute contribution, precise hourly estimates are not needed.

Survey questions on household labor vary widely on three dimensions: number of tasks, number of response categories, and question wordings. The number of tasks included varies from 1, "household role sharing" (R. Clark et al., 1978) through 8 (Blood and Wolfe, 1960; Presser, 1977), 20 (R. Stafford et al., 1977), 33 (Hoffman, 1963), and 60 (R. Berk and Berk, 1978). Scaling such items is a problem because the data are not interval-level. Tasks that vary widely in the time needed to do them should not be weighted equally. For example, Blood and Wolfe (1960) weight sidewalk shoveling and evening meal cleanup equally; they include no item for preparing meals. R. Stafford et al. (1977) try to decrease the problem by weighting tasks by frequency of occurrence.

Response categories and question wordings also vary. Least amenable to interpretation is Presser's (1977:3): "Does your husband ever help you with . . . .?" Richard Berk and Sarah Berk (1978:441) ask: "Who generally does . . . ." each task, allowing multiple actors. Hoffman (1963) used children's reports on "major" and "minor" actors for each task, coded two and one in her scale. Blood and Wolfe (1960) and Rebecca Stafford et al. (1977) used response categories ranging from one partner doing the task always, one partner doing it more often, to both equally, yielding five categories. Although clearly imprecise, such measures have been justified (R. Berk and Berk, 1978) on the grounds that they produce results similar to precise hour and dollar measures.

Our measure shares some of the problems just noted, but it can be justified on theoretical and empirical grounds. Doing the five tasks in our measures requires 72% of total housework time spent by all household members: meal preparation, 15%; shopping, 12%; physical and nonphysical care of family members, 12% each; regular housecare, 12%; and after-meal cleanup, 9% (Walker and Woods, 1976:57). Except for washing clothes, 5%, these tasks comprise all the "frequently" done tasks reported in that time-budget survey. Using survey rather than time-budget data makes our hypothesis tests more conservative since differences between levels of sharing a given task may not be reflected. However, our data have the advantage of including attitudinal and demographic measures not included in time-budget data sets.

Husbands' and wives' reports on the division of household labor are not totally consistent (Booth and Welch, 1978; Douglas and Wind, 1978; S. Berk and Shih, 1980), but we have found that reports of total contribution correlate highly and that inconsistent reporting is unrelated to demographic or attitudinal variables across individual items.

Table 4.2
UNSTANDARDIZED COEFFICIENTS PREDICTING MEAN OF HUSBAND AND WIFE DOHL REPORTS (STANDARDIZED COEFFICIENTS IN PARENTHESES)

Independent Variables	1^a	2^b
Wife EMPSTAT	.478 (.368)*	.425 (.327)*
Husband EMPSTAT	-.359 (-.170)*	-.352 (-.166)*
EARNRATIO	-.020 (-.028)	-.025 (-.036)
EARNMEAN	-.000 (-.021)	-.000 (-.051)
EDRATIO	-.110 (-.050)	-.125 (-.057)
EDMEAN	.042 (.162)*	.031 (.118)*
Wife DIVTHOUGHT	-.004 (-.007)	-.019 (-.029)
Husband DIVTHOUGHT	-.065 (-.080)*	-.064 (-.070)*
DECISION	.004 (.014)	.010 (.038)
Wife SRATT	-	.010 (.069)
Husband SRATT	-	.017 (.100)*
Wife HWTASTE	-	-.140 (-.103)*
Husband HWTASTE	-	.089 (.043)
RACE	.182 (.070)**	.156 (.060)
Husband AGE	-.003 (-.064)	-.001 (-.017)
a	1.551	1.10
R^2	.19	.23
$\overline{X}$	1.78	

* $p < .05$

** $p < .10$

N = 661

a Employment status, power, and control variables.

b Attitude and taste variables added to column 1.

Table 4.3

UNSTANDARDIZED COEFFICIENTS PREDICTING HUSBANDS' AND WIVES' PERCEPTIONS OF DOHL (STANDARDIZED COEFFICIENTS IN PARENTHESES)

Independent variables	Husband perception 1^a	Husband perception 2^b	Wife perception 1^a	Wife perception 2^b
Wife EMPSTAT	.540 (.373)*	.481 (.332)*	.417 (.293)*	.369 (.259)*
Husband EMPSTAT	-.344 (-.146)*	-.343 (-.146)*	-.374 (-.161)*	-.361 (-.156)*
EARNRATIO	-.020 (-.025)	-.022 (-.028)	-.020 (-.025)	-.029 (-.038)
EARNMEAN	-.000 (-.039)	-.000 (-.060)	.000 (.000)	-.000 (-.032)
EDRATIO	-.103 (-.042)	-.117 (-.047)	-.117 (-.048)	-.134 (-.055)
EDMEAN	.041 (.143)*	.030 (.104)*	.042 (.151)*	.031 (.111)*
Wife DIVTHOUGHT	.021 (.030)	.006 (.008)	-.030 (-.042)	-.043 (-.061)
Husband DIVTHOUGHT	-.051 (-.057)	-.051 (-.057)	-.079 (-.089)*	-.078 (-.088)*
DECISION	.013 (.047)	.019 (.069)**	-.006 (-.022)	-.000 (-.000)
Wife SRATT	-	.004 (.023)	-	.017 (.104)*
Husband SRATT	-	.025 (.133)*	-	.009 (.048)
Wife HWTASTE	-	-.138 (-.091)*	-	-.143 (-.097)*
Husband HWTASTE	-	.121 (.053)	-	.057 (.025)
RACE	.160 (.056)	.137 (.047)	.203 (.072)**	.174 (.061)
Husband AGE	-.004 (-.072)**	-.002 (-.032)	-.002 (-.043)	-.000 (-.000)
a	1.50	1.02	1.60	1.19
R^2	.18	.21	.15	.17
$\bar{X}$	1.89		1.67	

* $p < .05$

** $p < .10$

$N = 661$

[a] Employment status, power, and control variables.

[b] Attitude and taste variables added to column 1.

Hence we conclude that analyzing mean husband–wife responses reasonably solves the inconsistency problem. We also report results for each spouse's responses for comparison.

Table 4.2 shows regressions for housework on all relevant independent variables. Equations are estimated with and without attitudinal variables, reflecting our necessarily cautious stance toward their causal ordering. Table 4.3 shows similar results using each spouse's perception as a dependent variable. These results are similar for most independent variables. Differences will be noted.

FINDINGS

Our first hypothesis concerned the effect of available time on the division of household labor. We expected a slight increase in husband's housework with his wife's increased hours of market work, but we expected little or no change with decrease in husbands' market work. We found that both wives' and husbands' employment status affect the division of household labor (see Table 4.2). Betas for the wife's employment status are substantially larger, the largest in the equation. However, the metric coefficients imply only small substantive differences. Full-time employment of a wife (or nonemployment of a husband) would yield a change of .4–.5 on a scale of 1–5. As stated earlier, this effect probably reflects decreased input of wives rather than increases in husbands' housework, except perhaps in the case of nonemployed husbands. We have no way of distinguishing between these alternative interpretations.

Our second hypothesis concerned the effect of relative power or resources on the division of household labor. It was tested by using as variables the wife/husband education and earnings ratios, husband's and wife's perception of family decision making, and frequency of thinking about divorce. The hypothesis received less support than we expected (see Table 4.2). The wife/husband earnings ratio, education ratio, and perceptions of decision making failed to have significant effects. Mean education level, included as a control, had a large positive effect on the husband's contribution to the division of household labor, perhaps reflecting subcultural differences among couples. The only power variable to significantly affect the division was the husband's thought of divorce, which decreased his contribution. The wife's thought of divorce had no such impact. This outcome has common sense plausibility. A badly kept house might reflect on the wife, but not the husband. Hence a husband who dislikes his wife can withdraw from housework without loss of self-esteem.

The problems of causal ordering between attitudes and the division of household labor, noted earlier, also might be raised with regard to thinking about divorce. Conceivably an inequitable division of labor might cause the wife to think of divorce. However, the lack of an observed relationship between the two variables make such an interpretation improbable. Similarly, a rare husband, overburdened with housework, might contemplate divorce. Again, the observed relationship makes this interpretation unlikely.

Our third hypothesis predicted a moderate relationship between sex-role attitudes and the division of household labor. Husbands' attitudes were expected to be more influential than wives' attitudes. We found that husbands' but not wives' sex-role attitudes affected the division. As we suggested earlier, this may reflect a greater willingness of non-traditional husbands to pick up a more equal share of work, or it may reflect an attitudinal change in response to changes in household organization that resulted from the wife's employment. These effects will be discussed shortly when we compare husbands' and wives' perceptions of the division of household labor.

We also hypothesized that an interaction might occur between the wife's resources and nontraditional sex-role attitudes. In order to obtain a more equitable division of household labor, wives would need higher relative levels of resources, and one or both spouses would need to hold nontraditional attitudes. In other words, wives would need to believe that their demands for help were justified and have the resources to back them up. Although a high level of multicollinearity between and among interaction terms and their components made such tests difficult, we found no significant increase in explained variance when either interaction term was added (not shown).

Finally, we determined whether taste for housework might influence the division of household labor either directly or indirectly through time spent in market work. Again, causal ordering might be questioned since a relationship could arise due to rationalization. Anyone, particularly a wife, might choose to define herself as enjoying housework in order to feel more satisfied with her life. In fact, we do find an effect of wives' taste for housework and not of husbands' taste. Pragmatically, this variable reflects different choices for each spouse. Only 8% of the husbands expressed a preference for housework over job, whereas 43% of the wives did so. For husbands, this is clearly a nontraditional response. Again, it is difficult to arrive at a clearcut interpretation of the wives' response.

In addition to mean income and education, we included two demographic variables as controls: husband's age and wife's race. Both characteristics are so highly correlated between spouses that the inclusion of only one seemed adequate. Neither had a strong effect, but black couples tended slightly to have a more equitable division of household labor, consistent with past research.

In Table 4.3 we present the same analysis with husbands' and wives' perceptions, rather than their mean, as dependent variables. To the extent that they relate in a similar manner to the variables discussed earlier, we will have a greater degree of confidence that these effects do not result from biased perceptions.

Although two of the effects reported in Table 4.2, husband's race and thought of divorce, appear to arise more as a product of one spouse's perception than the other's, the differences in size of coefficients for husband's and wife's perceptions are not large. The only major difference between the two sets of equations is in the effects of sex-role attitudes. Only the husband's sex-role attitudes affect *his* perception of the division of household labor, whereas the wife's attitudes affect *her* perceptions. This may reflect two processes of rationalization: Each spouse may distort perceptions of the division of household labor slightly in order to make them conform to sex-role ideologies, but she or he may also do the reverse. Since other effects are similar and spouses' perceptions correlate .65, we would expect more of the latter to be taking place.[1]

Analysis by Wife's Employment Status

Since an equitable division of household labor presumably would be based in large part on available time and since many of the variables examined here (such as wife/husband earnings ratio and sex-role attitudes) are related to the wife's employment status, we further specify these effects by separating our sample by wife's employment status (see Table 4.4). Only full-time and nonemployed wives are included. The 8% of husbands who are not employed full-time are also excluded to clarify other effects.

We find that, for both groups, the explained variance is quite low, indicating that much of the previously explained variance related to the wife's employment status. Mean education level of spouses con-

---

[1]This analysis also sheds some light on the interpretation of survey data intended to test hypotheses about housework. Tests of hypotheses involving demographic variables appear to have the same results whether the husband or the wife is the respondent. Tests of attitudinal effects do not. Whatever discrepancy exists between husband and wife reports may relate to rationalizations on the part of one or both spouses, causing either attitude change or biased reporting of the division of household labor. Thus attitudinal hypotheses would be best tested using time-budget data for housework, with separate interviews of the husband and the wife for attitudinal data. Such data do not now exist. Future time-budget studies would do well to incorporate two additional features: (a) extensive interview data from both spouses for analyses in conjunction with data on hours; and (b) a longitudinal design for a panel of couples to determine under what conditions these behaviors shift over time.

Table 4.4

UNSTANDARDIZED COEFFICIENTS PREDICTING MEAN HUSBAND AND WIFE DOHL REPORTS BY WIFE'S EMPLOYMENT STATUS (STANDARDIZED COEFFICIENTS IN PARENTHESES)

Independent variables	Full-time employed wives[a] 1^b	2^c	Non-employed wives[a] 1^b	2^c
EARNRATIO	.015 (-.026)	.024 (-.040)	–	–
EARNMEAN	.000 (.068)	.000 (.032)	-.000 (-.099)	-.000 (-.099)
EDRATIO	-.375 (-.131)*	-.375 (-.131)*	.058 (.035)	.058 (.035)
EDMEAN	.048 (.182)*	.035 (.132)	.045 (.208)*	.042 (.194)*
Wife DIVTHOUGHT	-.026 (-.044)	-.038 (-.064)	.027 (.044)	.022 (.035)
Husband DIVTHOUGHT	-.070 (-.102)	-.067 (-.097)	-.032 (-.040)	-.038 (-.046)
DECISION	.007 (.027)	.015 (.053)	-.002 (-.009)	.000 (.004)
Wife SRATT	–	.010 (.070)	–	-.000 (-.001)
Husband SRATT	–	.026 (.155)*	–	.005 (.032)
Wife HWTASTE	–	-.061 (-.044)	–	-.123 (-.104)
Husband HWTASTE	–	.105 (.047)	–	.100 (.063)
RACE	.109 (.051)	.120 (.056)	.090 (.029)	.054 (.017)
Husband AGE	.002 (.044)	.005 (.088)	-.007 (-.149)*	-.005 (-.122)**
a	1.50	.79	1.28	1.21
R^2	.08	.12	.08	.09
$\bar{X}$	2.02		1.53	
N	257		270	

* $p < .05$

** $p < .10$

a Husbands employed full-time

b Employment status, power, and control variables.

c Attitude and taste variables added to column 1.

tinues to exert an effect for both groups, perhaps indicating subgroup cultural differences in norms. For employed wives, however, the education ratio also affects the division of household labor but in a counterintuitive direction. Wives with less education relative to their husbands receive more help from them. Apparently education does not function as a resource. On the contrary, the higher the husbands' education, the more they may contribute in the housework, regardless of their wives' educational attainment.

The effect of husband's thought of divorce is no longer significant, but it is of similar size as that reported in Table 4.2, probably reflecting the smaller sample. This effect is much larger for employed-wife couples than others, however, perhaps because housework is more likely to be negotiated in such families. Similarly, the effect of the husband's sex-role attitudes applies only to those families. The husband's attitudes may be irrelevant if the wife is not employed.

Finally, the husband's age comes into play for families with non-employed wives. Such families are likely either to be quite young with small children or to be much older, with the adults close to retirement age. In the former instance, the wife may be unable to do everything that needs to be done even if she is home full-time. Any recent change in norms regarding housework would also be highlighted in the contrast between these groups.

DISCUSSION

In this test of four hypotheses regarding the division of household labor, we have found that:

1. The wife's time (as measured by employment status) affects it more than does the husband's.
2. It relates to relative power only as reflected by the husband's thought of divorce.
3. It relates to sex-role attitudes of the spouse whose perceptions of the division of household labor are being measured, and most strongly to the husband's.
4. It relates to the wife's taste for housework.

This last effect disappears with controls for the wife's employment status; it therefore presumably results from its relation to her employment. Both attitudinal effects have unclear interpretations of causal ordering. There is no interaction effect between sex-role attitudes and relative resources. There are very slight race and age effects, and a relatively strong impact of mean educational level of both spouses.

Thus our expectations of a relatively strong impact of relative resource variables, based on the notion that housework represents menial labor performed by a less powerful person for a more powerful one was not borne out. This finding may imply that this view of housework is distorted or that our measures of relative resources are inadequate. It may also reflect the fact that, despite variation in relative resources of spouses, women rarely attain an equal footing with their husbands. Husbands can more easily survive a divorce financially than can wives, and husbands face a more favorable remarriage market because men's average age at death is lower than women's and men typically marry younger wives. As long as this combination of factors persists, it may be unrealistic to expect much variation in the division of household labor due to variation in women's lack of power.

Perhaps the fact that the division of household labor is more congruent with attitude–taste variables than with relative power should not be surprising, given the relatively static nature of our data. Most marriages are not, after all, permanent battlegrounds. People come into marriages with expectations as to how housework should be divided. They probably tend to marry persons who share those beliefs. If one spouse changes those beliefs, the ensuing negotiation may result in either a new consensus or, in some instances, a divorce. What we see here is, in the majority of cases, an equilibrium between attitudes and behaviors, with little evidence of any negotiation that may take place before or early in marriage.

We feel little cause for optimism here about future rapid change toward a more egalitarian division of household labor. Any change is likely to occur slowly as a result of a multitide of individual adjustments. Government policy can have little impact on the division of household labor. Even in those countries that officially endorse sharing of housework, such policies are viewed as unenforceable (Newland, 1980). Our government shows no interest in this type of "interference" in private affairs. The most likely source of change over the long run appears to be women's increased labor-force participation, which leads to necessary cuts in the hours of housework. The slack will be picked up either by husbands or by increased purchase of services.

Although we found no evidence here of any effect of relative income, perhaps women's attainment of actual parity with men's salaries may affect the division of household labor. We did not examine actual occupations here, but it is possible that decreases on sex segregation of jobs would lead to eventual changes in the division of household labor, since "women's jobs" have traditionally been more flexible than men's in relation to family needs. However, this long-term change is likely to occur at the expense of employed women in the interim.

CHAPTER FIVE

Considering Divorce: Toward A Sociological Theory of Marital Instability[1]

In this chapter we test the effect of individual self-interest on reported thoughts about divorce. In preindustrial society, marriage and reproduction tended to be governed by unconscious rationality—collective behavior patterns that benefit a species despite individual unawareness of them (Wrigley, 1978:135). Industrialization shifted the motivation for much individual behavior from collective folk wisdom to conscious self-interest. The theory of the demographic transition describes how reproductive behavior responded to increasing costs and decreasing rewards for childbearing in Europe during the nineteenth century.

In line with the popular belief that couples should marry for love, not to preserve or increase family wealth, individual self-interest has become a more dominant motive for marriage ever since the period of protoindustrialization. Today it is almost the only acceptable reason to get married. Indeed, the decline in family functions long ago led sociologists to conclude that personal relationships were the most important social contribution of the family (Ogburn and Tibbits, 1933:692).

[1]This chapter is a revision of an article published in the *American Journal of Sociology* 86 (1980):75–89. Jan Gorecki, William Form, Robert Schoen, and Linda Waite provided useful comments.

Beginning in the 1930s, social scientists vigorously but inconclusively sought the secret of marital adjustment (Kirkpatrick, 1968). Hence the attempt to formulate a satisfactory theory of marriage met limited success. In the 1950s a popular theory held that marriage fills complementary instrumental and expressive needs. By the 1970s this theory was discredited. Women's contribution to subsistence and men's contribution to expressive activities have been much greater than earlier theorists had supposed (Aldous, 1977:177). Empirical studies of the correlates of marital happiness also met difficulties. A recent sophisticated study reports that the lack of strong positive associations between reported marital happiness and a number of status variables unexpectedly casts doubt on a number of widely held generalizations about marriage (N. Glenn and Weaver, 1978:276). Yet the accelerating rise in divorces (Westoff, 1978a) indicates a need for a theory of marital stability.

A theoretical approach that may be fruitful because it includes factors that are historically associated with the rise in the divorce rate is Gary Becker's (1973, 1974, 1976, 1981) economic theory of marriage, based on individual-level empirical findings and also extended as a theory of marital instability (Becker et al., 1977). According to Becker, marriages dissolve when the utility expected from staying married falls below the utility expected from divorce. The theory assumes that individuals maximize utilities from commodities they expect to consume in a lifetime, ranking marital strategies by their full wealth and choosing the highest. Since uncertainty prevails, unfavorable outcomes may occur.

Becker predicts that dissolution probabilities are lowered by an increase in the expected value of positively sorted variables (e.g., men's earnings); an increase in the time spent seeking a spouse (age at marriage); and an increase in marital-specific capital (e.g., children), which increases with duration and decreases with order of marriage. Dissolution probabilities are raised by unexpected changes in values of positively sorted variables (e.g., husband's earnings), by an increase in the expected value of negatively sorted variables (e.g., wife's earnings relative to husband's), and by a larger discrepancy in mate traits (e.g., IQ, religion, race) than would occur in optimal sorting (Becker et al., 1977:1156–1157).

Becker's predictions are generally consistent with empirical findings. Husband's income relates negatively to marital dissolution (Cutright, 1971; Becker et al., 1977). However, recent research on the distinctive effects of husband's employment stability and income level—a

prominent topic during the Depression—shows that husband's employment stability decreases the probability of dissolution regardless of
income level (Cherlin, 1978; see also Ross and Sawhill, 1975). An increase in wife's income and the ratio of her earnings to family income
increases dissolution (Ross and Sawhill, 1975; Cherlin, 1976, 1978;
Moore and Waite, 1981). Age at marriage (Bumpass and Sweet, 1972;
Ross and Sawhill, 1975; Becker et al., 1977; Moore and Waite, 1981)
and duration of marriage relate negatively to the dissolution (Ross and
Sawhill, 1975; Cherlin, 1977), although duration does not predict
whether couples who apply for divorce will carry through or dismiss
the action (Levinger, 1979:148). Marital-specific capital deters dissolution when such capital takes the form of assets (Cherlin, 1977; Moore
and Waite, 1981), but the effect of the presence of young children is
unclear (Becker et al., 1977—but see Becker, 1981:224; Cherlin, 1977;
Moore and Waite, 1981). The relationship of childlessness to divorce
may be spurious since divorce occurs most often in the early years of
marriage (Monahan, 1955; cf. Kannoy and Miller, 1980). Indeed, recent
research based on Ryder and Westoff's 1970 sample of ever-married
women in childbearing ages reported no simple monotonic relationship. Dissolution rates were highest for couples with no children or
with fairly large families and lowest for couples with intermediate
numbers of children (Thornton, 1977). Discrepancies in spouse traits
such as age and religion increased dissolution (Bumpass and Sweet,
1972; Becker et al., 1977). Finally, marriages beyond the first are
slightly more likely to dissolve (Becker et al., 1977; McCarthy, 1978).

Although Becker's theory explains a variety of findings, it has several
problems from a sociological perspective. First, it fails to predict explicitly the utility of situations for the individuals experiencing them.
Economists take utility as a given because their deductive theories
cannot readily handle inexact variables (Maynes, 1978:391), hence
their utilities tend to be commonsense notions about typical human
preferences. Yet one cannot know why spouses decide to divorce unless one knows how they evaluate a particular situation.

Second, every divorce involves two people whose experience and
perceptions of benefits and costs may differ. In principle, Becker's theory could separate such effects, but in practice Becker makes no attempt to do so. Yet some variables could oppositely affect a husband's
or wife's desire for divorce. A wife's high earnings may motivate her to
end a bad marriage. This effect could be reinforced if the husband were
threatened by his wife's earnings (Komarovsky, 1973) or if he felt that
her earnings relieved him of financial responsibility. In contrast, the
wife might be a more attractive partner if she had higher earnings. Her

motivation to end the marriage might be offset by his desire to continue it. In sum, Becker's theory predicts that a particular event will increase the probability of dissolution, but it does not tell us why.

Nor is it known which sex is more likely to want a divorce. A recent study suggests that, as the grounds become more liberal, men are more likely to begin proceedings than women are. After the 1971 passage of a no-fault divorce law in Florida, about two-thirds of the petitioners were men. Before the law had been passed, two-thirds were women (B. Gunter, 1977). This report suggests the possibility that men may be more likely to seek divorce than women when the removal of social stigma permits the "true" preference to appear.

Third, because Becker's theory does not distinguish the ways husbands and wives may perceive costs and benefits, it cannot take into account new evaluations of the household division of labor. Although wives' employment has become acceptable because husbands like living in two-earner families, the division of household labor is now more likely to be contentious than it was in the past. Married women, fully employed or not, typically perform most of the daily care of house and children (Farkas, 1976; Walker and Woods, 1976). At the turn of the century, the typical husband was a manual worker or farmer. Today a majority of husbands work in white-collar jobs, doing labor that contrasts strikingly with the work that wives do at home. Hence women's household duties may seem relatively onerous to contemporary wives. Wives who reject traditional role definitions may evaluate their marriages according to whether they see their husbands doing a fair share of the daily housework. Indeed, sex-role attitudes may be so basic in marital interaction that major differences may influence both spouses to think more often about divorce. In sum, the basic problem with Becker's theory is that he fails to deal with individuals.

We shall therefore investigate individual motivations by testing husbands and wives separately. We shall also examine the effects of sociological variables in addition to the economic variables that Becker uses. We are thus able to examine individual motivations by testing the effect of divorce-related background factors on each spouse's thought of divorce. We are thus able to take into account the fact that marriage may differ markedly for men and women, something we could not do if we used the event of divorce itself as the dependent variable.

Our dependent variable is therefore the question used by Campbell et al. (1976:322): "Has the thought of getting a divorce from your husband/wife ever crossed your mind?" Choosing this wording in order to make it easy for respondents to indicate even ephemeral doubts, Campbell expected that many respondents would admit to having "ever" thought about divorce. Sociologists with whom we discussed the item were also certain that the thought of divorce must have crossed almost everyone's mind, but this expectation is wrong. About 64% of the women and 71% of the men in the Campbell study reported that they had never thought of divorce, and their response correlated highly with the degree of satisfaction with the marriage and with whether the respondent had ever wished to be married to someone else (Campbell *et al.*, 1976:322).[2]

Logically, marital satisfaction, thought of divorce, and divorce itself lie on a continuum, with fewer persons in successive categories. The propensity to end a bad marriage intervenes between marital satisfaction and divorce. Unhappily married people think of divorce only if it is possible for them, and presumably only a fraction of those who consider divorce translate thought to deed. Our measure separates spouses' motivations and sorts out persons who are not only dissatisfied in marriage but who are also willing to consider divorce; it should be quite stable since it concerns "ever" having thought of divorce. Measures of marital happiness are subject to short-term fluctuation (N. Glenn and Weaver, 1978:275). Perhaps the best reason for exploring the correlates of thinking about divorce is the need to know much more about the new realities of family life, especially because of their potential effects on children (Bumpass and Rindfuss, 1979:64).

HYPOTHESES

Because the most critical factors historically associated with the rise in divorce are the fertility decline and the increase in women's labor-

---

[2]The only study using a similar dependent variable is Booth and White's (1980) 1978 telephone survey of a Nebraska probability sample that included 1364 married respondents. The study tried to link marital satisfaction with thought of divorce. Respondents were asked if they had thought about divorce in the last two years. The proportion who had was lower than that of persons who had "ever" thought of it in Campbell's study: 8% of the men and 12% of the women. The independent variables were chosen on the basis of a review of the literature on marital satisfaction: marital duration, presence of children, age at marriage, education, values pertaining to marital sanctity, feelings of financial security, husband's and wife's employment, and income. Booth and White (1980) report that thinking about divorce had some of the same correlates as marital dissatisfaction but also some unique patterns. Age at marriage, marital duration, religiosity, and income affected marital dissatisfaction independently of their effect on thought of divorce. The wife's employment had no strong effect on marital dissatisfaction but importantly affected thought of divorce. Contrary to the Booth and White's expectation, the presence of preschool children was likely to lead to thought of divorce. Had this

force participation, we expect that the wife's work history and earnings, the presence of children, and the wife's definition of a fair division of household labor will most importantly affect thought of divorce. Specifically, we expect that:

1. Wives are more likely than husbands to think of divorce and to think of it more often because they are more likely to define the domestic division of labor as unfair. The costs of marriage are higher for women than for men.

2. We modify Becker's hypothesis that husband's earnings decrease the probability of divorce because it may be time-bound and better suited to a period when most wives of high-income husbands were not employed, making divorce costly for husbands and especially for wives and because at low-income levels, husband's employment stability is more important than his income level (Ross and Sawhill, 1975; Cherlin, 1978). Since we lack data on husband's work history, we hypothesize only that husband's income will insignificantly affect thought of divorce for both spouses.

In contrast, we expect the ratio of wife's earnings to husband's and also the wife's work history—her employment stability—to affect both spouses thought of divorce. The effects should be stronger for wives because the impact of their labor-force participation and earnings is direct, hence presumably stronger than it is for their husbands.

3. Persons who marry young are more likely than others to experience divorce because of the limited time invested in search. This should also affect thought of divorce for both spouses, but the effect may be greater for the husband since his ability to acquire information about his qualities relative to those of other potential spouses is less limited by early marriage than is the wife's, whose activity may be constrained by early pregnancy.

4. An increase in such marital-specific capital as young children should reduce the probability of thinking about divorce for both spouses, but more for the wife than for the husband, since she typically, if divorced, must care for the children and work outside the home.

5. A larger discrepancy in spouse traits (education, age, religion) should raise the probability of thinking of divorce for both spouses. Divorce may be contemplated more often by the spouse with the higher level of a trait that can be quantitatively evaluated (education).

---

report been available when we were formulating our hypotheses, some of them would have been altered, especially the one concerning the effect of the presence of young children on thought of divorce.

6. Thought of divorce will decline with marital duration, owing to the acquisition of marital-specific capital. We expect the effect to be greater for wives than for husbands because wives' value in the marriage market declines much more sharply with age. Also, women's investments in household or market skills appreciate much less over time than do men's market skills. Household skills reach maximum potential quickly, whereas women's market skills may depreciate or appreciate slowly because of discontinuous labor force participation and job choices made for family convenience.

7. Probability of thought of divorce is higher in marriages beyond the first, both because divorce-prone persons should be found in higher-order marriages and because such marriages accumulate less marital-specific capital (such as children) than first ones. If the major cause of this higher probability is "divorce proneness," thought of divorce should increase for previously divorced persons but not for their new spouses. If it is marital-specific capital, both a previously divorced person and a spouse in a second marriage should think of divorce more often. We test these alternatives by determining whether neither spouse, both, or only the previously divorced one is affected.

8. Differences in husband's and wife's attitudes on women's proper roles should increase thought of divorce for both spouses, but especially for wives.

9. Employed wives who feel that husbands should equally share housework but who also do most of the housework themselves will think of divorce more often than will other wives.

DATA AND METHODS

This study is based on telephone interview data obtained from 682 married couples (N = 1,364), part of a national probability sample of United States households (see Chapter 2). After deletion of missing data, the number was reduced to 1,288.

Our main dependent variable is a dichotomy (coded 1 = yes, 0 = no) in response to the question, "Has the thought of getting a divorce from your husband/wife ever crossed your mind?" Using regression analysis with splits near or outside the 25–75% range may bias findings because it violates several assumptions that the technique requires (M. Gillespie, 1977). We therefore use probit analysis, a maximum-likelihood technique suited to estimate a dichotomous dependent variable. We report probit slopes evaluated at the same point on the curve (P = .30) for husband and wife equations. These slopes can be compared across equations and interpreted similarly to unstandardized regression coefficients.

Our independent variables are in four categories. First, individual characteristics are measured for husband, wife, or both: age at marriage, coded in years; income, coded in dollars per year; previously divorced, coded 1 = yes, 0 = no. Two characteristics of wife's employment include current employment, coded 1 = current full- or part-time employment and 0 = no employment. The wife's employment history is measured by an index which includes number of years employed in the past 10, adjusted for part-time and part-year work.

Second, objective characteristics of the marriage include duration in years and age of youngest child (coded as two dummy variables, one for 0–5 years, another for 6–11 years). Spouse's age and education differences are computed by subtracting the wife's years from the husband's. Religious difference is coded as a dummy variable (1 = difference, 0 = both protestant, Catholic, Jewish, other, or no religion). We also included wife's earnings as a percentage of family income.

Third, subjective characteristics of the marriage include both spouses' perceptions of who prepares meals, shops for goods, cares for children or old people, does daily housework, and cleans up after meals—the five tasks that comprise the bulk of the time spent in housework (Walker and Woods, 1976). An index is based on the number of these tasks for which the husband does half or more of the work. We also include spouses' responses to the question, "If a husband and wife both work full-time, do you think that the wife should be responsible for the housework (coded 0), that the husband should help her (also coded 0), or that the husband and wife should share daily housework equally (coded 1)?"

Fourth, two questions measure spouses' sex-role attitudes: "A married woman should be able to have a job even if it is not always convenient for her family," and "By nature women are happiest when they are making a home and caring for children." These two items were recoded so that 4 indicated the liberal response and 1 indicated the most traditional. Responses were summed, then we constructed a difference score between husband and wife.

Several variables were eliminated after preliminary runs revealed problems of multicollinearity. We could not include both husband's and wife's earnings and wife's percentage of family income. Since absolute earnings were less important theoretically (and also had no effect), they were omitted from the equations. Also, we could not include wife's employment history and current employment status in the same equations. Since current employment status could be a response to as well as a cause of thoughts of divorce, it was omitted in favor of the more straightforward employment history measure.

FINDINGS

As expected, more wives (30%) than husbands (23%) had ever thought about divorce, and they had thought of it more often. Of husbands who said yes, 51% of their wives also said yes. Of wives who ever thought of divorce, 8% had done so often; 11%, sometimes; 21%, once in awhile; and 60%, hardly ever; and of husbands, 6%, 8%, 16%, and 70%, respectively (see Table 5.1 for means and standard deviations of all variables).

The absolute level of the husband's earnings, as predicted (in contrast to Becker), had no effect on either spouse's thoughts of divorce, nor did the absolute level of the wife's earnings. We expected wife's earnings as a percentage of family income to affect wives' more than husbands' thoughts of divorce, but it affected neither spouse's thoughts (see Table 5.2). Although the wife/husband earnings ratio may affect the decision to dissolve a marriage, it apparently fails to affect initial thoughts of divorce.

We also tested the effect of the wife's history of employment in the past 10 years. The number of years she was employed (adjusted for full-time and part-time employment) positively affected the wife's thought of divorce, about one percentage point for each year of employment. However, the effect on husband's thought of divorce is significant only at the .13 level and only when the wife's earnings as a percentage of total family income has been removed from the equation (since they are highly correlated). Apparently the wife's potential for economic independence affects wives more than it does husbands. This finding is consonant with those of an 8-year panel study showing that employed women experience more marital dissatisfaction than either housewives or employed husbands (Haynes and Feinleib, 1980:135). One cannot, of course, deduce the wife's reasoning from these data. Possibly her ability to support herself is decisive. On the other hand, the stress resulting from a double workload may heighten her feelings of dissatisfaction.

Age at marriage negatively affected wives but not, unexpectedly, husbands. For every additional year of age at marriage, the wife is 1% less likely to have thought of divorce. Women who marry young have spent less time searching for a spouse and are more likely to have married to cover a pregnancy. We expected age at marriage to affect the husband since he can more easily continue to gather information about alternative mates. Possibly, the earlier a woman marries, the more likely are her sex-role attitudes to diverge from her husband's over time.

The effect of the age of the youngest child is partly as expected. The presence of a child under 6 years has a negative effect (7%) on the husband's thought of divorce (significant only at the .11 level). A negative effect makes some sense: when a marriage dissolves, young children typically live with the mother. A husband who does not want to be separated from a young child would therefore tend not to consider divorce during this period. Divorced women are not usually separated from their children, hence they bear a double burden of market work

Table 5.1
MEANS, STANDARD DEVIATIONS, AND VARIABLE DESCRIPTIONS

Variable	Mean	S.D.	Description
Husband's Div. thought	.23	.46	Has the thought of getting a divorce from your husband/wife ever crossed your mind, coded 1=yes, 0=no.
Wife's Div. thought	.30	.42	
Wife's earnings/fam. income	.18	.21	Wife's earnings as percentage of total family income.
Wife work past 10 years	4.56	3.66	Adjusted (part-year, part-time) number of years wife worked in past 10.
Husband's age at marriage	25.28	6.87	Husband's age at marriage in years.
Wife's age at marriage	22.60	5.74	Wife's age at marriage in years.
Youngest child under 6	.25	.43	Youngest child less than 6, dummy variable.
Youngest child 6-11	.21	.40	Youngest child 6-11, dummy variable.
Education difference	.42	2.35	Years difference in husband/wife education levels.
Age difference	2.68	4.60	Year difference in husband/wife age.
Re igious difference	.22	.42	Husband/wife in different categories, Protestant, Catholic, Jewish, other, none, dummy variable.
Marital duration	15.12	11.50	Years duration, present marriage.
Husband previous divorce	.14	.34	Husband divorced at least once, dummy variable.
Wife previous divorce	.13	.34	Wife divorced at least once, dummy variable.
Sex-role att. difference	.19	1.38	Negative value=husband more liberal than wife, 0=both the same, positive value= wife more liberal, with a range of -6 to 6.
Division of housework	.98	1.22	Number of household tasks (preparing meals, food shopping, childcare, daily housework, meal cleanup) for which husband does equal share or more.
Husband housework att.	.78	.42	Husband/wife believe that housework should be shared equally if spouses work full-time, 1=yes, 0=no.
Wife housework att.	.78	.42	

Table 5.2
PROBIT SLOPES (EVALUATED AT P = .30) TO PREDICT WHETHER RESPONDENT HAS EVEN THOUGHT ABOUT DIVORCE FROM CURRENT SPOUSE (N = 644)

	Wives	(t-value)	Husbands	(t-value)
Wife's earnings/family income	-.062	-.70	.039	.42
Wife work past 10 years	.014*	2.30	.007[a]	1.11
Husband's age at marriage	---	---	-.001	-.16
Wife's age at marriage	-.010*	-2.61	---	---
Youngest child under 6	-.016	-.36	-.074[b]	-1.60
Youngest child 6 to 11	.130*	2.75	.036	.73
Education difference	.0001	.05	.011	1.30
Age difference	.004	1.02	-.010*	-2.17
Religious difference	.038	.86	.104*	2.26
Marital duration	-.004*	-2.28	-.005*	-2.75
Husband previous divorce	.003	.53	.016	.25
Wife previous divorce	-.005	-.65	-.138**	-1.74
Sex-role attitude difference	.001	.73	-.001	-.09
Division of housework	-.030**	-1.87	-.025[c]	-1.50
Wife's attitude housework	.095*	2.04	.077[d]	1.57
Husband's attitude housework	-.032	-.73	-.070[c]	-1.51
Variance explained	.09		.09	

* p < .05

** .05 < p < .10

[a] p=.13 when wife's earnings ratio is omitted. The correlation between wife's earnings/family income and wife's employment in past 10 years is .59.

[b] p=.11

[c] p=.13

[d] p=.12

and child care. The positive impact on the wife of having a youngest child 6–11 years old may reflect the tendency for this burden to decrease when children reach school age. A woman may begin to think of divorce when single-parenthood appears more feasible.

Spouse education discrepancy affects neither spouse. Age differences affect only husbands, who think less of divorce if they are older than their wives. Religious differences greatly increase (by 10%) husband's thought of divorce, especially if he is Protestant married to a wife with no religion or to a Roman Catholic (see Table 5.3). Why do religious differences affect husbands but not wives? Perhaps such husbands resent a wife's influence on the children or her nonparticipation in her husband's religious network. For wives, tolerating a husband's participation in his own network is more normative.

As expected, marital duration decreases thought of divorce for both spouses but, unexpectedly, men's thought of divorce decreases about as much as women's, .5% for each year of marriage. Wives' investment in housewife or hostess skills is not significant. Perhaps the thought of losing a longstanding spouse-specific social network—and the prospect of forming another—strikes husbands and wives alike as being just too much work.

Like Becker, we expected thought of divorce to increase in marriages beyond the first, but it did not. About 13% of both husbands and wives had experienced divorces, but this failed to affect the previously divorced person's or spouse's thought of divorce, with one exception. It negatively affected thought of divorce for husbands of previously divorced wives. Thus our findings support neither the "divorce-prone person" nor the "marital-specific capital" explanations of the effect of an earlier divorce. However, Becker's (1976:1179) empirical findings are mixed. When the large 1967 sample for the Survey of Economic Opportunity was appropriately standardized for age and for age at contracting current marriage, the findings did not support Becker's prediction that the duration of marriages is shorter in higher-order marriages. Perhaps many people find the experience of divorce so painful that,

Table 5.3
THINKING ABOUT DIVORCE BY RELIGIOUS COMBINATIONS*

Husband's religion	Wife's religion	Percent husbands thinking of divorce	Percent wives thinking of divorce	N
Protestant	Protestant	.19	.30	366
None	Protestant	.23	.42	43
Protestant	Catholic	.35	.40	20
Catholic	Catholic	.24	.28	117
Jew	Jew	.20	.25	20
Protestant	None	.38	.42	26
None	None	.24	.31	26
TOTAL		.23	.30	618

* Combinations with an N less than 20 are omitted.

even if they have traits—such as genius—that make a good mate hard to find, they avoid thinking of divorce.

Unexpectedly, spouse differences in sex-role attitudes had no affect on thought of divorce. We expected that employed wives with non-traditional sex-role attitudes who also saw the domestic division of labor as unfair would be more likely to think of divorce than other wives would, but no such interaction effects (2-way or 3-way) occurred (not shown). Yet the test of this hypothesis revealed several interesting findings. Both the wife's perception of the actual division of labor and her attitudes about a fair division for a two-earner family affect her thought of divorce. For each of the five daily household tasks that the husband performs at least half the time, the wife is about 3% less likely to have thought of divorce. The husband is also less likely to have thought of divorce but not significantly so. Also, if the wife believes that housework should be divided equally in families with two full-time earners, she is 10% more likely to have thought of divorce and her husband is almost (8%) as likely (but not significantly so) to have thought of it. Since about 80% of both men and women hold this view, our findings may simply reflect the extreme conservatism of the other 20%, who believe in a rigid division of household labor and in the sanctity of marriage. Since husbands rarely perform more than half the housework, the husband's life may be less affected by existing varia-tions in the division of labor. In contrast, wives may be more aware of minor differences and consider themselves lucky if the husband per-forms even one daily task, such as child care or mealtime cleanup.

CONCLUSIONS

We have tried to develop a sociological theory of marital instability by examining the possibility that spouses' perceptions of costs and benefits may differ, adding to the Becker variables the spouses' sex-role attitude differences and their definitions of a fair division of household labor. Before drawing conclusions, we compare our findings with those of Becker et al. (1977) in order to show the extent to which economic factors also influence thoughts of divorce. The comparisons must be interpreted cautiously because (a) we do not know precisely how thought of divorce relates to divorce; and (b) attitudes on marriage and divorce are changing so rapidly that comparisons at different times may be misleading.

Becker et al. (1977) predicted a negative effect on divorce for the husband's earnings, a positive effect for the wife's; we found no effects for the earnings of either spouse. However, following Becker's reasoning, we found that the wife's employment history positively affected thoughts of divorce for both spouses. Becker predicted a negative effect for age at marriage. We found a negative effect for wives but no effect for husbands. Becker predicted that the presence of children would negatively affect the probability of divorce. We found that the presence of a child under 6 years negatively affected the husband's thought of divorce but that there were no negative effects for wives. Instead, the presence of a child aged 6–11 positively affected wives' thoughts of divorce. Becker predicted that spouse trait differences would positively affect divorce. We found no effects for education, age, or religious differences for wives. For husbands, only religious differences had the predicted effect. Becker predicted that marital duration would negatively affect divorce. We also found a negative effect.

Tests of hypotheses new to this research show that women think more about divorce than men do and that certain sex-role attitudes fail to affect thought of divorce. Yet the wife's perception of the division of labor for employed spouses does affect her thought of divorce. Our findings suggest, first the possibility that in the future a husband's high income will not have as important an affect on marital stability as it has had in the past.[3] Should our finding also appear in studies of divorce, it could affect the rate of normative change of customs concerning divorce and child custody. In our view the slow development of norms for divorced persons results partly from the fact that divorce has been relatively uncommon, historically, among groups with the most resources and influence to affect social patterns.

In industrial societies, the husband's income has been critical to divorce or separation for several reasons. The higher the husband's income, the less likely was the wife to be employed, a result of the vast expansion of the middle classes during industrialization. Ambitious couples emulated upper-class behavior patterns; the middle-class wife aspired to the role of gracious hostess and companion, producing a few high quality children on the side. Since emulating an upper-class life without an army of servants downstairs was quite labor intensive, a middle-class wife could be more than fully occupied meeting rapidly changing standards of child care, companionship, household sanitation, and gracious living. In turn, law and custom gave economically dependent wives little choice but to remain married, even if they heart-

---

[3]However, the husband's employment may affect divorce at low-income levels. Cherlin (1978) shows that the husband's employment stability negatively affects divorce for low-income respondents.

ily disliked their husbands. Very few divorced wives received alimony (United States Bureau of the Census, 1979a:5). The wife's dependency also constrained the husband—especially if she had put him through college or professional school—if he wanted to divorce her (see also Gorecki, 1966:611). Thus, both husbands and wives in high-income families had reason to avoid divorce.

Today, women's economic roles are changing faster than men's. Women's massive entry into the paid labor force parallels men's during industrialization. High-income husbands are now much less likely than in the past to have nonemployed wives. In 1950 only 16% of wives in the top 5% of family income were employed; by 1970, 41% were employed, and the number continues to rise (United States Bureau of the Census, 1975b:295). More wives can now weigh the costs and benefits of housework and market work. Shifting the balance of women's self-interest in turn shifts the balance for men. In the long run, as more wives enter the paid labor force, an important factor in the stability of the dual-earner couple may be the extent to which dual earnings imply dual domestic labor.

A second finding suggesting change in factors that affect marriage is that the presence of children of any age fails to deter mothers' thoughts of divorce and only the presence of young children deters fathers' thoughts. Should this finding occur in future studies of divorce, as we now expect, it may make people nervous to think that parents may care more about their own personal happiness than about their children's welfare. Changes in family norms arouse anxiety, even among social scientists, because such norms, critical to the survival of any society, are so deeply embedded. For example, the received wisdom typically describes the rise in the divorce rate as alarming. Perhaps we should question the received wisdom and be worried, instead, about the number of unhappy couples who, failing to attain divorce, continue to live miserably together. Similarly, if the presence of children fails to deter divorce, this may not imply that parents care less for their children; it may mean, instead, that parents can find alternatives to subjecting their children to life in an unhappy home.

One outcome seems probable if the presence of children fails to affect a rising divorce rate: The norms that guide divorcing parents should experience vigorous growth. As all divorced and divorcing parents know, norms in this area, are poor guides to behavior. Enormous energy is needed to solve daily problems. More than 30 years ago Kingsley Davis (1949) noted the lack of institutionalized patterns for dealing with children of divorce, and the situation persists today (Cherlin, 1978). The growing number of divorces and the rise in the status of divorcing couples should stimulate development of norms concerning children of divorce in the near future.[4]

Finally, our findings imply that an adequate sociology of marriage and family should begin by examining historical changes in how people make a living. The study of personality and sexual adjustment may provide useful information for therapists, but it cannot explain long-term shifts in marriage patterns. In preindustrial societies marriage was situated in a web of economic reciprocities. Tearing that web decreased the durability of marriages—not because contemporary husbands and wives get along less well, but because they have other options if they grow to dislike one another. The task for the sociology of marriage and family is to examine how these options emerged and to predict how women and men will react to them. Becker's focus on economic factors in marital instability paves the way for a sociological theory of marriage that, like the theory of the demographic transition, will explain how populations come to change their behavior when they confront a changed environment.

[4]However, public anxiety about divorce may slow the development of new norms. The great majority of our respondents disagreed that divorce should be easier to attain (see Chapter 8) as did the great majority of respondents in the 1975 General Social Survey (T. Smith, 1980:43). Moreover, women's (but not men's) approval of the Equal Rights Amendment was negatively affected by their belief that its ratification would make it easier for men to divorce their wives (Spitze and Huber, 1982).

CHAPTER SIX

Fertility

Chapter 1 describes the historical context for current norms, policies, and attitudes on fertility in the United States. We argued that the United States can now be described as being structurally antinatalist. A number of trends, themselves the unplanned consequences of technological change, have increased the costs and decreased the rewards of childrearing. Such trends include women's rising levels of education that, in turn, increase the opportunity cost of remaining home; women's rising rates of labor-force participation and husbands' increasing approval of wives' employment; the rising divorce rate; the rising cost of child care for preschoolers and of college education for grown children; the widespread job retirement plans that sever links between childrearing and economic security in old age; and the development of increasingly effective contraceptives that sever links between sexual activity and impregnation. In principle, these structural trends should exert antinatalist effects.

This chapter presents empirical evidence from past research and from our 1978 data on attitudes related to fertility. To what extent do these attitudes comprise an antinatalist climate of opinion? Although we agree with those who hold that such attitudes result from behavior and available choices more than the other way round (Easterlin, 1978b; Ryder, 1979), we suggest that attitudes are important because the range of acceptable government policies and their effects on individual behavior will be limited by public opinion.

We are especially concerned with the following questions. Is American public opinion toward childbearing positive, neutral, or negative? Can opinion trends be identified? If so, how fast are they moving? Are public perceptions of the consequences of childbearing consistent with the evidence? What types of fertility-related policies are currently acceptable to the public? Which ones are most strongly supported by groups with the most political clout—and therefore more likely to be carried out?

We begin by examining structural factors and policies that may affect fertility. We then review the literature that forms the basis for our hypotheses. This literature bears on attitudes about the desirability or undesirability of having children and on fertility-related practices that are potentially amenable to public policy regulation—practices such as birth control and provision of care for children and old people. Finally, we present our findings.

SOCIAL STRUCTURE, PUBLIC POLICY, AND FERTILITY

Until very recently American norms typically favored fertility (Ryder, 1978:361). Only a decade ago Blake (1972) described American society as being pervaded by time-honored pronatalist forces, especially the prescribed primacy of parenthood for adult sex roles and the prescribed congruence of personality traits with the demands of motherhood. People made "voluntary" choices, Blake wrote, in a context that constrained them not to remain single, not to choose childlessness, not to bear only one child, and even not to limit themselves to two. Sex-role socialization represented the enforcement of society's commitment to reproduction. Blake (1972:87) argued that prescribing the maternal role for all women made no sense in a low-mortality society.

We shall argue that the "coercive pronatalism" that Blake described has been attenuated, yielding to the impact of structural factors that may in turn affect attitudes about fertility-related issues. We briefly review these factors (see also Chapter 1) and then analyze public policies that may affect fertility.

A number of interrelated trends spawned by industrialization have increased the costs and decreased the rewards of childrearing to individual parents. The direct cost has risen with the increased investment in the child's human capital that is needed to enable the child to 'inherit' its parents' status. The indirect cost, basically the mother's opportunity cost of foregone earnings, rises with women's increasing level of educational attainment. The rewards of having children have been eroded by the establishment of government and private pension plans for retirement. Such plans make children irrelevant to financial security in old age. Rates of geographical mobility decrease the ability of children to provide psychological support to elderly parents. None of these trends seems likely to be reversed.

Whether the total mix of federal policies ever favored fertility is open to question. Like fertility policies of other developed countries, the American policy mix is only partly conscious and deliberate (Blake, 1971a; H. Scott, 1974). The laws that benefit and burden reproduction are typically twentieth century in origin, statutory in form, and economic in immediate impact (Noonan and Dunlap, 1972). The government policies that most obviously affect fertility concern taxation and welfare.

Impressionistic evidence indicates that, to the extent that people think about the relation of taxation to fertility, tax policy is thought to encourage fertility, at least for the middle class. Such taxes are relatively new. Of the wide variety of taxes that characterize industrialized countries, most developed after the turn of this century (Pechman, 1971:245). Although international comparisons are difficult (Rolph, 1968:528), in most developed countries the income tax—the major or the only progressive tax—is thought to exert pronatalist effects by permitting deductions or exemptions for minor dependents. The more children, the greater the tax relief.

Yet it seems unlikely that tax deductions for dependents can exert much pronatalist effect in the United States. Such deductions cannot induce poor people to have children because the incomes of the poor are too low to take advantage of the deductions. The tax savings for middle- and upper-income families are too low to offset much of the actual cost of rearing children. Moreover, the effects of local and state taxes are likely to offset any pronatalist effects of the federal income tax because real estate and sales taxes (the major taxes at the local and state levels) are regressive in effect. Indeed, the combined effect of local, state, and federal taxes, contrary to popular belief, is only mildly progressive. An extremely detailed study showed, for example, that the lowest group of income receivers paid 23% of their incomes in taxes, whereas the highest group paid 39% of theirs (Musgrave, 1955:96ff). On balance, one is inclined to agree with Noonan and Dunlap (1972:127) that American tax law neither consistently rewards nor penalizes parenthood.

Impressionistic evidence also indicates that welfare policies are believed to encourage lower class fertility. As with tax structures, the effect of welfare policies in industrialized countries' is difficult to analyze and compare because the programs are so complex (Organisation for Economic Co-operation and Development, 1976:11). The patchwork of social programs that blanketed Europe by the turn of the twentieth century (Rimlinger, 1971) are somewhat more pronatalist than those in the United States. Most countries instituted programs in roughly similar sequence. Compensation for work injuries has usually been first, followed by pensions for the aged, widows, and invalids, and then by early forms of sickness and maternity benefits. National programs for the unemployed came later. Family allowances tend to be fairly recent additions (Heidenheimer et al., 1975:188). All western European countries (and Canada, but not the United States) provide family allowances. Benefits are small, however, compared to the benefits for old-age pensions and health care (Huber, 1978:113). Benefits to single-parent families are also relatively small, although they are larger in Europe than in the United States. Most European countries use a mix of non-means-tested programs to aid such families. Public assistance is used only as a last resort (Heidenheimer et al., 1975:106ff). In the United States, aid to children and their caretakers is means-tested, and the size of grants is relatively low. The average per person grant under the Aid to Families with Dependent Children (AFDC) program is about half that of a public assistance grant to an elderly person. Although AFDC grants vary enormously by state, the average grant enables a family of four to subsist at a level that is about half the poverty line (Levitan and Taggart, 1976:57).

However hard it is to compare welfare programs and assess their effects, it is safe to conclude that no industrialized country has a welfare program with clearly pronatalist effects. The antinatalist effects of some popular welfare programs probably offset any pronatalist effects that others could have. For example, well-funded programs for medical care and retirement income for the elderly should, in principle, reduce the rewards of rearing children. Hence their long-run effect should be antinatalist. Well-funded programs for child or maternal allowances should have a pronatalist effect. In practice, the funds provided for retirement pensions and medical care for the elderly are much larger in all countries than are sums allotted for rearing children. Furthermore, the absolute size of grants given to families with children living at home is so small as to have no discernible effect on fertility, as shown by a number of United States studies (Placek and Hendershot, 1974; Ross and Sawhill, 1975; P. Rossi and Lyall, 1977:127). On balance, then, especially in the United States, the effect of welfare policy seems to tip toward antinatalism.

Moreover, the effects of the private sector, an almost completely un-researched topic, are often overlooked as a factor that might affect the birthrate. For example, age was excluded as a category in the Equal Accommodations Sections of the Civil Rights Act of 1964. As a result, 27% of United States rental housing now excludes children in contrast with 17% only a few years ago (Sullivan, 1981). Interest rates that make buying a house difficult for most young couples also exert antinatalist effects. The availability of adequate housing is often overlooked as a highly significant factor that affects fertility (Rindfuss, 1982).

The probable outcome of current structural trends and public policies is not a topic of consensus. Some demographers support a cyclical fertility theory (Easterlin, 1969; 1978b; Sklar and Berkov, 1975). As the current baby boom cohort ages, the relatively small cohorts that enter the labor market will experience higher job demand, just as the cohorts that entered the labor force after 1940 experienced high demand. The better jobs that would be available to smaller cohorts would in turn stimulate marriage and family formation.

The trouble with the cyclical fertility theory is that it links men's prospects to their numbers on the assumption that the traditional sex division of labor will persist unchanged (Ryder, 1979:360). A booming labor market would presumably attract women as well as men. In the absence of adequate child-care facilities that would help to make parental employment easier, it is difficult to see why a strong labor market would induce higher fertility.

In contrast to the cyclical theorists, we expect fertility rates to continue to decline on a fluctuating, gentle slope below zero population growth (ZPG) on toward zero. This prediction is not inconsistent with those of many demographers (Ward and Butz, 1978; Butz and Ward, 1979a, 1979b; Bogue, 1980; DeVaney, 1980; Westoff, 1980). A leveling off at zero population growth would be convenient (Ryder, 1979) but contrary to the experience of many western European countries (Alan Guttmacher Institute, 1980a; H. Scott, 1974). Their population policies have become more explicitly pronatalist as fear of depopulation grows (Butz and Ward, 1979b.

Do declining fertility rates pose problems? No one seems certain. Historically, economic growth has not occurred simultaneously with population decline, but that does not imply it could never occur.

Spengler (1979:337) notes that the French experience—they have worried about population decline for three centuries—little supports the view that slow population growth leads to unemployment or slow income growth. Implicit in the belief of most experts, however, is the idea that policies are available to maintain national growth at replacement level, even with a voluntaristic approach. However, current conditions such as contraceptive availability, legal abortion, and increasing marital instability have become so institutionalized as to make government actions less effective (Myers, 1979:vii). What seems more probable is that government intervention in family policy will increase, whether stimulated by fear of population decline or fears about the state of the traditional family. It is therefore important to know something about public attitudes on such issues.

FERTILITY-RELATED ATTITUDES

This section discusses a series of attitudes that are related to fertility. We review relevant literature and then present the items used in this study and, finally, the coding we used. We discuss in turn items referring to women's "proper" place, world overpopulation, voluntary childlessness, the effect of children on happiness and satisfaction, abortion, free abortion for women on welfare, free child care, and the proper residence for elderly parents. We begin with an attitude basic to fertility, the natural happiness of house-bound mothers.

Women's Place

We found only one national sample survey item that focused on women's "proper" place: "Women are much happier if they stay home and take care of their children" (Mason and Bumpass, 1975:1,219); 51% of blacks and 40% of nonblacks agreed. This item appeared in the National Fertility Survey in 1970, a study based on a national probability sample of ever-married women under age 45 (Westoff and Ryder, 1977). A rationalizing belief about the nature of women (Mason and Bumpass, 1975:1,215), the item was included in an attitude scale with four other items covering potential conflicts between employment and maternal roles. When the scale was regressed on a series of dummy variable classifications representing 10 sociodemographic characteristics, education had the strongest effect. Race and religion had more modest effects.

Although this item seemed a prime candidate for replication, we changed the wording to stress that women's happiness at home resulted from innate characteristics. We feared that lower-income respondents might feel that women would be happiest if they *only* had to stay home with their children instead of combining child care with low-wage market work. We therefore asked whether respondents agreed or disagreed that "By nature, women are happiest when they are making a home and caring for children."

We expected women to disagree more than men with the item. With the exception of the setback in the liberalism of women's opinion in the 1960s (see Chapter 8), women are typically less traditional than men are on sex-role items. In line with the usual response, we also expected the strongest effects from age and education and, for women, employment. We expected race to have no significant effects because we had reworded the question to stress biological factors. We could think of no reason why race should make a difference.

Childbearing

Considerable evidence supports the view that American attitudes about childbearing have long been pronatalist. Some recent studies, however, show evidence of change (Peck and Senderowitz, 1974; Polit, 1978; Blake, 1979; Veevers, 1979; Fried and Udry, 1980).[1] Tom Smith (1980:21), for example, using data from a number of national sample surveys, shows that the proportion of respondents who said that three or more children was ideal has decreased in the last several decades. In 1936, 58% agreed, rising to a high of 78% of 1959, then declining in a jagged line to 43% in 1978. A decline in pronatalism may also be inferred by comparing findings from two national sample surveys conducted in the early and later 1970s. Griffith (1973) reports that 78% of

---

[1]Another indicator of change is the appearance of the National Alliance for Optional Parenthood (1979). It aims to persuade people that choosing to be childfree—its preferred term for those who oppose pronatalism—does not mean that one is selfish, immature, or evil. Pronatalism, said to be akin to sexism, is any policy or attitude that exalts parental status and encourages reproduction for everyone. This approach has problems. It implies that some talented women should be childfree whereas others (presumably less talented) should cope with children. We also believe that parenthood should be a choice. However, unless one is prepared to let the human race just die out, it seems more fair to everyone to make childrearing for men and women consonant with unrestricted participation in major human activities.

the respondents to a 1972 national sample survey of ever-married women and men had experienced pronatalist pressure from parents and close relatives. There was no evidence of a major trend toward weaker social pressures for having a first or second child. However, Fried and Udry (1980), reporting on data collected in 1976–1977, found unexpectedly high levels of discouragement, even at zero parity, reported by 39% of white women and 35% of white men. For blacks, discouragement at parity levels zero and one combined were also substantial, 38% for women and 17% for men. Beyond parity one, antinatalist pressure was surprisingly high. Fried and Udry concluded that attitudes were becoming less pronatalist.

Several types of questions tap attitudes about the desirability of bearing children. At the most abstract level the concern is with world or national rates of population growth or decline. A number of surveys have asked respondents if they worry about a world population increase. The worry levels reported by American Institute of Public Opinion polls in 1960, 1963, and 1965 seem modest. In 1960, 21% of the respondents were worried; in 1963, 25%. In 1965, 30% were worried but, unlike the procedures used in the two earlier polls, only those respondents who had heard or read of an increase were asked if they were worried about it. Hence the base was only 70% of the total sample (Erskine, 1966:491). We thought this level of worry rather low, probably because we have been well-exposed to demographic literature. About half of the world's people live in countries where rates of increase come close to doubling every 29 years. The potential for famine and political unrest seems great.

An opposite version of the same question was asked about the United States in 1971. Respondents to a national probability sample survey were asked if they were worried about the slow-down and leveling off of population growth in the United States (Wolman, 1972). Only 26% of the respondents would be concerned if population growth leveled off. Other questions in the survey helped to explain this low level of worry. Many respondents thought that population growth had bad consequences: 64% thought it made for social unrest; 57% thought it caused a country to use its natural resources too fast; 48% thought it caused water and air pollution. About a third of the respondents thought population growth was good; 36% thought it kept the country prosperous, and another 36% thought it was important in maintaining military strength.

The low level of worry about the leveling-off of United States population growth surprised us less than did the low level of worry about too

rapid world growth. The most recent birthrate decline had been under-
way only a decade. Moreover, pollution and too rapid use of natural
resources were becoming topics of increasing concern.

At the world level, the majority response to the possibility of rapid
population growth appears to be pronatalist by default, as it were,
exhibiting a benign indifference. At the national level, the majority
response seems neither pro- nor antinatalist.

Our question on global birthrates (Question 2.1) included a factual
statement intended to make respondents aware of the predicted rate of
increase: "Population experts predict that the world population will
double in 40 years. Are you very worried, somewhat worried, not very
worried, or not at all worried about this population increase?" We
expected that the general worry level would have increased since the
earlier AIPO polls because the item indicated the actual rate of increase
and because of increasing concern about pollution, energy reserves,
and Third World political unrest. We expected education to have the
strongest effects, followed by income. We would have liked to ask
respondents how they would feel about the possibility of a decline
below replacement in the United States birthrate. We did not do so,
however, because we expected that the level of concern would be too
low to yield much variance to analyze.

A second type of question about the desirability of having children
shifts to the individual level and alters the question by asking whether
it is undesirable to have few or no children. Veevers (1979) suggests
several reasons why voluntarily childless persons (VCs) could be
viewed negatively: They could have undesirable traits such as being
selfish that, along with their lack of desire for children, could arise
from psychological maladjustment. Voluntarily childless people could
come to be labeled as deviates and therefore acquire other undesirable
traits. Or perhaps interaction with children might be needed for mature
adjustment.

Extant research tends to support the view that the public sees voluntary childlessness as evidence of character deficiency. Polit's (1978)
findings confirm Rainwater's (1965) findings from the early 1960s. People who voluntarily have fewer than two children were viewed as less
socially desirable, less well-adjusted, and less nurturant than other
people. Parents with as many as eight children were viewed positively.
However, involuntarily childless persons were viewed as being well-
adjusted and socially desirable, perhaps indicating that, in the popular
view, maladjustment is indicated by lack of desire for children rather
than caused by lack of interaction with them.

Polit (1978) also reported that such perceptions relate significantly to respondent characteristics. Favorable judgments of voluntary childlessness and unfavorable judgments of parents of eight children were commonest among the young, the highly educated, and those with small families. They were least common among Roman Catholics.

In contrast, the findings of Mason et al. (1976) imply greater approval of voluntarily childless women. Respondents to two sample surveys of ever-married women of childbearing ages were asked if they agreed or disagreed that women who do not want at least one child are being selfish. In regression standardized percentages, 73% disagreed in 1970 and 86% in 1973.

The first national survey of attitudes toward childlessness, conducted as a 1977 Gallup poll, was Blake's (1979) investigation of perceptions of the positive and negative consequences of being childless. Blake felt that children no longer represent a financial hedge against old age, nor do they share the characteristics of consumption goods as economists suggest. She therefore hypothesized that respondents would tend to see children as social investments. Of the suggested negative consequences of being childless, the largest proportion of respondents (64%) agreed that being childless resulted in loneliness. The smallest proportion (15%) agreed that being childless resulted in financial problems later in life. Other disadvantages of being childless (empty lives, unfulfillment for women, and increased chance of divorce) received 34–45% agreement. Only 13% and 14% of the respondents agreed with the two advantages of being childless that were mentioned in the survey: couple intimacy and having a good time in life. The inclusion of items on the financial advantages of being childless or the work-life advantages for women might have elicited more agreement.

Blake (1979) reported that attitudes toward childlessness were more positive among women, the young, the highly educated, the single and divorced, and those with no religious affiliation. Respondents most likely to view children as social investments had less education, were middle-aged or old, religious, were married or widowed, had low incomes, were Southerners, or lived in places with a population of less than 100,000 (Blake, 1979:247). The relatively favorable attitudes about childlessness among the young today are consistent with Griliches' (1974) contention that today's young adults have few children because they recognize the relatively low rate of return experienced by their own parents.

Thus the evidence suggests continued (albeit possibly decreasing) existence of pronatalist attitudes and pressure on young American adults. Pronatalist pressures appear to be justified by beliefs that being childless or having a very small family will have negative consequences for adults, such as loneliness in old age.

We assessed attitudes toward voluntarily childless couples with this question (Question 2.2): "Married couples who do not want children are being too self-centered." We used the strongly agree–strongly-disagree format. We also would have liked to know if respondents differentiate men and women on this issue, but available time did not permit another question. We expected that the strongest effects would result from age, education, income, and wives' employment. Because only the older respondents (the age factor) have had time to invest heavily in their children, we thought persons who have so invested would have an incentive to believe that adults who purposely avoid such an investment are being self-centered. Education and income typically exert antinatalist effects because they make people more aware of the costs of childrearing, as does the wife's employment. We expected women to be less likely than men to think that voluntary childlessness was self-centered because women are more aware of the daily costs of parenthood. Nonetheless, we expected substantial majorities of both sexes to agree that voluntarily childless people are self-centered.

The next three items concerning childbearing addressed the psychological consequences of having or not having children.[2] Veevers' (1979) comprehensive literature review suggests that being childless or having few children may be related to a variety of psychological states such as general mental health, happiness, and satisfaction with life. We will first review the literature relating childlessness to mental health; then we will discuss the literature bearing specifically on happiness and satisfaction with life in order to provide the background for our two items on these topics. Last, we will introduce a question asking respondents to compare their pleasure in childrearing with that of their parents.

A summary of the evidence relating childlessness to mental health shows differences between parents and childless persons to be nil or to favor the childless (Veevers, 1979:11). Childless adults tend to be more satisfied with life as a whole and to have higher levels of psychological well-being than parents. This may be particularly true when the chil-

---

[2]Being childless or having few children also relates to women's activities outside the home. Even a primitive theory on the effects of discretionary time would predict that women with no or few children would have higher rates of labor force participation (Cain, 1966; Oppenheimer, 1970; Sweet, 1973), higher occupational achievement (Treiman and Terrell, 1975; Veevers, 1979), more participation in professional occupations (Silka and Kiesler, 1977), and higher incomes (Suter and Miller, 1973).

dren are young. The presence of children, especially young ones, decreases women's sense of well-being (Bolt et al., 1979:12), especially if the women are not employed (Gove and Geerken, 1977). Thus the studies that Veevers discusses imply somewhat different consequences for being childless than Blake's respondents expected. Kessler and McRae (1981:444) also report that a number of studies consistently show that children negatively affect women's mental health. In the area of mental health, then, a causal ordering from family size to psychological well-being would seem more convincing than the reverse unless one suggests that wanting children stems from having poor mental health.

The presence of children, especially young ones, seems to have other unfavorable consequences. Young children detract from marital happiness, according to two comprehensive literature reviews (N. Glenn and Weaver, 1978; Veevers, 1979). Even job satisfaction may be in part a function of the family-life course, in parallel with high happiness levels reported by young single adults and childless couples and the lower happiness levels reported by couples with preschoolers (Wilensky, 1981:241).

Turning specifically to the study of happiness, we find that one item has been used in a number of surveys. Early on, Bradburn (1969), using a question from the first major study of quality of life experience (Gurin, Veroff, and Feld, 1960), asked respondents to an area probability sample survey of a number of communities how happy they were. The response was then related to a number of background variables.[3] In the lowest income category, having more than two children under age 21 at home reduced reported happiness levels. Bradburn (1969:99) concluded that, unless the number of children drained family income, it was not related to parental well-being.

Yet a summary of a number of national probability surveys that had used the happiness item reports nothing about the effect of children on happiness. Campbell et al. (1976:26) analyzed response to the happiness item because it is almost the only generalized assessment of quality of life that has long-term United States trend data. The authors note a number of regularities: happier respondents tend to be married, higher in socioeconomic status, younger, and to be living in small towns or rural areas. Few persons describe themselves as not too happy. Al-

[3]George Gallup (1977) reports that, at a global level, happiness varies with national economic level. The proportion of very happy respondents was 40% in North America, 37% in Australia, 20% in Eastern Europe, 32% in Latin America, 18% in Africa, and 7% in the Far East. The proportion of respondents who were not too happy was 8% in North America, 6% in Australia, 18% in Europe, 28% in Latin America, 31% in Africa, and 50% in the Far East.

though Campbell *et al.* (1976:26) report that United States happiness levels declined from 35% very happy in 1957 to 22% in 1972,[4] Tom Smith (1980:64), extending the analysis to 1978, found no clear trend. Happiness levels zigzagged, beginning with 35% very happy in 1957 and ending with 34% in 1978.

We replicated the question used by Gurin, Veroff, and Feld (1960:41) and Campbell *et al.* (1976:557), discussed earlier: "Taking all things together, how would you say you are these days? Would you say you are very happy, pretty happy, or not too happy?" (Question 2.3). We expected the main impact on happiness to come from family income, race, and marital status, in line with past findings. We expected no effects from sex or from number or ages of children. Our literature review provided scant support for the proposition that people with children are happier than those without children. Neither did it support the view that people without children are happier than those with children. In sum, we predict that the presence or absence of happiness and the presence or absence of children are unrelated events.

Another way of finding out how people feel about themselves is to ask how satisfied they are. Campbell *et al.* (1976:6–9) were more interested in satisfaction with life than in happiness because satisfaction had less ephemeral mood connotations, fewer differences in meaning, and depended more on a comparative judgment of personal circumstances than on immediate feelings. In our view feelings of satisfaction should be more sensitive than feelings of happiness to the number and ages of children. One might be very happy staying home with small children but still feel relatively constrained in relation to other adults.

Respondents to a national sample survey were asked how satisfied they were with their lives as a whole. Satisfaction was affected both by the number and ages of the children. General life satisfaction for both women and men increased sharply upon marriage but then decreased sharply for respondents with a child less than 6-years-old. Married respondents whose youngest child was between 6 and 17 were about as satisfied as those whose youngest child was over 17 or as older married respondents with no children. Higher satisfaction levels were reported by respondents with no children in the home and declined moderately but consistently among both husbands and wives as the number of children increased (Campbell *et al.*, 1976: 398, 328, 325).

Moreover, married women in the empty-nest stage showed high lev-

---

[4]Tom Smith (1979:27) reports that Campbell (personal communication) found slightly lower happiness levels in telephone interviews than in personal interviews. Bradburn (1969), comparing in-person and telephone reinterviews, reported no difference.

els of well-being. Men at this stage were also more satisfied than were other categories of men. Campbell et al. (1976:411) concluded that any remorse these people feel at no longer having children at home did not affect their outlook on life. In addition, older wives who had not borne children viewed their lives just as positively as did other wives. The financial consequences of childlessness may be insufficiently appreciated. In relation to their needs, the incomes of childless couples are the most adequate of all the life-course groups (Campbell et al., 1976:417).[5]

All parents were asked if they had ever wished they could be free from the responsibility of parenthood. Despite the threatening form of the question, two-fifths of the mothers of small children admitted that they sometimes wished they could be free of maternal responsibility, in contrast to one-fifth of the mothers of children between ages 6 and 17, and less than a tenth of the mothers of older children. The fathers' pattern was similar but the proportion who wanted to be free of responsibility was lower. Only a fifth of fathers of children under 6 for example, admitted that they often or sometimes wished they could be free of responsibility (Campbell et al., 1976:408).

Young parents also reported feeling various pressures. Except for divorced or separated women, young parents were more likely than other life-course groups to report experiencing more stress. The contrast between young married women with no children and young mothers a few years older was remarkable, especially in their fears of nervous breakdown, admitted by 19% of young mothers and 7% of young married women. Young fathers were as likely as young mothers to describe their lives as stressful, although they did not so often worry about nervous breakdowns (Campbell et al., 1976:409).

We examined the effect of children on life satisfaction (Question 2.4) by replicating the item in Campbell et al. (1976:554): "We have talked about various parts of your life. I would like to ask you about your life as a whole. How satisfied are you with your life as a whole these days? If you had to pick a number from 1 to 7 with 1 being very dissatisfied and 7 being very satisfied, which number would come closest to how

[5]In an attempt to replicate Campbell et al. (1976), we tested the effects of having a youngest child preschool age, in grade school, older than grade school versus having no children on income adequacy, controlling for level of family income. (A summated scale was constructed from items 46a, b, and c in the Appendix.) For both sexes, income was perceived as being most adequate when the youngest child was in grade school; then with no children; then with having a youngest child older than grade school age; and it was least adequate when the youngest child was preschool age. This seems to be due to differences in age and career stage of respondents whose children are differing ages. We do not have enough childless respondents to separate them by age group, however.

satisfied or dissatisfied you feel?" As with the happiness question, we expected a major effect from income. We also expected that both men and women would be negatively affected by the presence of children, especially young ones because such persons, especially women, have less discretionary time, less freedom for social and work activities, and more hourly responsibility than do other adults. These disadvantages are structural, not individual.

Our next item in this series, new to this study, concerns enjoyment of children. Although this study is cross-sectional, we tried to tap a sense of temporal change from one generation to another. On rational grounds, one would expect parents to enjoy children more when there was less danger of the child's death or of the child's being crippled by illness, when food and clothing were more easily available, and when the number of children tended to be planned. In sum, we expect material well-being to affect enjoyment of children.

To assess perceptions of change in enjoyment of children (Question 2.5), we asked: "Compared to the way your own (mother/father) felt, have you enjoyed your children more, about the same, or less than (she/he) did?" For both sexes we expected a positive effect for level of family income on the assumption that the capacity to enjoy children, like that of enjoying social interaction, is a randomly distributed characteristic subject to marginal effects from income. We expected that most respondents would report enjoying their children more than did their own parents because of the temporal increase in real income in the United States. However, we have no estimate of the respondents' parents' income and cannot, therefore, assess individual effects.

Fertility Policies

Governments wishing to promote or discourage childbearing may choose from a number of alternative strategies. Implementation and success of such policies would depend on public acceptance and the relation of a policy to existing social patterns. We discuss three such policies.

First, governments can limit access to some of the means of birth control: appliance and pharmacological contraceptives, abortion, and sterilization (Wulf, 1980) and to information about them. Second, they can manipulate the opportunity costs of bearing and rearing children by promoting or discouraging women's educational and labor force opportunities through tax incentives and other legislation. Probably more important, they can make child care more or less accessible and adequate.[6] Third, societies can manipulate monetary costs and incentives for childrearing. The cost can be decreased by family allowances and adequate public education. The benefits may be decreased by improving retirement plans and providing adequate care for the aged (Alan Guttmacher Institute, 1980a). We will discuss these issues in turn along with a question bearing on at least one aspect of each issue.

The term birth control, coined by Margaret Sanger in 1914, denoted both male and female methods of preventing conception. It now includes all methods of fertility control including abortion and sterilization (Draper, 1974:1067). In common sense language, contraception includes methods that use appliances and drugs to prevent conception. Abortion refers to the termination of the pregnancy before the fetus can live independently. Some oral contraceptives may be abortifacients in effect. In the following discussion, however, we follow the common-sense usage.

Historically, contraception has been vigorously opposed by almost everyone, at least by everyone who said anything about it in public. Only the users presumably favored it, and they kept their views to themselves. For example, although physicians were among the first to limit the size of their own families, the English medical press long took an anticontraceptive point of view. The expected ritual condemnation of contraception was omitted in the presidential address to the meeting of the British Medical Association only in 1913 (Peel and Potts, 1969:6). Physicians had opposed it because the effects, they thought, included cancer, sterility, and nymphomania in women, and mental decay, amnesia, and cardiac palpitation in men. In both sexes the practice was thought to produce a suicidal mania (Peel and Potts, 1969:12). In the 1920s American physicians opposed contraception because they thought it represented social and moral degeneration (Gordon, 1977:259). Hence research on birth control was long neglected (Draper, 1974:1069). Socialists opposed contraception because they thought that equitable economic conditions would make women willing to have as many children as came naturally (Gordon, 1977:241). Only in the last decade, for example, has the French Communist Party slowly ceased to suspect family planning as a bourgeois plot to eliminate the working class (Stoddart, 1978:66).

Birth control began to become respectable in the 1920s when it was separated from issues of sexual or feminist liberation. The term "family planning" came into use, followed by "planned parenthood" (Draper,

[6]Housing availability is often overlooked as a factor that affects the decision to have children (Rindfuss, 1982; David, 1982).

1974:1065). In 1930 the Federal Council of (Protestant) Churches ruled that careful and restrained use of contraception by married couples was valid and moral. Although the Lambeth Conference of Anglican bishops had condemned contraception in 1908 (many years after Great Britain experienced the demographic transition), they gave such methods limited approval in 1930. They gave full approval only in 1958. Roman Catholics were slower to come round. They formally approved the rhythm method of birth control in 1930. In 1968, however, even after much evidence of growing uncertainty among Roman Catholic moralists, Pope Paul VI failed to approve the use of appliance and pharmacological methods of birth control. This set off controversy in the Church. By the early 1970s American Catholic laity were using the same methods of birth control as did other Americans (Westoff and Bumpass, 1973; Greeley, 1979:99). Similarly, Roman Catholic opinion did not differ significantly from that of Protestants as to whether free birth control services should be provided for teenage girls who requested them (Blake, 1973a). Today Roman Catholic lay opinion on such issues continues to differ from that of the hierarchy, at least from its formal statements. Birth control does not seem to be an issue in the United States today. A number of national probability sample surveys show that public opinion increasingly favors making information about it available to anyone. In 1959 73% of the respondents to the General Social Survey thought that birth control information should be available to anyone who wanted it. This proportion rose to 91% in 1977 (T. Smith, 1980:139). The proportion who favored sex education in the public schools also rose, from 56% in 1970 to 77% in 1977 (T. Smith, 1980:195).

Abortion is more controversial than contraception. Until the middle of the nineteenth century, the United States followed the British Common Law tradition. Abortion was not a crime until quickening (at about the fifth month, the first certain evidence that a woman was pregnant), and the aborted woman was immune from prosecution (Tietze, 1981:8). Mohr (1978) explains in detail how and why the situation changed. We follow his account.

In the first third of the nineteenth century, abortion was not defined as a means of limiting the family size of married couples. Rather, it was a last resort of poor, destitute, unmarried, or deserted women. From 1840 to 1880, however, the abortion rate increased dramatically when middle- and upper-class women began to use it as a supplementary means of birth control, along with whatever other means were available.

The great upsurge in the abortion rate of "respectable" married women occurred just when the medical "regulars" were trying to oust the "irregulars" from practice. This task was not easy. Until Lister's 1865 breakthrough on the nature of sepsis, one could well argue that going to a physician, whether regular or irregular, was bad for the health. The regulars tried to persuade state legislators to make abortion a criminal offense since the regulars faced not only a loss of fee but also a long-term loss of general practice. The regular physicians therefore began to campaign against abortion, warning of the dire consequences of women's self-indulgence. Abortion was thought to signify a woman's rejection of her traditional role. Women who had abortions were domestic subversives.

The state medical societies therefore pressed the legislatures to make abortion illegal and to prosecute the woman as well as the abortioner. The fight in Ohio exemplifies the arguments used. The physicians stressed that quickening had no real biological meaning and that abortion was dangerous. Their most telling argument, however, was based on racism and sexism. The final report to the Ohio Legislature asked whether native American women realized that in avoiding duties and responsibilities of married life, they were living in a state of legalized prostitution—should the broad and fertile prairies of Ohio be settled only by the children of aliens? If not, then the Legislature should suppress so prevalent a crime (Mohr, 1978:206). By 1900 every state in the union had outlawed the practice. Between 1880 and 1900, however, abortion declined. Abortion again came to be associated with poor, socially desperate, and unwed women, but the laws remained on the books.

Early in the 1960s public opinion on abortion came to interest pollsters. Although the level of tolerance is sensitive to the phrasing of the question, similar patterns of response have been observed in relation to social and economic background characteristics (Westoff and Ryder, 1977:163). We will report first the findings of seven national sample surveys (an 11-year span) that used identical questions and then discuss the findings of a variety of surveys that have used different questions with various populations.

Public opinion on the acceptability of abortion has been evaluated with the use of quite similar questions in a series of five Gallup polls between 1962 and 1969, in two National Fertility Studies in 1965 and 1970, and in the Population Growth Study conducted in 1971 for the Commission on Population Growth and the American Future. However, only the NORC 1965 survey and the General Social Survey in each year from 1972 through 1976 used precisely the same lead-in questions, the same selection and wording of items, the same interview context, and the same target population, according to Evers and McGee (1980) who analyzed these surveys. Because we used the same items, we will review the Evers and McGee (1980) analysis. The general response was similar across the six items. Approval increased substantially from 1965 to 1972; smaller increases occurred between 1972 and 1973. Approval for the "hard" reasons (mother's health, pregnancy resulting from rape, serious defect in child) decreased after 1974. Approval for "soft" reasons (low income, mother unmarried, wanting no more children) decreased after 1975. Specifically, from 1965 to 1977, approval increased from 73% to 90% for reasons of the mother's health; from 57% to 86% for defect in the baby; from 60% to 84% for rape; from 22% to 53% for low income; from 18% to 50% for not being married; and from 16% to 46% for not wanting any more children. Evers and McGee (1980:263) concluded that their findings pointed to a continuing strong relationship of education, race, religion, and age with approval of abortion. Education effects were strongest for white non-Catholics, who were more approving than were their counterparts.

Other studies also show that United States attitudes toward abortion became more liberal during the 1960s (Blake, 1971b; E. Jones and Westoff, 1973). Approval peaked in 1973, the year of the United States Supreme Court decision, and decreased or leveled off since then (Tedrow and Mahoney, 1979; Ebaugh and Haney, 1980).[7] Approval decreased least for the "hard" reasons. CBS and NBC polls in the fall of 1979 were consistent with GSS data; 90% of the respondents approved abortion to save the mother's life, two-thirds would leave the decision to the woman and her physician, and about half agreed that every woman who wanted an abortion should be able to have one. In the NBC poll about 70% agreed that the Roman Catholic Church should reverse its stand (Alan Guttmacher Institute, 1980a).

Over time the effect of most background variables on abortion attitudes has decreased. The effects of sex and age have tended to reverse. Although religion predicts abortion attitudes in most recent United States studies—Roman Catholics were least liberal (Blake, 1971b; Rao and Bouvier, 1974)—its effects decreased from 1972 to 1978 (Ebaugh and Haney, 1980). Jews overwhelmingly favored abortion. Protestants favored it less, only slightly more than did Roman Catholics. Baptists and members of "other" denominations were the least liberal Protestants; Presbyterians and Episcopalians, the most liberal. Attendance at

---

[7]Support for legal abortion grew since the late 1960s in Great Britain, France, the Netherlands, and West Germany. In Denmark it grew rapidly in the early 1970s (de Boer, 1978b).

services has also been linked to negative attitudes on abortion (Welch, 1975; Alan Guttmacher Institute, 1980a).

Higher educational levels are linked to attitudes favoring abortion (Rao and Bouvier, 1974), although the effect has decreased over time. Grade school educated respondents became increasingly liberal, whereas the attitudes of persons in other categories remained relatively constant (Ebaugh and Haney, 1980). A nationwide survey of health professionals in medicine, nursing, and social work reported that more than two-thirds of the respondents in each category would be willing to help a client obtain an abortion under some circumstances. Social workers were the most liberal; nurses, the least, perhaps because nurses have to work with the fetus and social workers, with family problems resulting from the birth. Fewer Roman Catholic health professionals favored abortion on demand than did the general Roman Catholic public at each educational level, but students favored abortion more than the faculty did (Rosen et al., 1974).

In the early 1960s older respondents tended to favor abortion more than did younger ones (Blake, 1973b). Using data from 1970 and 1971, Zelnik and Kantner (1975) reported that female teenagers were somewhat more conservative on abortion than were women, although the never-married, sexually experienced, and older teenagers showed the greatest approval. By the mid 1970s younger respondents tended to be more liberal than older ones (Welch, 1975). The middle-aged group, 30–45, experienced the greatest increase in approval (Ebaugh and Haney, 1980).

In the 1960s men tended to approve abortion more than women did (Blake, 1971b), particularly men with high levels of education and income. Blake suggested that advantaged men had much to gain and little to lose by abortion reform and contraceptive improvements. Such men tend to prefer small families and to take an instrumental view of teenage sexual behavior. Modern birth control methods, expecially abortion, tend to pass the risk and inconvenience to women. Thus it is not surprising that men would more readily approve such measures. Moreover, men are much less likely than women to experience the ambivalence and conflict that women feel over being aborted—even those women who most strongly approve of abortion. More recent evidence, however, shows that the sex difference is reversing, inconsistent, or disappearing (Blake, 1973b; Ebaugh and Haney, 1980).

Black women have long disapproved of abortion more than white women did, but this difference is also disappearing. Elise Jones and Charles Westoff (1973) reported that at all education levels the opposition of black women under age 35 is indistinguishable from that of whites. Behavior by race also differed. Before 1969 black women were less likely than white women to resort to legal abortion but more likely to use illegal abortion despite their negative attitudes about abortion. Between 1972 and 1974 the ratio of black to white abortions increased from being 1.3 times greater to 1.9 times greater than that of whites. Thus, despite their greater disapproval (linked to fears of genocide), blacks were using abortion at about twice the rate of whites. This disproportionate use has increased since the 1973 Supreme Court decision (Cates, 1977).

Thus the overall picture of abortion attitudes is one of basically stable approval levels in the 1970s and of decreasing subcategory differences. It is not clear whether such differences are becoming sharper or more blurred among the youngest age cohorts. Finally, no research since Blake's (1971b) has spelled out the relation between social power, these attitudes, and the potential consequences for the future of legal abortion.

Our first question on abortion (Question 3.1) is a variant of the one used in the National Fertility Survey, 1965 and 1970, and a replication of the item in the NORC Amalgam Survey in 1965 and the GSS, 1972 through 1978. It consists of six questions on the conditions under which abortion should be available: "Please tell me whether or not you think it should be possible for a pregnant woman to obtain a legal abortion if:

1. The woman's own health is seriously endangered by the pregnancy
2. There is a strong chance of serious defect in the baby
3. She became pregnant as a result of rape
4. The family has a very low income and cannot afford more children
5. She is not married and does not want to marry the man
6. She is married and does not want any more children."

We expected significant effects for education, age, and income but not for race and religion. The Evers and McGee (1980) analysis pointed to continuing effects for race and religion. However, we expected the rising rate of abortions for blacks (as compared to the rate for whites) to induce blacks to bring their opinion into greater conformity with their behavior. We expected religion to have no significant effects on Protestant–Roman Catholic opinion because a substantial body of research shows that the opinions of Roman Catholic laity come more and more to resemble those of their counterparts at equal levels of education and income. (We will explore this issue in more detail in Chapter 8.) We expected, however, that Jews might continue to be more liberal on abortion than persons in other religious groups.

We expected the usual strong effects for education because, historically, groups with more education have been more open to various forms of family limitation. We expected strong effects for age because our analysis, as we explain later, focuses on the "soft" reasons. In principle, approval of abortion should be highest among those who most strongly perceive the tension between moral norms and instrumental behavior, that is, young men and women who may be faced with an unwanted pregnancy.

We expected significant effects for income, despite the fact that other studies reported no such effects. The current rate of inflation, the climate of economic uncertainty, the increase in the two-earner family all imply an increase in the number of persons who may come to view abortion instrumentally.

Our second abortion question (Question 3.2) asked respondents whether they agreed or disagreed that "Women on welfare who become pregnant should be able to get an abortion at no cost to themselves." We expected strong effects for education and smaller effects for income. High income receivers' fears about paying taxes for the poor may be offset by their fears about the increase in the number of children living in female-headed households that are also supported by taxes.

Turning from birth control to another public policy that can affect fertility, we now examine opinion on the provision of child-care services. Societies can discourage fertility by encouraging women to work for pay (Blake, 1965) without providing child-care services. Pronatalist policies, in contrast, would constrain women's labor force participation or provide extensive child-care services such as maternity or paternity leaves with pay.

No matter how concerned the public becomes at the prospect of declining fertility—and they certainly are not much concerned right now—it seems unlikely that keeping women out of the labor force could readily become federal policy. It would be too unpopular with husbands and wives. It would deprive society of workers in such sex-segregated occupations as nursing, office work, and teaching. Even if such occupations were masculinized over time, restricting women's labor force participation would only further increase the dependency ratio that already looms large as the baby boom cohorts reach middle age.

Support for day-care centers and other child-care policies was rarely measured before the 1970s, judging from the list of sex-role attitude items in Mason's (1975) compendium. The Mason and Bumpass (1975) analysis of 1970 data for women of childbearing age revealed that a majority (59% of nonblacks, 80% of blacks) supported the provision of maternity leaves (of unspecified length); about half supported the provision of free day-care centers (44% of nonblacks, 80% of blacks). A 1972 survey of women in a midwestern college town reported that 79% supported government-provided day-care centers (Welch, 1975). Little evidence shows how favorable attitudes toward free day care relate to a wide range of background variables.[8] The findings for race in Mason and Bumpass (1975) suggest that persons who most perceive the need for child care do support it, but they tend to be those with just about the least political clout.

Our question on child care (Question 3.3) was like the item Mason and Bumpass (1975) analyzed from the National Fertility Survey (Westoff and Ryder, 1977), except that we used the word "can" instead of "could." Using the agree–disagree format, we asked whether "there should be free child-care centers so that women can take jobs." On theoretical grounds, one would expect that women (and their spouses) who might benefit from such services would be most favorable to them. Black women should therefore favor them more than white women because they are more likely to be employed and more likely to be single parents. Family income might have slight effects because women who are employed when their children are small include poor women who head families and highly educated women who command high salaries. The effect of education, however, should be positive, since more highly educated women are more likely to be employed than less well-educated ones. Last, we expected women to favor free child care more often than men did. Typically, the burden of arranging child care falls on employed mothers rather than on employed fathers in dual-earner families.

Because the respondent's experience might shed light on her attitude about the provision of free child care, we asked all employed mothers who had children under age 12 living at home: "Who usually takes care of your child(ren) while you are working?" We also asked the same

---

[8]A French study (Alan Guttmacher Institute, 1980b) suggests that, as awareness of a declining birthrate increases, the public more readily accepts policies that let women combine employment and childrearing in preference to limiting their access to birth control measures. Of the three-fourths of French respondents who were aware of the falling birthrate, a majority favored some form of government intervention to reverse the trend. Only a third favored restrictive abortion laws. Large majorities favored guaranteed jobs for mothers, more part-time employment, and increased family allowances.

women: "How difficult is it to arrange for this child care?" (Questions 3.4 and 3.5).

The third public policy issue we inquired about concerns the care of aged parents. A major incentive in the past for rearing children has been a belief that grown children should care for their parents when the parents were too old or too ill to care for themselves. The enactment of the Social Security Act in 1935 dented this norm. The retirement provisions ultimately covered about nine-tenths of United States employees (and some self-employed) and their dependents. Another factor that eroded grown children's responsibilities to their parents was the affluence of the 1950s. The supply of nursing and retirement facilities increased because more older people had enough money to live independently of their children. Finally, the increasing number of employed women effectively reduced the supply of caretakers for elderly parents.

Not surprisingly, surveys show that Americans think that financial independence has positive psychological consequences for aged parents (Kreps, 1977). Indeed, both financial and residential independence have come to be valued and expected. A National Council on Aging (1976) survey in 1974 showed that only 10% of the respondents believed that children should provide for elderly parents; only 5% of those under age 65 and 7% of those over aged 65 believed that moving in with the children was an important step in preparing for old age. Over three-quarters of respondents of all ages felt that economic support for the elderly should be a function of government. Most respondents specifically supported the Social Security retirement provisions as a way to do this. On the other hand, when the GSS asked respondents whether it was a good or bad idea for older people to share a home with their grown children, the proportion who thought it was a bad idea declined from 65% in 1957 to 48% in 1978 (T. Smith, 1980:7). Possibly the inflation rate during the 1970s had an effect.

Our question was more specific than the GSS item: "Do you think that elderly people who can no longer fully care for themselves would be better off living in a good nursing home or living with their children?" (Question 3.6). We expected the strongest effect from family income, since nursing homes, especially "good" ones, are expensive. We also expected strong effects from the wife's employment, since caring for someone at home is much harder for employed than non-employed women. However, caring for an elderly person who needs hourly assistance is confining work, whether the caretaker is employed outside the home or not. Since women usually perform these roles, we expected that women would be more likely than men to feel that elderly people belong in "good" nursing homes.

DATA AND METHODS

Data for this chapter come from a national probability sample of United States households (N = 2,002). Respondents were interviewed by telephone late in 1978 (see Chapter 2).

In order to test the hypotheses presented in the preceding section, we regress the fertility-related attitudinal variables on the following set of independent variables. Age and education are coded in years. Race is coded 1 = black, 0 = other. Family income is coded from 1 = less than $5,000 to 7 = more than $30,000. Religion is coded in 4 dummy variables for Roman Catholic, Jewish, other, and none, with Protestant as the omitted category. We include employment status (for women) and the presence of an employed wife (for men) because of the relevance of women's market status to fertility; it is coded 1 = employed, 0 = non-employed. Finally, we included several measures of marital and family status. Marital status is coded 1 = currently married, 0 = other. Ever-divorced is coded 1 = yes, 0 = no. Number of children is coded in actual number. Age of youngest child is coded in dummy variables for ages 0–5, 6–11, 12 and over, with no children the omitted category. Due to problems of multicollinearity between the number of children, their ages and the respondent's age, the age-of-children dummy variables are not included in the equations we report. The few significant coefficients will be reported in the text.

The dependent variables were balanced as to direction (liberal versus illiberal) in the questionnaire, but they have been recoded, as needed, so that the liberal response is high. "By nature, women are happiest at home" was coded on a scale of 1–4, from strongly agree to strongly disagree, with the liberal response as 4. "Worried about doubling world population" was coded on a scale of 1–4, with 1 = not at all worried to 4 = very worried. "Voluntarily childless couples are self-centered" was coded on a scale of 1–4, with 1 = strongly agree to 4 = strongly disagree. "Happiness" was coded on a scale of 1–3, with 1 = not too happy to 3 = very happy. "Satisfaction" was coded on a scale of 1–7, with 1 = very dissatisfied to 7 = very satisfied. "Respondent's enjoyment of own children compared to respondent's parent's enjoyment" was coded on a scale of 1–3, with 1 = enjoyed children less to 3 = enjoyed children more.

The abortion items were coded as dichotomies, with 1 = approve, 0 = disapprove. Because respondents overwhelmingly approve abortion for the three "hard" reasons, we do not analyze these items, but we do combine all six into a scale. We use the Evers and McGee (1980) mnemonics.

The item on free child care was coded on a scale of 1–4, with 1 = strongly disagree to 4 = strongly agree. The item on care of children while mother works was open-ended. "How difficult is it to arrange childcare" was coded on a scale of 1–4, with 1 = not at all difficult to 4 = very difficult. The item on care of aged parents was coded as a dichotomy, with 1 = good nursing home, 0 = live with children.

FINDINGS

Women's Place

The pronatalist attitude that women by nature are happiest at home is less common, as predicted, among women than men; 53% of the women and 43% of the men disagreed (see Table 6.1). Age, education, family income, religion, and number of children affect men's attitudes. Being younger, having more education, higher family income, no religious preference, and fewer children elicit a more liberal response (see Table 6.2). Age, education, family income, religion, and employment status affect women's response. Being younger, having a higher level of education, higher family income, being Jewish or of no religion (in contrast to being Protestant) and being employed elicit a more liberal response (see Table 6.3).

The effects of sex, age, education, race, and (for women) employment on this item were as predicted. We had not, however, predicted income or religious effects. The effects of age, education, and employment lead to the prediction that increasing proportions of men and women will come to disagree that women's proper place is at home. Compositional changes in the population in the next few decades should tend to make the liberal response a strong majority response.

Doubling World Population (2.1)

A majority of both sexes are unworried about the possibility of a doubling of world population every 40 years. About 10% were very worried and an additional 30% were somewhat worried (see Table 6.1). The worriers tended to be more highly educated and younger, as predicted, but family income failed to have the effect we expected. Blacks worry significantly less than whites do. Among women, Roman Catholics are less worried than are Protestants, but religion has no effect on men's opinion.

Table 6.1
NATALISM ATTITUDES BY SEX (IN ROUNDED PERCENTAGES)

Women happiest at home	Strongly Agree	Agree	Don't Know	Disagree	Strongly Disagree	N
Men	6	43	10	38	5	905
Women	6	35	5	43	10	1,091

Worry over world overpopulation	Very Worried	Somewhat Worried	Don't Know	Not very Worried	Not at all Worried	N
Men	10	30	1	21	38	908
Women	10	31	2	24	32	1,091

Childless couples selfish	Strongly Agree	Agree	Don't Know	Disagree	Strongly Disagree	N
Men	4	24	6	53	13	908
Women	4	17	5	52	22	1,090

Happy	Very Happy	Pretty Happy	Not too Happy	N
Men	41	51	8	901
Women	42	51	7	1,089

Satisfied	Least 1	2	3	4	5	6	7 Most	N
Men	0	0	2	7	23	36	31	908
Women	1	1	2	7	26	31	32	1,092

Enjoy children	More than Parents	Same	Less than Parents	N
Men	50	48	2	640
Women	42	55	4	816

We had predicted that worry levels about world population would have increased from the 1960s because of concern over world energy supplies and because our item was more specific than the earlier one. An increase from about one-fourth to about two-fifths of the population who are worried is not dramatic. To the extent that United States public opinion is antinatalist, concern about world population growth seems to play only a minor role.

Voluntary Childlessness (2.2)

In line with earlier findings, we predicted that respondents would tend to agree that voluntarily childless couples were being too self-centered, but only about a fourth of the respondents agreed, men somewhat more than women (see Table 6.1). Yet a similar question in the National Fertility Study ("Women who do not want at least one child are being selfish") drew an opposite response. In 1970 72% of a sample of ever-married women in childbearing years agreed; in 1973 in a somewhat different sample 86% agreed (Mason et al., 1976) in contrast to 21% of the women in our sample.

How can we account for so sharp a difference in response? The two items differed in several ways. Our item referred to couples. The National Fertility Study item referred to individual women. Possibly respondents are more critical of women than of couples who do not want children. A second difference is the time the items were presented. So

Table 6.2
REGRESSIONS FOR MEN'S NATALISM-RELATED ATTITUDES (STANDARDIZED COEFFICIENTS IN PARENTHESES)

Category High=	Women happiest at home SD	Population very worried	Childless selfish SD	Happy very	Satisfied very	Enjoy kids more
Age	-.006(-.113)*	-.014(-.173)*	-.010(.178)*	-.000(-.003)	.008(.097)*	-.006(-.140)*
Education	.044(.199)*	.026(.075)*	.037(.153)*	.006(.028)	.006(.015)	-.013(-.074)
Race	.009(.004)	-.328(-.079)*	.046(.016)	-.185(-.074)*	.006(.001)	-.095(-.045)
Family income	.065(.169)*	.030(.049)	.041(.099)*	.010(.029)	.059(.093)*	.005(.015)
Catholic	.071(.043)	-.103(-.040)	-.046(-.026)	-.025(-.016)	-.173(-.064)	.099(.074)
Jew	.193(.059)	-.202(-.039)	-.057(-.016)	.007(.002)	-.472(-.088)*	-.132(-.047)
Other	.055(.009)	.130(.001)	-.112(-.017)	.000(.000)	.299(.030)	-.099(-.020)
None	.165(.093)*	-.197(-.007)	-.029(-.015)	-.002(-.001)	-.166(-.057)	-.106(-.067)
Ever-divorced	-.014(-.009)	-.102(-.039)	.022(.012)	.058(.037)	-.051(-.019)	-.163(-.126)*
Wife employed	.083(.063)	.047(.023)	-.022(-.016)	.060(.049)	-.044(-.020)	.025(.023)
Number of children	-.025(-.072)*	.017(.032)	-.027(-.071)	.001(.003)	-.004(-.007)	.021(.069)
Marital status	-.127(-.070)	-.091(-.032)	-.054(-.028)	.209(.123)*	.132(.044)	-.165(-.085)
N	905	908	908	901	908	700
a	1.92	2.31	2.65	2.02	5.20	2.98
R^2	.17	.05	.11	.03	.04	.06
$\bar{X}$	2.46	2.12	2.78	2.34	5.84	2.44

* $p < .05$

Table 6.3
REGRESSIONS FOR WOMEN'S NATALISM-RELATED ATTITUDES (STANDARDIZED COEFFICIENTS IN PARENTHESES)

Category High=	Women happiest at home SD	Population very worried	Childless selfish SD	Happy very	Satisfied very	Enjoy kids more
Age	-.008(-.141)*	-.012(-.153)*	-.011(-.196)*	-.001(-.015)	.006(.062)	-.003(-.057)
Education	.074(.023)*	.051(.119)*	.045(.143)*	.023(.091)*	.019(.037)	-.018(-.074)
Race	-.077(-.027)	-.270(-.071)*	-.196(-.070)*	-.236(-.102)*	-.505(-.112)*	-.037(-.018)
Family income	.055(.127)*	.030(.053)	.039(.093)*	.027(.078)*	.050(.073)*	-.002(-.005)
Catholic	.005(.003)	-.202(-.085)*	-.117(-.067)*	-.033(-.023)	-.041(-.015)	-.020(-.016)
Jew	.341(.086)*	.002(.000)	.085(.022)	-.228(-.071)*	-.036(-.057)	-.097(-.034)
Other	-.037(-.006)	-.141(-.017)	.016(.003)	-.002(-.000)	.368(.037)	.151(.031)
None	.386(.149)*	.059(.017)	.186(.073)*	.026(.012)	.127(.031)	-.104(-.048)
Ever divorced	.090(.049)	.103(.042)	-.027(-.015)	.097(.065)*	-.108(-.037)	-.032(-.024)
Employment status	.144(.095)*	-.036(-.018)	.039(.026)	-.073(-.059)	-.153(-.064)*	-.010(-.009)
Number of children	-.002(-.005)	-.019(-.035)	-.019(-.047)	-.002(-.007)	-.000(-.000)	-.003(-.010)
Marital status	-.100(-.056)	-.091(-.038)	-.159(-.091)*	.388(.266)*	.423(.149)*	-.003(-.002)
N	1091	1091	1090	1089	1092	851
a	1.74	2.12	2.86	1.73	4.95	2.75
R^2	.21	.08	.14	.12	.08	.01
$\bar{X}$	2.60	2.21	2.95	2.34	5.76	2.37

* $p < .05$

large a difference is surprising, however, for so short a time period. Yet when one considers the speed with which Roman Catholics shifted their views on various sexual behaviors during the 1960s, a rapid opinion shift seems more plausible. A fourth difference is that the National Fertility Study sample included only ever-married women of child-bearing age. Our sample represents all United States women. However, including older women should reduce the liberality of the response, not increase it.

It seems most probable that the large difference in response to the two items stems from two factors. First, referring to the selfishness of couples rather than of individual women may increase the liberality of response. Second, the liberality of response to our item may represent an important opinion shift. Both of these propositions will be easy to test in subsequent studies. It seems fair to conclude, however, that the response indicates reduced social pressure to have children. However much voluntarily childless couples may have been defined as maladjusted in the past, public opinion hardly defines them as antisocial today.

Men who tended to disagree that voluntarily childless couples were self-centered were younger and had higher levels of education and income, as expected. For obvious reasons, men who had no children were more likely to disagree than were men whose youngest child was more than 6 years old. However, the opinion of men whose youngest child was 5 or less did not differ from that of men with no children (not in tables). Women who tended to disagree that voluntarily childless couples were self-centered were younger, more highly educated, white, unmarried, and had higher incomes. Roman Catholic women were less liberal and women of no religion were more liberal than Protestant women (see Table 6.3). Women whose youngest child was 5 or less were less liberal than women with no children (not in tables).

Thus the least pronatalist opinion tends to be held by women and men in the more powerful social groups, that is, by persons with higher levels of education and income. Although women as a group are less powerful than men, women's unique ability to bear children may give them some influence on fertility decisions in individual families. However, evidence on decision making among voluntarily childless couples is mixed (Silka and Kiesler, 1977).

Happiness and Having Children (2.3)

One indicator of a pronatalist climate of opinion is the extent to which the absence of children lowers self-ratings of happiness. Conversely, an antinatalist indicator would be the extent to which the presence of children lowers happiness ratings. Although the happiness question might not be answered with total honesty, there is no reason to suppose that candor varies with the number or ages of children. We expected the main effects on self-rated happiness would come from family income, race, and marital status. We expected no effects from the presence or ages of children or from sex.

As expected, men's and women's happiness levels were about the same. Two-fifths were very happy and about half were pretty happy (see Table 6.1). For men, race and marital status had expected effects.

Black men and unmarried men were less happy than their counterparts
(see Table 6.2). Unexpectedly, family income had no effect. Men with
children under 6 were less happy than men with no children. For
women, race, marital status, and family income had expected effects.
Also as expected, the presence or absence of children of any age had no
effects. Why the presence of children under 6 would reduce men's but
not women's happiness is not intuitively obvious since women are
more constrained than men by the presence of preschoolers. Perhaps
some men resent their wives' being so preoccupied with others. Education had positive effects. Protestant women were happier than Jewish
women. Unexpectedly, ever-divorced women were happier than the
never-divorced. Many ever-divorced women have presumably remar-
ried. Perhaps the category "never-divorced" includes a number of
women in unhappy marriages who lack the resources or the inclination
to terminate the marriage (see Table 6.3).

Children and Life Satisfaction (2.4)

We now ask whether the presence or absence of children or their ages
affected a respondent's satisfaction with life. We expected family income to affect satisfaction positively and the presence of young children to affect it negatively, especially for women because of the typical
constraints on the mothers of preschoolers.

The proportion of respondents who were satisfied with their lives
was much like that reported in Campbell et al. (1976:423): 91% of the
men and 89% of the women scored in the top three (of seven) categories. For both men and women, income had its expected positive effects. Other findings were unexpected. Men's and women's satisfaction
seems to stem from different factors. Older men were more satisfied
than younger men, but age had no effect for women. Married women
were more satisfied than other women, but marital status had no effect
for men. Jewish men were less satisfied than Protestant men, but religion had no effect for women. Black women were less satisfied than
other women, but race had no effect for men. Employed women were
less satisfied than nonemployed women. Perhaps employed women
feel dissatisfied because they bear a disproportionate share of housework, or perhaps they may feel underpaid in relation to their training
and experience.

Most important, satisfaction was not affected by the presence, absence or ages of children (see Tables 6.2 and 6.3). Unlike the findings
reported by Campbell et al., (1976:423), these findings point to no

sharp decrease in reported satisfaction levels of parents of young children. On the other hand, neither does the presence of a child of any age increase satisfaction. In sum, with the exception of men with children under 6, the relationship of happiness and satisfaction to the presence or absence of children seems neither pro- nor antinatalist.

Enjoyment of Children (2.5)

Forty-five percent of respondents reported enjoying their children more than did their own parents; 52%, about the same; 3%, less (not shown). Younger and never-divorced men tended to enjoy their children more than their parents had. Probably women's custody of children affects divorced men's enjoyment. No background variables affected women.

Abortion (3.1)

Response to the abortion items tended to cluster into the so-called hard and soft reasons (see Table 6.4 for frequencies). A strong majority (85–93%) favors legal abortion for reasons of the mother's health, pregnancy resulting from rape, or the possibility of serious defect in the child. Only a little over half (51–58%) favor legal abortion if the mother is unmarried, has a low income, or does not want the child. Sex differences are slight. About 2% more men favor abortion for each reason.

We will report significant background effects roughly in order of their frequency for the three soft reasons and for the total score. (We omitted the hard reasons from the regression equations because there is so little variance to explain.) Number of children negatively affected all soft reasons except MONEY for men and all except UNMARRIED for women. Family income positively affected all the reasons for both men and women. Education positively affected all the reasons for men. It affected only MONEY for women, although the coefficients for UN-MARRIED and NOMORE children were of borderline significance. Being currently married affected all the soft reasons negatively for both men and women. Age had no effects for men, but it negatively affected UNMARRIED for women. Effects for religion were spotty. Jewish women were more liberal than Protestant women for all the reasons, and Jewish men were more liberal than Protestant men for all the reasons except MONEY. Roman Catholic men were less liberal than Protestant men with respect to MONEY. Men and women of no religion were more

Table 6.4
FERTILITY POLICY ATTITUDES BY SEX (IN ROUNDED PERCENTAGES)

Percent approving abortion under each condition (N in parentheses)

	HEALTH	RAPE	DEFECT	UNMARRIED	MONEY	NOMORE
Men	93 (897)	87 (884)	86 (887)	52 (876)	58 (881)	54 (875)
Women	92 (1070)	85 (1056)	85 (1062)	52 (1064)	56 (1067)	51 (1055)

Free abortion for welfare mothers

	Strongly Disagree	Disagree	Don't Know	Agree	Strongly Agree	N
Men	25	28	4	28	14	910
Women	29	28	5	22	16	1,092

Child care should be available

	Strongly Disagree	Disagree	Don't Know	Agree	Strongly Agree	N
Men	10	41	4	41	4	908
Women	7	37	3	43	9	1,090

Elderly better off with children or nursing homes

	Children	Don't Know	Nursing Home	N
Men	40	14	46	892
Women	44	12	44	1,076

liberal than Protestants for all the reasons (see Tables 6.5 and 6.6). These findings point to the importance of the effects of family income and education, especially for men. Since men are typically the legislators and judges in the United States, and since such occupations tend to recruit persons with high levels of education and income, we predict that those who oppose legal abortion will encounter great difficulties.

Free Abortion for Women on Welfare (3.2)

Approval of free abortion for welfare clients is lower than for abortion that is not charged to the taxpayers. Of those respondents who expressed an opinion, 28% disapproved and 28% strongly disapproved of free abortion for welfare clients. The background variables significantly affecting men's approval are education, race (blacks are more liberal), income, being Jewish or of no religion, ever-divorced, and not being currently married. For women, education, being Jewish, and (negatively) number of children are significant (see Tables 6.5 and 6.6).

It is interesting that black men (but not black women) favor free abortion for welfare women more than do their counterparts. Traditionally, blacks connected abortion with genocide and viewed it more negatively than whites did. Black men's greater approval of free abortion may reflect the recent dramatic rise in the proportion of blacks obtaining abortions, but this does not explain why black women's approval of abortion has not increased in response to their behavioral

Table 6.5

REGRESSION ON ABORTION QUESTIONS FOR MEN (STANDARDIZED COEFFICIENTS IN PARENTHESES)

High=	ABORTION total scale yes	MONEY yes	NOMORE yes	UNMARRIED yes	Welfare mothers abort. available strongly agree
Age	.005(.031)	.001(.022)	.002(.058)	.002(.051)	-.001(-.007)
Education	.075(.118)*	.013(.081)*	.015(.092)*	.020(.120)*	.046(.136)*
Race	.306(.040)	.122(.062)	.075(.038)	.120(.060)	.301(.074)*
Family income	.213(.195)*	.039(.137)*	.052(.183)*	.053(.184)*	.085(.145)*
Catholic	-.351(-.074)*	-.085(-.070)*	-.074(-.060)	.000(.000)	-.110(-.044)
Jew	.697(.074)*	.136(.056)	.214(.088)*	.260(.106)*	.598(.120)*
Other	.500(.029)	.124(.028)	.217(.049)	.071(.016)	.170(.019)
None	.511(.100)*	.118(.090)*	.180(.136)*	.133(.100)*	.196(.072)*
Ever-divorced	.159(.033)	.049(.039)	.019(.015)	.062(.050)	.200(.079)*
Wife employed	-.194(-.052)	-.036(-.036)	.014(.014)	-.040(-.041)	.051(.026)
Number of children	-.132(-.132)*	-.028(-.107)	-.028(-.110)*	-.025(-.095)*	-.037(-.070)
Marital status	-.498(-.096)*	-.148(-.110)*	-.161(-.119)*	-.114(-.098)*	-.231(-.083)*
N	910	910	910	910	910
a	2.81	.37	.19	.09	1.55
R^2	.14	.10	.13	.12	.12
$\overline{X}$	4.17	.57	.54	.52	2.33

* $p < .05$

Table 6.6
REGRESSION ON ABORTION QUESTIONS FOR WOMEN (STANDARDIZED COEFFICIENTS IN PARENTHESES)

High=	ABORTION total scale	MONEY	NOMORE	UNMARRIED	Welfare mothers abort. available
	yes	yes	yes	yes	strongly agree
Age	-.011(-.068)*	-.002(-.039)	-.002(-.040)	-.003(-.084)*	-.002(-.021)
Education	.030(.035)	.014(.068)*	.012(.058)	.013(.064)	.060(.135)*
Race	.174(.023)	.091(.049)	.037(.020)	.036(.019)	.087(.022)
Family income	.198(.174)*	.043(.151)*	.042(.149)*	.043(.152)*	.029(.049)
Catholic	-.218(.047)	-.031(-.026)	.002(.002)	-.018(-.016)	.040(.016)
Jew	1.132(.109)*	.258(.100)*	.353(.136)*	.309(.119)*	.850(.155)*
Other	-.275(-.017)	-.019(-.005)	.069(.017)	.156(.038)	-.195(-.022)
None	1.075(.157)*	.283(.167)*	.283(.166)*	.270(.158)*	.602(.167)*
Ever divorced	.533(.109)*	.132(.109)*	.120(.099)*	.079(.065)*	.116(.045)
Wife employed	.093(.023)	.003(.003)	.005(.005)	.001(.001)	.034(.016)
Number of children	-.099(-.090)*	-.022(-.082)*	-.022(-.083)*	-.013(-.047)	-.046(-.080)*
Marital status	-.591(-.126)*	-.137(-.117)*	-.124(-.106)*	-.161(-.137)*	-.029(-.012)
N	1092	1089	1089	1089	1092
a	3.80	.37	.33	.41	1.46
R^2	.15	.13	.13	.12	.11
$\bar{X}$	4.09	.56	.51	.51	2.27

* $p < .05$

change. Perhaps black women are more concerned with the issues of sexual morality implied by this question.

Free abortion for women on welfare probably taps complex conflicting feelings about taxes, race, and sexual morality. Although the item does not explicitly refer to race, it probably evokes racial images. Although it refers to giving poor women a free service, the alternative for the taxpayer is (presumably) a higher welfare grant. This alternative is not attractive. A majority of respondents (62% of men, 67% of women) feel that women on welfare have babies to increase their incomes (see

Chapter 8). Altogether, the response to this question provides question-able evidence on natalist sentiment.

Free Child Care (3.3)

Women are a little more likely than men to agree that child care should be free, 52% versus 45%. For men, favoring free child care is

Table 6.7
REGRESSIONS ON CHILD CARE AND NURSING HOMES BY SEX AND BY DIFFICULTY IN FINDING CHILD CARE FOR EMPLOYED MOTHERS OF CHILDREN UNDER 12 (STANDARDIZED COEFFICIENTS IN PARENTHESES)

| | Males | | Females | | |
| | Nursing home | Child care | Nursing home | Child care | Child care hard to obtain |
High=	nursing home better	Strongly agree	nursing home better	Strongly agree	very difficult
Age	.004(.108)*	-.003(-.056)	.002(.063)	-.007(-.109)*	-.036(-.207)*
Education	-.004(-.025)	-.009(-.037)	.001(.006)	-.011(-.034)	-.010(-.018)
Race	-.023(-.012)	.578(.200)*	-.155(-.088)*	.537(.189)*	.963(.287)*
Family income	.026(.094)*	-.040(-.097)*	.008(.028)	-.009(-.020)	-.018(-.026)
Catholic	-.050(-.043)	.192(.107)*	-.005(-.049)	.105(.059)	.459(.170)*
Jew	.055(.024)	.363(.102)*	-.009(-.035)	.496(.125)*	.564(.074)
Other	-.301(-.071)*	.114(.017)	-.173(-.044)	.282(.045)	----
None	.020(.016)	.140(.072)*	-.054(-.033)	.251(.096)*	.799(.203)*
Ever divorced	.037(.031)	.022(.012)	.045(.039)	.035(.019)	-.045(-.019)
Employment status	.068(.073)	.129(.090)*	.044(.047)	.018(.012)	----
Number of children	-.004(-.015)	-.018(-.047)	-.002(-.008)	-.028(-.067)	.039(.054)
Marital status	.029(.023)	-.107(-.054)	.030(.027)	-.141(-.078)*	-.060(-.022)
N	892	908	1076	1090	188
a	.27	2.78	.35	3.02	2.98
R^2	.04	.08	.02	.09	.18
$\overline{X}$	.53	2.42	.50	2.56	1.97

* $p < .05$

related to being black, Roman Catholic or Jewish, having a low income, and having an employed wife. For women, it is related to being young, black, Jewish, having no religion, and not being currently married (see Table 6.7).

Obtaining Child Care (3.4 and 3.5)

In order to help explain women's response to the issue of free child care, we asked employed mothers (with children under age 12 at home) who cared for their children and how difficult it was to arrange it. Relatively few employed mothers used day care or nursery school. Some of the 198 employed mothers used more than one type, hence the total types added to 230 rather than to 198 (not shown)—38 mothers used a baby sitter; 28, the child him- or herself; 28, the husband; 24, the mother-in-law; 19, an older child; 11, nursery school; 8, a relative; 8, a friend; 6, day care; and 60, some other means. Difficulty in arranging child care was reported by 14% of the employed mothers; 16% reported it was somewhat difficult; 21% reported it was not very difficult; and 49% reported that it was not at all difficult.

The regression analysis helps to explain why some women favor free child care (see Table 6.7). Young women, black women, and women of no religion were significantly more likely to agree strongly that child care should be free; they were also more likely to report that it was very difficult to obtain. However, although Roman Catholic women found it harder to obtain, they were not more likely to think it should be free. Conversely, Jewish women and women not currently married favored free child care but did not report that they found it hard to obtain.

The response to the free-child-care question seems antinatalist. This conclusion must be tempered, however, by the fact that half of the employed mothers with children under 12 report that obtaining child care is not at all difficult. However, it seems unlikely that free child care will soon be a hot item on someone's political agenda. Most of the people who favor it tend to lack political clout: the young, the black, and the poor.

Where Should the Elderly Live? (3.6)

Whether aged parents who can no longer care for themselves are better off in a good nursing home or living with their children is a question that elicits some uncertainty. Of respondents who replied (2%

refused), 45% thought that elderly parents were better off in a good nursing home; 42% thought they should live with their children; and 13% were undecided (see Table 6.4). Of those who had an opinion, 53% of the men and 50% of the women, thought elderly parents were better off in a nursing home.

For men, being older and having a higher income were related to approving nursing home care. Being of "other" religion—a tiny category—rather than Protestant related negatively to approval of nursing home care (see Table 6.7). For women, only being white related positively to approving nursing homes. However, the variables we used explain only 4% of the variance for men and 2% for women. Probably the main significance of this item is that it indicates that about half of the respondents see the link between rearing children and being cared for by them in old age as being broken.

CONCLUSIONS

The purpose of this chapter has been to assess the United States climate of opinion on fertility. It has generally been assumed to be pronatalist.[9] We argue, instead, that the increasing cost of and decreasing rewards for rearing children tegether with the ease of fertility control comprise a set of factors that should so act as to reduce pronatalist sentiment. On the whole our findings indicate a climate of opinion that cannot reasonably be described as pronatalist.

A majority of respondents denied the natural happiness of housebound mothers. Although only a minority were worried about the rapid rate of world population growth, a majority favored legal abortion under all circumstances as an individual right in the United States. The presence or absence of children was irrelevant to respondents' perceptions of personal happiness or satisfaction with life. A large majority of respondents did not see voluntarily childless couples as being self-

[9]How pronatalist must structural factors and opinion be to maintain fertility? Presumably, some must be favorable if a population is to replace itself. Blake (1969:529) argues that population replacement would not occur among humans were it not for the complex social organization and system of incentives that encourage mating, pregnancy, and the care, support, and rearing of children. Lorber (1975) similarly argues that it is impractical to assume that children will be reared for 15–20 years without strong social pressures. Even van den Berghe (1979:195, 192), who argues that all humans are programmed to maximize their fitness (i.e., to want children), is concerned that the rise in divorce and sharp increase in the number of unmarried persons living together have thrown the American family into "crisis."

centered. Finally, they tended to favor policies that have antinatalist effects.

Three-fifths of the women and about half the men do not believe that women are by nature happiest when they are home, caring for their children. It is reasonable to suppose that belief in this proposition has decreased over time. We cannot know for certain because the level of belief at earlier periods must be inferred from literary and journalistic sources. Since younger or more highly educated persons are less likely to believe in the happiness of the house-bound mother, one would expect the belief to become even less widely held in the future.

Only two-fifths of the respondents were worried about the rate of world population growth. As expected, the more worried respondents were younger or more highly educated. In contrast, large majorities favored legal abortion if the mother's health was endangered, if the pregnancy resulted from rape, or if there was a chance of serious defect in the child. A majority (men more than women) favored legal abortion under any circumstances.

Except for the lesser happiness of men whose children were less than six, neither the presence nor the absence of children affected respondents' feelings of happiness or satisfaction with their lives. Children seem irrelevant to the perception of individual well-being. One cannot therefore argue that the beneficial effect of children on individual well-being may offset antinatalist structural factors. Furthermore, the public apparently does not disapprove of couples who do not want children. Large majorities of both sexes disagreed that voluntarily childless couples were being self-centered. This may be one of the most important findings of this study.

Respondents split 50–50 in support of free child-care centers. The opposition tended to come from persons with higher levels of education or income, indicating that support for free child care may encounter difficulty in the legislative arena.

Respondents were also divided on the question as to whether elderly people were better off with their children or in a good nursing home. However people feel about it, caring for the aged at home will probably become more difficult in the future. Old people are living longer, hence they experience increasing periods of frailty before they die. Ever fewer middle-aged women are at home full-time to care for others. It is therefore plausible that support for free child-care centers may increase while support for caring for old people away from home also increases.

The politics of fertility are currently a confused mixture of pro- and antinatalist positions. Since population maintenance is not seen as a problem, political groups hold opinions that are consistent with their views on other issues. Whether or not liberals and conservatives see the separation of sexual pleasure and reproduction as a positive good, both tend to feel that government regulation of individual sexual behavior is hard to enforce and unjustifiably restricts individual privacy. In contrast, Far Right groups are so concerned about the morality of separating sexual pleasure and reproduction that, like the bureaucrats in a number of communist countries, they favor government regulation of the means of fertility control. However, liberals tend to favor (and conservative and Far Right groups tend to oppose) policies that would ease the burden of childrearing for individual parents.

However confused public opinion may be on pro- and antinatalism, one cannot doubt that the current social structure is strongly antinatalist. Trying to show the ineffectiveness of the family planning approach to fertility control, Kingsley Davis (1967:783) described a realistic government policy that would reduce fertility: Squeeze consumers through taxation and inflation; make housing scarce by limiting construction; force wives and mothers to work outside the home to offset inadequate male wages while providing few child-care facilities; encourage cityward migration by paying low wages in the country and providing few rural jobs. Increase city congestion by starving mass transit systems, increase personal insecurity by encouraging conditions that produce unemployment and haphazard political arrest.

The communist countries appear to meet all of these conditions. The Western democracies meet all of them with the important exception of haphazard political arrest. One hopes that many of these structural conditions will improve. When and if they do, then we can see clearly the extent to which couples prefer to invest the wife's human capital in the children or in the couple's own standard of living.

CHAPTER SEVEN

Wives' Employment, Household Behaviors, and Sex-Role Attitudes[1]

The massive increase in women's labor-force participation (LFP) during recent decades is having major consequences for United States society in such seemingly diverse areas as fertility rates (Ward and Butz, 1978), the reappearance of the women's movement, and the rise in property crime rates owing to the increase in the number of dwellings unoccupied during the day (L. Cohen and Felson, 1979). Norms for men's and women's behavior are also changing (Mason et al., 1976), presumably due in large part to new work patterns. Just how these trends relate to behavior and attitude changes of individuals in households remains unclear. Do people who experience new patterns also change other behaviors and attitudes or are the consequences of these trends more diffuse and long term?

Research on the consequences of women's labor-force participation for individuals has tended to focus on effects of their current employment status on attitudes (Mason and Bumpass, 1975, Huber et al., 1978) or on household behaviors (Bahr, 1974). Yet current employment status is only one aspect of a woman's labor-force participation that could affect spouses' behavior and attitudes. In our view at least three aspects of wives' labor-force participation could have important indi-

[1]This chapter is a revision of an article published in Social Forces in September, 1981.

148

vidual effects: current employment status, work attachment during a given period, and level of earnings.

First, a wife's current employment could induce pragmatic changes due to rescheduling of household activities and time constraints. A husband might wash the supper dishes and bathe the children because his wife had a night job. Hence her current employment status might exert mainly a temporary effect on the household division of labor rather than a longer term effect that would include attitudes about role obligations. Family differences therefore would be most clear between those in which the wife was currently employed and those in which she was nonemployed, whatever her past labor force status.

Second, wives' employment could cause gradual and cumulative changes such that wife's work attachment over time would affect household behaviors and attitudes more than would her current employment status. A woman's current labor force status, unlike a man's, may not adequately indicate her labor market behavior over time (Maret-Havens, 1977). In contrast, a work attachment index could reflect seasonal, part-time, discontinuous aspects of women's labor-force participation patterns. A woman's current employment status might imply little about her participation next year or last. An overall female labor-force participation rate of 50% might imply that half the women work continuously or that every woman works half-time. If wives' employment induces behavioral and attitudinal changes that persist even if they are not employed currently, family differences would occur mainly between those in which the wife had been employed a major portion of a recent time period and those in which she had not, whatever her current status.

Third, a wife's employment may have few effects unless her earnings are high enough to affect the family balance of power. If so, a wife's earnings or earnings potential would relate more strongly to attitudes and behaviors than either her current employment status or work attachment, implying that attitude and behavioral change needed for women's social equality may depend more on their chances to enter the best-paid jobs rather than on their chances to do market work.[2]

Using a national probability sample of married couples, our purpose is to test the effect of work attachment, current employment status, and earnings on both spouses' attitudes and behaviors. We now outline a theoretical rationale for the specific hypotheses tested in this study.

---

[2]Farkas (1976) argues that the ratio between husband's and wife's earnings is a more important determinant of the balance of power, but he finds no effect of that ratio on the division of household labor (nor do we in Chapter 4).

HYPOTHESES

The Relation of Work Attachment and Current Employment

Past research reports that women's past and current labor-force participation relate strongly (Mahoney, 1961; Ben Porath, 1973; Waite, 1978). This finding seems trivially true, but in fact it implies either that factors determining past employment remain unchanged or that past labor-force participation itself affected current employment status, reinforcing the likelihood that a woman will or will not work for pay.

The factors that affect women's labor-force participation are less stable than those affecting men's because of women's domestic responsibilities: current family status, including ages and number of children (Sweet, 1973); husband's income (Cain, 1966); his attitudes about her employment (J. Morgan et al., 1966); her marketability—education, job training, experience (Sweet, 1973); local labor market conditions (Bowen and Finegan, 1969); and her personal market work preferences (Dowdall, 1974; Waite, 1978). Although education may remain constant after a certain age, job skills may improve or deteriorate (Rosenthal, 1978). Women may move to regions with different employment opportunities (Long, 1974). Children age; new ones may be born. Furthermore, some of these factors may respond to labor force experience: a wife's or her husband's preferences, the presence of preschoolers, increased labor market knowledge, or the opportunity cost of nonemployment (Waite, 1976).

The potency of work attachment to predict current employment status should depend on the stability of the factors just noted, on other unmeasured factors, and on the quality of the work attachment measure. The first part of our analysis will therefore examine the relation between work attachment and current employment status. We expect to find that a wife's work attachment will affect her current employment status independently of the relatively stable factors captured by the measure.

Household Behaviors

Next we will examine the extent to which women's current employment status, work attachment, and earnings affect marital decision making and the division of household labor. Studies of decision making or "family power" have been plagued by methodological problems with substantive consequences. Typically, only wives are interviewed; resulting biases are then incorporated into the research (Safilios-Rothschild, 1969). Moreover, decision-making scales have often combined trivial daily decisions, such as what to serve for supper, with major infrequent ones, such as whether to move to another city (Safilios-Rothschild, 1970; Blood and Wolfe, 1960). Not surprisingly, analyses of the relation between decision making and wives' employment report mixed results; many researchers report more power for employed wives (Bahr, 1974; Blood and Wolfe, 1960), although the latter stress generally high levels of egalitarianism.

Due to time constraints, employed wives should make fewer trivial daily decisions than do nonemployed wives, but time constraints should not affect major decision making. On common sense grounds, we would expect that the higher the absolute value of the wife's earnings and the longer her record of work attachment, the more voice she would be perceived to have in family decisions. We thus expect wife's earnings and work attachment to affect perception of decision making most, and wife's current employment status to affect it least.

We will then examine the effect of wives' employment on the division of household labor (see also Chapter 4). Research based on time-budget studies shows that employed wives' husbands spent little more time doing housework than do other husbands, and neither group does very much (Vanek, 1974; Walker and Woods, 1976). However, employed wives work fewer hours at home than do nonemployed wives, hence their husbands' relative contribution is higher (Pleck, 1977). Since time-budget data are costly to collect, such studies to date have included few other variables—at most, a few demographic but not attitudinal ones (R. Berk and Berk, 1979; F. Stafford and Duncan, 1979).

We expect that wives' employment will affect husbands' and wives' relative contributions to household tasks for several reasons. First, a currently employed woman, having less time at home, may cut corners or receive more help from her husband, changing their relative contributions. Second, her long-term employment may affect spouses' attitudes about appropriate household work roles for husbands and wives such that one or both favor a more equal division of labor. Third, the absolute level of her earnings (for the effect of wife/husband wage ratio, see Chapter 4) may give her the bargaining power to demand more help from her husband, whatever his attitudes or preferences (Farkas, 1976). As with our decision-making hypothesis, we expect current employment status to exert the weakest effects and wife's earnings and work attachment, the strongest.

Sex-Role Attitudes

Last, we examine effects of current employment status, work attachment, and earnings on five sex-role attitudes. A wife's employment may change her own or her husband's attitudes about sex roles for several reasons. An employed wife or her husband may be cognitively uncomfortable if he opposes married women's employment. Particularly if the household needs her earnings, the husband may change his views; hence, the higher her earnings, the more likely such a change might be. Furthermore, attitudes may change gradually but permanently over time as a woman's employment becomes more acceptable to her family and as their definitions of women's roles broaden. We expected long-term consequences to be more diffuse than immediate ones from current employment, perhaps ranging over a wider set of issues.

We examine five issues ranging from those specifically related to a wife's employment to general sex-role issues. First, a husband's attitude to his wife's employment is both immediate and specific and should respond to both her current and past employment (Ferber, 1982). Second, each spouse's attitudes toward married women's employment are more general but still pertinent to the wife's current employment status (Mason and Bumpass, 1975; Mason et al., 1976). Third, a norm on family financial support as part of a wife's role may have begun to develop. If wives' employment promotes such a norm, we would expect the change to occur over the long run, not in response to brief fluctuations in her labor force status.

The fourth and fifth issues are more remote from household affairs. The Equal Rights Amendment relates to women's employment as well as to other general issues. Indeed, a wife's current employment status affects her husband's but not her own ERA attitude (Huber et al., 1978). Whether ERA attitudes are affected by work attachment or earnings would again be determined by how diffuse such effects are. Finally, abortion availability, which feminists and many social scientists see as a necessary condition for women's equality, may also be a religious issue. Attitudes about abortion may be an ultimate test of how diffuse are any effects of work attachment on current attitudes.

The causal order of current sex-role attitudes and current employment behavior must be justified because although women's employment decisions cannot be affected plausibly by attitudes on such issues as the ERA or abortion, they could be affected by attitudes toward maternal employment. The only adequate nonrecursive test of this relation reported no significant effect in either direction but a near-significant path from labor force status to sex-role attitudes (Molm, 1978).[3] On logical grounds, we also assume that any impact runs from current or past employment to household division of labor and decision making, rather than the reverse.

In sum, this research tests five hypotheses:

1. A wife's work attachment affects her current employment status independently of the stable factors measured.
2. A wife's current employment status will have the least effect and her work attachment and earnings the strongest effects on spouse decision making.
3. A wife's current employment status will have the least effect and her work attachment and earnings the strongest effects on the division of household labor.
4. A wife's current employment status will have the least effect and her work attachment and earnings the strongest effects on sex-role attitudes.
5. Husbands' attitudes will be less affected by wives' employment than will wives' attitudes.

DATA AND METHODS

Our data come from a national United States probability sample (N = 2002) interviewed by telephone in November 1978. If possible, both husbands and wives were interviewed. This chapter uses data only from these 682 couples because we want to test the effect of wives' employment on both husbands and wives. The wives ranged in age from 18 to 66 years, with about one-third under 30—thus with less than 10 years potential work time, particularly for the college-educated. The late twenties are also likely years out of the labor force for those who remain nonemployed when preschool children are present. This would present problems if some of the variables used here interact with age in their effects on attitudes or behavior—that is, if the meaning of work varies during different life stages. When equations in the present analysis were reestimated including work experience–age interaction terms, none of these terms was significant, but this problem should be kept in mind when interpreting the findings.

[3]One other nonrecursive test (Smith-Lovin and Tickamyer, 1978) found a near-significant path in the opposite direction, but their measures make this path hard to interpret. Employment behavior was measured for years since the woman married; sex-role attitudes, at age 30. Hence the authors assumed that attitudes retroactively affected behavior.

Another interpretation problem concerns the use of cross-sectional data. Ideally, we would examine *changes* in attitudes and behavior over a time period from work experience during that period (e.g., Macke *et al.*, 1977; Spitze and Waite, 1980); however, no such data are available for the variables we used or for a sample of married couples. Thus when we discuss effects of work attachment on attitudes and behavior, this limitation must be kept in mind.

We predict three separate sets of equations with the following dependent variables: wife's current employment status; husbands' and wives' perceptions of household decision making and the division of household labor; and both spouses' attitudes on issues related to women's employment. We use regression analysis; the only equations with dichotomous dependent variables (ERA attitudes) have splits well within the range in which regression and other techniques have similar results (Goodman, 1976). Unstandardized regression coefficients are reported to allow cross-equation comparisons.

An adequate measure of a woman's work attachment should reflect a relatively long period of time so as not to be affected by a single brief labor force absence; it should also reflect seasonal and part-time variations (Maret-Havens, 1977). The first characteristic can be determined by years worked over a period (J. Morgan *et al.*, 1966;) and the second, by months (Mahoney, 1961) or weeks (Shaw, 1980) worked over the period. Using 1967–1971 data for the National Longitudinal Survey of Mature Women 30–44, Maret-Havens captured all three characteristics by calculating an index based on number of years worked between leaving school and 1967 (maximum contribution to index = .50) and on number of hours per week and weeks per year between 1967 and 1971 (maximum combined contribution to index = .50). Although the index varies nicely between 0 and 1, it has no direct intuitive interpretation.

Our index, based on a recent 10-year period, is more easily interpretable and varies between 0 and 10. Full-time, year round (i.e., over 6 months, over 35 hours per week) work for one year counts as 1, whereas one-third of a point is subtracted for part-year work and one-third of a point for part-time work for a year. These somewhat arbitrary choices resulted in only a 9% decrease from total years worked.

Current employment status is coded 1 for full-time, .5 for part-time, and 0 for not employed. Wife's current earnings and past earnings are coded from 1 = less than $5,000 to 7 = more than $30,000. In the equation for current employment status, control variables are wife's age and education in years; race (1 = black, 0 = other); husband's earnings (coded same as wife's); and dummy variables for age of youngest child,

0–2, 3–5, and 6–11 (the omitted category includes the childless and those with youngest child over 11). Control variables for attitudes and behavior include the respondent's age, education, race, age of youngest child (as just described), and husband's earnings. These equations are predicted alternatively including wife's current employment status, work attachment, and earnings. Their relative predictive power is determined by the increment in R^2 when each is added to the equation.

Other dependent variables are measured as follows. Perception of marital decision making was the sum of the husband's (H-DECISION) or the wife's (W-DECISION) responses to the following questions, coded 1 = wife always; 2 = wife usually; 3 = both equally, other, not applicable; 4 = husband usually; 5 = husband always:[4] "We'd like to know who makes the following decisions in your family. Who decides: (a) where to go on vacation; (b) what job the husband should take; (c) what house or apartment to live in; (d) whether the wife should have a job; and (e) whether to move if the husband gets a job offer in another city?" These infrequent issues are of major importance to the family; they are therefore unlikely to be delegated by a more to a less powerful family member.

Reported perceptions of the household division of labor by the husband (H-HOUSEWORK) or the wife (W-HOUSEWORK) were measured as the sum of responses to the following items, which account for about three-quarters of the weekly time spent in housework (Walker and Woods, 1976), coded the same as the question on decision making. "Certain things have to be done in every household. Please tell me who does the following tasks in your family. Who (a) prepares regular meals for your household; (b) shops for food for your household; (c) takes care of the children or old people in your household; (d) does the daily housework; (e) cleans up after meals?"

Husband's attitude about his wife's employment (WIFEWORK) was measured by the following item, coded from 4 = strongly opposed to 1 = strongly in favor: "Overall, how (do/would) you feel about your wife's working?"

Sex-role attitudes focusing on employment (SRATT) are measured as

[4]A number of researchers have documented the moderate to high levels of inconsistency found between husband and wife responses to questions about household functioning (S. Berk and Shih, 1980; Douglas and Wind, 1978; Booth and Welch, 1978; and see Chapter 3). These responses are similar in the aggregate. Inconsistencies do not appear to relate systematically to couple characteristics. Researchers do not yet agree as to how dual responses should be handled analytically (Burr et al., 1977). Here, we analyze husband's and wife's responses separately and describe them as each spouse's perception of household functioning.

the sums of responses (strongly agree, agree, disagree, strongly disagree) to the following questions, recoded so that 1 = traditional, 4 = nontraditional response.[5]

1. It would be better for American society if fewer women worked.
2. A woman who works can be just as good a mother as one who does not.
3. A married woman should be able to have a job even if it is not always convenient for her family.
4. It is more important for a husband to have a good job than for a wife to have a good job.
5. There should be free child-care centers so that women can take jobs.
6. By nature women are happiest when they are making a home and caring for children.
7. A preschool child is likely to suffer if his or her mother works.
8. It is much better for everyone involved if the man is the achiever outside the home and the woman takes care of the home and family.

Attitudes regarding normative pressures for women to work for pay (SHOULDWORK) were measured by total positive responses to the following four questions, new to research in this area: "In our society most people think that any able-bodied man should have a job. Do you think that an able-bodied women should be *expected* to work if she is (a) unmarried and has completed school; (b) married and has no children; (c) married and has no children under age 18; (d) married and has no children under age 6."

Attitudes about ERA, coded 1 = favor, 0 = opposed, .5 = don't know, were measured by this item: "Do you favor or oppose the Equal Rights Amendment?"

Attitudes about abortion were measured as total positive responses to "Please tell me whether or not you think it should be possible for a pregnant woman to obtain a legal abortion:

1. If there is a strong chance of serious defect in the baby
2. If she is married and does not want any more children
3. If the woman's own health is seriously endangered by the pregnancy
4. If the family has a very low income and cannot afford more children

---

[5]All had a minimum .40 loading on a principal components factor analysis.

5. If she became pregnant as a result of rape
6. If she is not married and does not want to marry the man."

FINDINGS

Current Employment Status and Work Attachment

As expected, work attachment strongly predicts current employment status. For each year of the past 10 that a woman was employed, she is 7% more likely to be in the labor force currently (see Table 7.1, column 2). This relation is not perfectly linear but is monotonic (see Table 7.2). Why does past labor force behavior so potently predict current status? Is it because the causes are fairly stable or does employment simply perpetuate itself? The answer is some of each. A number of the standard predictors of women's labor force participation lose their predictive capacity when work attachment is included in the equation:

Table 7.1
UNSTANDARDIZED REGRESSION COEFFICIENTS
PREDICTING WIFE'S CURRENT EMPLOYMENT STATUS

Independent Variables	1	2
Age	-.010*	-.010*
Race	.193*	.072
Youngest child 0-2	-.496*	-.423*
Youngest child 3-5	-.271*	-.168*
Youngest child 6-11	-.137*	-.056
Education	.273*	.010
Husband's income	-.033*	-.015
Work index	----	.067*
R^2	.14	.37

* $p < .05$
Column 1 omits work attachment; column 2 includes it.

Table 7.2
WIVES' CURRENT WORK STATUS BY 10-YEAR WORK ATTACHMENT (IN PERCENTAGES)

Years Worked of Past Ten	Employed	Unemployed	Not Employed
0	3	3	92
1	26	12	60
2	40	4	55
3	58	8	33
4	58	19	23
5	60	4	35
6	62	13	20
7	72	12	14
8	72	15	13
9	75	4	21
10	90	6	4

race, husband's income, and education (see Table 7.1, columns 1 and 2). Presumably these factors are relatively stable in adulthood. Factors that fluctuate over time (age and age of youngest child) still operate, even with work attachment in the equation. Thus work attachment predicts effectively in part because it captures effects of potent stable predictors. Yet adding work attachment to the equation increases the explained variance from 14% to 37%, indicating either that important, unchanging causal factors have been omitted (e.g., regional or areal factors) or that employment is in some sense self-perpetuating; it may affect factors that are unmeasured here, such as wage potential, that tend to perpetuate a woman's being in or remaining out of the labor force.

Decision Making

We expected that the wife's current employment status would affect decision making least and that the effects of all three variables would be stronger for wives than for husbands. We found, however, that current status, work attachment, and earnings affect only husbands' but not wives' perceptions of the relative decision making power between spouses and that all three variables exert about the same effect on husbands (see Table 7.3, columns 1 and 2). Husbands' and wives' perceptions diverge; the correlation between the two scales is .27. This divergence may result from the influence of unshared norms between spouses. Husbands may feel that they earn the right to dominate decision making by supporting the family and that wives earn the right to share decisions if they also work for pay. Wives, in contrast, may feel that their housekeeping contribution entitles them to as much decision

Table 7.3
UNSTANDARDIZED COEFFICIENTS PREDICTING HUSBANDS' AND WIVES' PERCEPTIONS, DECISION MAKING, AND DIVISION OF HOUSEHOLD LABOR[a]

Independent Variables	H-DECISION	W-DECISION	H-HOUSEWORK	W-HOUSEWORK
Age	-.025*	.016	-.007	-.023
Education	-.084*	-.068	.160*	.140*
Race	.448	-.270	.942	.921
Husband's earnings	.081	-.123*	-.153	-.012
Youngest child 0-2	-.004	.601*	-.810*	-1.551*
Youngest child 3-5	.004	.918*	-.965*	-1.504*
Youngest child 6-11	.005*	.240	-.660*	-.987
R^2	.04	.04	.09	.10
Wife's current employment	-.756*	-.161	2.434*	1.750*
R^2 increment	.02	.00	.11	.05
Wife's work attachment	-.087*	-.023	.224*	.155*
R^2	.02	.00	.06	.03
Wife's earnings	-.296*	-.073	.766*	.606*
R^2 increment	.02	.00	.08	.04
N	681	681	682	681
Mean of dependent variable	16.2	16.2	9.9	8.9
Range of scale	5-25	5-25	5-25	5-25

a. Coefficients for Age through Youngest child are taken from equations which include current work but neither the significance of coefficients nor the signs of significant coeffieients differ when employment history or income is substituted.

*p < .05.

making power as would employment. However, we cannot assess which perception is more accurate.

Significant effects of other demographic variables on spousal perceptions of decision making are also inconsistent. Less educated husbands are more likely to see decision making as husband-dominated; such perceptions are shared by younger husbands. Wives whose husbands earn less view their husbands as more dominant, inconsistent with the power-conferring function of earnings, but their husbands do not share this perception. Finally, wives see themselves as less powerful if preschool children are present—a view not shared by husbands.

Household Labor

We expected current employment status to exert weakest effects and wife's earnings and work attachment, the strongest effects on the division of household labor. However, for both husbands and wives, wife's current status influences household labor more than do her earnings or past employment, consistent with a pragmatic interpretation of the situation. Wives working for pay, particularly if full-time, must cut down their housework hours. Whether husbands in turn perform more housework due to a shift in relative power or ideology is not clear from these data (see Table 7.3, columns 3 and 4).

However, perceptions of household labor are more highly correlated between husbands and wives ($r = .65$) than are perceptions of decision making, reflecting the more objective basis for them. Consistent with past research using this type of scale (Pleck, 1977), wife's employment is related to husband's relatively higher contribution, but husbands' perception of contribution is more influenced by wives' employment than wives' perception is: Effects of wife's current status are greater for husbands' than wives' perceptions, and wives' current status explains consistently more variance for husbands' than wives' perceptions. Again, whether this reflects over-estimation of their own performance by husbands of employed wives or under-estimation by wives is unknown. A few more hours of work a week may seem like a lot to husbands but little to employed wives. In any event the differences reflected here are not great.

Sex-Role Attitudes

The effects of wives' employment variables on husbands' and wives' sex-role attitudes can be summarized briefly. First, attitudes most closely related to wives' employment are most strongly affected by wives' employment. Husbands' attitudes toward their wives' working and both husbands' and wives' attitudes to married women's employment are affected positively by the wife's employment. Attitudes less clearly related to employment are less affected (see Table 7.4). Second, differences in explained variance between wives' current status, work attachment, and earnings are small and thus imply only slight differences in predictive power. Third, wives' employment effects on husbands' and wives' attitudes are similar for employment-related attitudes but differ for peripheral issues. Both husbands' ERA attitudes and wives' attitudes toward abortion are affected by wives' current status. Although these effects are small enough that they should not be overinterpreted, it seems reasonable that wives would more readily perceive a relation between abortion availability and employment since they are more likely than husbands to be aware of the consequences of an unwanted pregnancy. We have no explanation for the positive effects of wives' employment on husbands' but not wives' ERA attitudes. Wives' current earnings do, however, affect their own ERA attitudes.

Effects of demographic variables on sex-role attitudes are relatively consistent for husbands and wives. Husbands' attitudes toward wives' employment and both spouses' attitudes toward married women's employment are more favorable among the young, the highly educated, and households in which husbands' earnings are higher. Husbands' attitudes toward wives' employment are less favorable when a very young child is present. Only race predicts a newly developing norm regarding women's employment as a responsibility. Blacks favor it more, probably because black women have borne, historically, more responsibility for family support. ERA and abortion availability are supported more by husbands who are more highly educated or who have higher earnings, and ERA by black husbands. Highly educated women are more favorable to the ERA, and women whose husbands have high earnings are more favorable to ERA and abortion.

Analysis by Current Work Status

Since the high intercorrelations among current employment status, work attachment, and wife's earnings (ranging from .44 to .59) make it hard to compare their effects, we reestimate these equations separately for currently employed and nonemployed wives, using work attachment and earnings as a predictor for both groups. For the currently nonemployed, work attachment and past earnings affect wives' sex-role

Table 7.4
UNSTANDARDIZED COEFFICIENTS PREDICTING ATTITUDES OF HUSBAND AND WIFE[a]

Independent Variables	Husband Attitudes					Wife Attitudes			
	WIFEWORK	SRATT	SHOULD WORK	ERA	ABORTION	SRATT	SHOULD WORK	ERA	ABORTION
Age	-.009*	.064*	.007	-.001	-.010	-.092*	-.007	-.002	-.010
Education	.057*	.244*	-.013	.015*	.157*	.387*	-.029	.018*	.035
Race	.097	.687	.464*	.192*	.138	.687	.911*	.058	.123
Husband's earnings	.035	.225*	-.014	.005	.142*	.297*	-.045	.033*	.260*
Youngest child 0-2	-.367*	.028	-.089	.031	-.464	-.556	-.133	.071	-.244
Youngest child 3-5	-.284	.362	.121	-.002	-.170	-.483	-.229	-.007	-.446
Youngest child 6-11	-.211	-.563	.012	.001	-.432*	-.254	-.225	-.024	-.260
R^2	.07	.16	.02	.02	.10	.02	.01	.03	.01
Wife's current employment	.529*	1.557*	.041	.086*	.038	1.328*	.208	-.070	.434*
R^2 increment	.04	.03	.00	.01	.00	.02	.01	.00	.01
Wife's work attachment	.059*	.187*	-.001	.010*	.019	.213*	.005	.005	.047
R^2 increment	.03	.03	.00	.01	.00	.03	.00	.00	.01
Wife's earnings	.215*	.529*	.019	.040*	.039	.726*	.031	.043*	.211*
R^2 increment	.04	.03	.00	.02	.00	.04	.00	.01	.01
N	679	669	682	664	682	678	682	666	682
Mean of dependent variable	2.84	19.60	1.26	.63	4.04	20.49	1.36	.59	3.98
Range of scale	1-4	8-32	0-4	0-1	0-6	8-32	0-4	0-1	1-6

[a]Equations include either wife's current employment, wife's employment history, or wife's income. Coefficients for Age through Youngest child are taken from equations which include current employment. However, neither significance of coefficients nor signs of significant coefficients differ when employment history or income are substituted.
*$p < .05$.

Table 7.5
UNSTANDARDIZED COEFFICIENTS, ATTITUDES, AND PERCEPTIONS OF HUSBANDS AND WIVES, CONTROLLING FOR WIVES' CURRENT EMPLOYMENT[a]

Independent Variables	DECIDE	HOUSE WORK	WIFE WORK	SRATT	SHOULD WORK	ERA	ABORTION
				HUSBAND'S ATTITUDES			
Wife not employed							
Wife's work attachment	-.031	.031	.008	.096	-.018	.005	.044
Wife's past earnings	-.205	.532*	.016	.267	-.061	.043	-.258
N	304	304	302	295	304	295	304
Wife employed							
Wife's work attachment	-.033	.133*	.016	.145*	-.004	.005	-.004
Wife's earnings	-.203*	.380*	.091	.242	.013	.029	.067
N	377	378	377	374	378	369	378
				WIVES' ATTITUDES			
Wife not employed							
Wife's work attachment	.037	.050		.248*	-.030	.005	.039
Wife's earnings	-.246	.110		.727*	-.157	-.028	.116
N	304	304		301	304	294	304
Wife employed							
Wife's work attachment	-.018	.064		.183*	.007	-.002	.047
Wife's earnings	.002	.432*		.831*	-.019	-.002	.290*
N	377	377		377	378	372	378

[a] Control variables and method of analysis same as in Tables 3 and 4.

*p < .05

attitudes, whereas past earnings affect husbands' perceptions of household labor (see Table 7.5). For the currently employed, effects resemble those in the previous analyses with two interesting exceptions. Husbands' perceptions of decision making are affected by wives' current earnings but not their work attachment, supporting a power interpretation of earnings effects. In contrast, sex-role attitudes for husbands is affected only by work attachment, implying a gradual, cumulative attitude shift. For employed wives, both perceptions of housework and abortion attitudes are influenced by earnings but not by work attachment. Thus from a wife's viewpoint, earnings may allow her to demand household help in a way that work attachment does not. On the other hand, this may simply imply that wives with high earnings decrease their own housework time due to job demands, with a consequent increase in husbands' *relative* time. However, the effect of non-employed wives' *past* earnings on husbands' perceptions of housework would tend to support the notion that earnings potential increases wives' power to make demands, even during periods of nonemployment.

It is instructive to compare the effects of the absolute level of wife's earnings with the effect of the wife/husband wage ratio (see Chapter 4). At first glance the relation between the husband's contribution to housework and the wife's earnings reported in this chapter appear inconsistent with the lack of relation between spouse earnings ratio and the division of household labor reported in Chapter 4. We have several explanations for these seemingly discrepant findings. First, equations in Chapter 4 include wife's employment status, which is correlated .45 with earnings ratio and would thus detract from its potential effect. However, when we run separate regressions for employed and nonemployed wives (Tables 4.4 and 7.5), the effect of wife's earnings but not the earnings ratio remains.

Second, wife's earnings and earnings ratio may operate rather differently. Perhaps a high level of earnings is the crucial factor allowing women either to demand more participation by husbands in housework or allowing women to purchase more goods and services to replace their housework time—or both. A high earnings ratio may make little difference in the ability to buy released time from housework when total family income is low.

DISCUSSION

Women's massive entry to market work has had major social consequences. In this chapter we try to determine household-level counterparts in attitudes and behavior by examining whether differences related to wives' labor-force participation tend to be specific or diffuse, and pragmatic, or longer lasting and cumulative, or whether they tend to occur mainly in families in which wives' earnings are higher. Our main hypothesis was that wives' work attachment over time, because it reflects part-time and discontinuous aspects of women's labor-force participation, would have more effect than their current employment status on household behaviors and sex-role attitudes. We also expected wives' earnings to affect behaviors and attitudes more than would their current employment status on the grounds that level of earnings should affect power and prestige in the household as it does in the larger society.

As expected, we found that a measure of wives' work attachment over a recent 10-year period captured effects of stable predictors of women's labor-force participation such as race, education, and husband's income as well as effects of unmeasured variables such as wage potential and areal factors.

Unexpectedly, we found that wives' current employment status, work attachment, and earnings similarly affected husbands' perceptions of decision making. Yet these variables had no effect on wives' perceptions. Controlling for wives' current employment status, we found that only wives' earnings affected perceptions for husbands of employed wives, supporting the notion that earnings, not just employment per se, positively affected husbands' perceptions of wives' decision-making power.

Although work attachment, current status, and earnings all affected both spouses' perceptions of the division of household labor, the effect of wives' current employment status was, unexpectedly, greater than the effects of work attachment and earnings. Although these effects are hard to separate, it appears that past work attachment does not induce more help from husbands of currently nonemployed wives, but for employed wives, the longer their work attachment and the higher their earnings, the less housework they do relative to that done by their husbands. Yet translated into actual tasks, these effects are minimal.

Unexpectedly, work attachment, current status, and earnings differed only slightly in predicting sex-role attitudes although, as expected, both spouses' attitudes were more strongly affected the more they specifically pertained to women's employment, consistent with the attitude–behavior literature (Schuman, 1978; Fishbein, 1978). More diffuse effects were limited.

Finally, our expectation that husbands' attitudes would be affected less than wives' attitudes by wives' employment was not supported. With a few exceptions, effects were similar for husbands and wives.

These findings imply that attitude and behavior change tend to occur on pragmatic rather than on ideological grounds. As Converse (1964) observed, nicely developed ideologies occur mainly among intellectuals and academics. Wives do market work because the family needs money; their husbands do a little housework to enable the household to continue to function. Approval of married women's employment increases because, otherwise, the wife's daily market work would make both spouses uncomfortably aware of inconsistency in belief and behavior, and both spouses come to approve married mothers' employment—the idea that such work harms children declines. The husband's attitude toward his own wife's employment is more favorable.

Family comfort, however, does not require that attitudes change on issues less closely related to women's market work; it is easier for spouses not to see them as related. As other studies have noted (Mason and Bumpass, 1975; Welch, 1975), sex-role attitudes are multidimensional. Women's labor-force participation affects attitudes about employed women but not about the ERA or abortion. Furthermore, it is not pragmatically necessary that decision making become more equal, and, indeed, wives do not perceive that it does become so. Presumably, for sex-role attitudes not directly related to women's employment to change, or for the household division of labor or decision making to become more equal, other changes must occur in people's lives, changes that force them to confront these issues. For example, a woman who lives alone after a divorce, who is forced to make all decisions for a time, might prefer to continue doing so upon remarriage.

Thus, we expected wives' work attachment and earnings to affect household behaviors and attitudes more than would their current employment status because strong work attachment indicates commitment to steady employment outside the home and earnings indicate the level of reward, but we were wrong. That current employment generally has more effect implies that married couples are remarkably resistant to changing household norms and behaviors. This implies, in turn, that women's social equality remains a distant goal. Perhaps this should not be surprising. For husbands, the temptation to preserve current household norms must be overwhelming. As Gilman (1903/1972) observed nearly 80 years ago, the present system gives each husband a whole, live, private cook to himself. Why would any sensible man want to change? An important question for future investigation, therefore, is whether the current division of household responsibility is somehow fixed for all time, and if it is not, what kinds of economic and demographic conditions might induce change?

CHAPTER EIGHT

Religion and Sex-Role Issues[1]

This chapter examines the effect of religion on attitudes concerning two broad topics: first, issues associated with women's rights and responsibilities for work outside the home; seond, issues that tap concern for the traditional male-dominated family. Some of the issues associated with this second theme are currently topics of vigorous debate.

Religion should be an important variable in the study of sex-role attitudes and behaviors because it legitimates marriage and fertility patterns that affect collective survival. In the United States one would expect religious norms to support male dominance because the Judeo–Christian tradition inherited by western industrial societies (as well as the Islamic tradition) notably lacks feminine symbolism (Pagels, 1976:293). Women seemingly have been defined as male property (Driver, 1976)—as in the Ten Commandments: Thou shalt not covet thy neighbor's ox, nor his ass, nor his wife, nor any other thing that is his.

The Ten Commandments reflected a definition of women's place that responded to subsistence conditions in herding societies. Since grazing animals must be tended far from home over long periods of time, the

[1]We are indebted to Robert Alun Jones and Mary Jo Weaver for suggestions that improved this chapter. We thank Carolyn White for analyzing the trends in attendance at religious services.

functional requirements of herding fit poorly with the requirements of pregnancy and lactation. Morever, competition for good grazing land and water rights made law and order a constant problem. Whenever warfare significantly helps to maintain a food supply, women's status is low. Men's larger average size and greater strength give them an advantage over women (particularly over women carrying children) in hand-to-hand combat. The Old Testament illustrates the squabbles over grazing rights in the dry hills, gulches, and plains of ancient Israel. The American wild West film illustrates a more recent version.

The New Testament introduced an ethic of universal love that tended to put women on more equal footing. Indeed, the political success of Christianity early in the fourth century was partly based on its appeal to women in the competitive battles it fought with pagan cults and mystery religions. Christianity uniquely recognized the dignity and equality of women before God and was in turn anathematized by its competitors as a women's religion. This accounts for the fact that so many early converts were women, as were so many early martyrs (R. Jones, 1982).

However, all religions must confront particular subsistence conditions. Christianity emerged among the natives of a minor Roman colony, an erstwhile herding society. It spread to European plow cultures that also subordinated women. When land is the chief form of wealth, the heirs must be identifiable and their number must be controlled. Therefore, agricultural societies tend to encourage monogamous marriage and to constrain women's premarital and marital sexual behavior. The early Gnostic Christian tradition that included feminist symbolism therefore encountered a type of subsistence technology that encouraged rigid sexual stratification. By A. D. 150–200 the Gnostic tradition was rejected (Pagels, 1976:293). The writings of the church fathers from the second to the eighth centuries therefore continued the Old Testament tradition, treating women as subordinate creatures. Not a single prowoman statement occurs in the entire patristic literature (Daly, 1975).

Conceivably, however, the Judeo–Christian tradition may have improved women's lot relative to men's more than did other religions in agricultural societies. Compared to men, were women better or worse off in the great kingdoms and empires of Egypt, Greece, India, China, or Europe? No one knows for sure. Although the degree of subtle or overt control over women's behavior varies from one society to another, no one has systematically analyzed the part that religious beliefs might have played.

Several gross cross-cultural comparisons of systematically induced female suffering make it plausible that the Judeo–Christian tradition may have been a factor (whether strong or weak) in ameliorating women's lot relative to men's in Europe. In China for nearly a thousand years, the feet of most little girls were bound when they were 3–5 years old. The bindings were progressively tightened for 10–15 years to give women the hobbling gait that was sexually attractive to men. If her family were rich enough to dispense with her labor, then a woman could aspire to attaining the esteemed 3-inch lotus foot, named for its resemblance to that flower. A woman with a pair of perfect lotus feet could not walk at all. In India a major form of suffering—notably elitist—was less prolonged. Widows of wealthy men were expected to climb atop the husband's funeral pyre, there to be incinerated. According to Hindu precept, a widow's sins in an earlier incarnation caused her husband to die first. Whatever the religious justification, the widow's death gave the husband's brothers a free hand in dealing with the estate and the children. In Europe, with the exception of the witch craze, it is hard to find examples of controlling women by systematically maiming or killing them. Some writers take a functional view of witch-hunts, seeing them as being useful in shifting responsibility for the crisis of late medieval society from church and state to imaginary demons, using defenseless old women as the most convenient scapegoats for a corrupt clergy and a rapacious nobility (Harris, 1964:237; Garrett, 1977:461). Others writers find it odd that so many scholars ignore the essential responsibility of the Christian religion and its institutions (Moia, 1979:799). Horsely (1979:692) is probably correct in claiming that the critical social history of witch-hunts remains to be written.

Yet even if women suffered less, compared to men, in Europe than in Asia and even if the Judeo–Christian tradition played a part in improving their lot, that tradition still clearly subordinated women to men. One would therefore expect that persons who took the beliefs of that tradition to be literally true would tend to approve the continued subordination of women. In the United States the Protestant fundamentalists are the largest group of such persons. In principle, such fundamentalists could be Jewish, Roman Catholic, Protestant, or adherents of any historic religion. For practical purposes, they are mostly Protestant in the United States. Jewish fundamentalists are too few to count in a national sample. It is difficult to know how much Roman Catholic charismatics and pentecostals resemble Protestant fundamentalists in their social attitudes, but whatever their attributes, their proportion is small in the church. Greeley (1979:107) notes that in 1974 only 5% of United States Roman Catholics had attended charismatic meetings. Roman Catholics tend to remain more closely akin to their coreligionists than do Protestants, whose history legitimates the right to separate from a parent body. Conversely, one would expect persons whose religious views had been attenuated by the secular culture to hold more liberal opinions on women's roles.

From these two general propositions, we derive the two main hypotheses of this chapter: first, that Roman Catholic sex-role attitudes will be more liberal than those of Protestants and, second, that among Protestants the views of the fundamentalists will be more conservative than the views of others. In order to place these hypotheses in context, we first discuss why Protestant–Roman Catholic attitude and behavior differences have so interested American sociologists. We then explain why, on theoretical grounds, we expect their differences to be overshadowed by the differences between fundamentalist Protestants and all other persons. After reviewing the empirical literature and presenting data on attendance trends that tend to support our theoretical perspective, we test our hypotheses, using data from a national sample survey supplemented by earlier data collected by Gallup, the National Opinion Research Corporation (NORC) and the General Social Survey (GSS).

THE PROTESTANT ETHIC

American fascination with Roman Catholic–Protestant differences stems from the work of Max Weber. His thesis on the influence of the Protestant ethic on the rise of modern industrial society has been the single most influential hypothesis in the sociology of religion (Bellah, 1968:412). Unlike Marx, Weber claimed that ideas can affect human organization independently of material factors. Few scholars would dispute this claim, but probably what gave Weber's thesis so much vigor—no book in sociology of religion ever aroused more commentary than this one (Yingh, 1974:610)[2]—is that extremely popular ideas typically resonate with the culture in subtle ways.

Weber's thesis resonates harmoniously with two widespread American beliefs. First, the thesis implied that Marx was wrong to lay so much stress on material factors. Second, the thesis implies that being a Protestant is better than being a Roman Catholic: The Protestant ethic motivates people to do well, whereas the Roman Catholic ethic motivates them only to do good. This difference implies that the Roman

---

[2]Samuelsson (1957:26, 154) argues that there is nothing to explain. No empirical evidence supports the thesis.

Catholic ethic lacks some needed ingredient—or, worse, that it includes a pernicious element that makes for intellectual or political incompetence in the modern world.[3] Even Roman Catholic intellectuals insisted on the anti-intellectualism of their own religion (Greeley, 1979:94). In the United States the belief in the superiority of the Protestant ethic has been reinforced by a 300-year Protestant status advantage—a result of their earlier arrival. It has therefore been part of the dominant culture to believe in the beneficial effect of the Protestant ethic on attitudes and behaviors.

One of the most extensive empirical studies in the Weberian tradition was Lenski's (1961) analysis of the religious factor in Detroit (Yinger, 1974:612). It typified the trend toward the empirical study of religion that occurred after the early 1950s (Smart, 1974:620), and it inspired a flurry of research (Riccio, 1979:200). Lenski's study was based on a 1958 Detroit-area survey. It was designed with the Weberian concept in mind, not to unravel the historical problem of the origin of the capitalist spirit but rather to examine the relationship of religion and the spirit of capitalism at the date of the study (Lenski, 1961:6).

The historical context of the study was a widespread belief that religious groups were becoming more important in American life (Lenski, 1961:40). Just a few years earlier Herberg (1956:69ff) had reported an all-time high in religious identification. His widely read book, Protestant, Catholic, Jew, attributed the increase to individuals' efforts to find places for themselves in society, to a basic character change from inner- to other-directedness, and to the contemporary crisis of western civilization that increased individual need for security. Herberg thought the increase was possibly linked to what he saw as a sensational reversal of long-term population trends and the sudden rise of the birthrate among college graduates and professionals. In the family-togetherness context of the affluent 1950s, Herberg's ideas seemed plausible.

Lenski (1961:289) found that religion still influenced individuals in a number of ways. Roman Catholics were intellectually disadvantaged. They remained less likely than Protestants or Jews to do well in science because obedience outranks autonomy in Roman Catholic values (Lenski, 1961:225). However, Schuman's (1971) 1966 re-study of parts of the 1958 Detroit-area study suggested that Lenski's conclusions about Roman Catholic–Protestant differences were too sweeping. Schuman (1971:47) questioned whether attitudes related to religion

---

[3]Theodore Adorno (1950:734), known for his work on the authoritarian personality, states this position forthrightly: "It is not accidental that Nazism arose in southern Germany with its strong Roman Catholic tradition."

could change so much in only 8 years. In reply, Lenski (1971:50) pointed out that some of the most important religious changes were of a kind that few persons would have predicted as recently as the early 1960s.[4] Lenski concluded that earlier differences had been seriously eroded and were likely to diminish even more. Lenski's (1961) study of the religious factor pictured at best an era that had ended.

THE SPIRIT OF SECULARISM

To the extent that there was an era when the Protestant ethic inspired special behaviors and beliefs, why would it end? On theoretical grounds Roman Catholic–Protestant differences in beliefs and behaviors should decrease over time for two reasons.

First, the problem of developing effective bureaucracies tends to make all highly organized religious bodies more alike than different, as Niebuhr (1929/1957:124) noted more than 50 years ago. In distinction from the sects of the poor such as the Brethren, Mennonites, and Quakers, the churches of the Reformation share with the Roman Catholic Church more or less the same institutional principles of social organization. Lutherans, Anglicans, Presbyterians, and Reformed denominations all belong in this category, along with the Catholic Churches of the East and West. In their conceptions of the sacraments, of conversion and education, and of the office of the ministry, they represent the institutional and authoritarian as opposed to individual and democratic conceptions of Christianity. Such differences as occur do not obscure the underlying unity of the conception of the church as an institution rather than as a voluntary society. This conception is connected to the idea of the church as the coordinate of the state. In later Protestantism the church accepts the view of the state it identifies with. Thus the spread of bureaucratic structures through religious institutions makes them increasingly resemble each other (MacIntyre, 1967:66). The traditional terminology pertaining to styles of polity usually obfuscates this fact (P. Berger, 1969:139).

However, the sects of the poor of the past have moved into the bureaucratic mainstream. Although their values still differ significantly from those of the state on pacifism, the Quakers, Mennonites, and Brethren today are hardly poor. The sects that heavily stress the need

---

[4]Lenski (1971:50) notes that almost the only sociologist who anticipated the changes precipitated by Vatican Council II was Joseph Fichter, who predicted an early victory for the liberal theologians over the conservative bishops.

for individual salvation, after the fashion of the early Anabaptists, tend to include some Baptists and most of the small sects that comprise the sizable "other Protestant" category.

The second reason that Protestant–Roman Catholic differences should decrease is that over time all major religious bodies tend to converge in the direction of the secular culture. They must all operate in a milieu that no longer takes for granted their definitions of reality. Modern religious institutions therefore have two basic options: accommodation with or resistance to the massive impact of the environment (P. Berger, 1969:156). The pressure for accommodation occurs because religions that could previously be imposed authoritatively must now be marketed, and "sold" to a clientele no longer constrained to "buy" (P. Berger, 1969:138).

From the perspective of the religious organizations themselves, neither accommodation with or resistance to the secular environment is an inviting option. Both may result in loss of members. To the extent that large-scale religious organizations resemble other large-scale organizations, they lose their distinct attractiveness. To the extent that they resist, they tend to lose those members who find a sectarian interpretation of reality to be incredible. Hence those who remain in the sect huddle together for mutual support. The sect is the form par excellence for huddling (P. Berger, 1980:85).

In the United States the mainstream Protestant denominations have adapted to the secular environment much more rapidly than has the Roman Catholic communion. This is hardly surprising. Mainstream Protestanism has long been dominated by social and economic elites. More recent immigrants, poor and not well-educated, tended to comprise the bulk of Roman Catholic membership. Since World War II, however, Roman Catholics have been increasing their status. The Church has now clearly been affected by secularism (D'Antonio, 1980). Vatican II signalled that great changes in Roman Catholic lives and consciousness had already occurred. Today many Roman Catholic theologians are experiencing the cognitive miseries long familiar to their Protestant colleagues (P. Berger, 1980:53). The social gospel movement that swept the Protestant denominations in the 1920s and 1930s now sweeps through the Roman Catholic Church. One supposes that the social gospel will meet much the same fate in one communion as in another. It is not easy to make ancient theological solutions relevant to the twentieth century without relativizing them into triviality. In the long run the religious differences that in the past fueled so much ethnocentrism will doubtless diminish further as large-scale religious organizations continue to adapt themselves to the spirit of secularism.

EMPIRICAL STUDIES

Recent empirical studies on the effect of the Protestant ethic support the view that Roman Catholic–Protestant differences are declining with respect to family, occupational, educational, and sex-role issues. Indeed, even in the 1960s some studies had suggested that differences among Protestants were greater than Roman Catholic–Protestant differences (Glock and Stark, 1965:121).

On marital issues Westoff and Bumpass (1973) and Westoff and Jones (1977) report considerable convergence in Roman Catholic and non-Catholic attitudes toward divorce and contraception. Blake (1973a) reported that in 1972 71% of men and women responding to a Gallup survey approved birth control education in the public schools; Roman Catholics did not differ significantly from non-Catholics. Although the research literature of the 1940s, 1950s, and 1960s consistently found Roman Catholics to be considerably less likely to divorce, the evidence was flawed by the use of inadequate samples (McCarthy, 1979:180). The first adequate data source, the 1970 National Fertility Study of ever-married United States women aged 45 or younger reported smaller religious differences (Bumpass and Sweet, 1972). Roman Catholics differed from Protestants by only three percentage points, and there was much variation among Protestants.

A recent comprehensive review of major studies of the relationship between religious affiliation and socioeconomic achievement reports that they were plagued by serious conceptual and methodological deficiencies (Riccio, 1979). Some studies used nonprobability samples and most failed to include some important controls. Hence the net differences might well be attributed to noncontrolled variables. Yet despite differences in samples, research designs, and variable measurement, these studies generally pointed to the conclusion that religion explained little of the variance in socioeconomic achievement (Riccio, 1979:226).

One of the few studies that used a national probability sample and controlled for parental socioeconomic status found no evidence that a Roman Catholic education hindered occupational or educational achievement (Greeley and Rossi, 1966:146). Greeley (1973) later pointed to strong evidence that the number of Roman Catholic academics was increasing. The breakthrough for (male) Jewish faculty members at elite schools took place for those who were aged 45–60 in 1969—that is, those who had been graduate students between 1935 and 1950. The breakthrough for Roman Catholics at elite schools occurred for men under age 40 in 1969—that is, for those who attended graduate school from 1955 to the early 1970s. Greeley (1973:1,253) questioned that anyone should take the absence of Roman Catholics in scholarly careers as proof of their intellectual inferiority whereas the absence of women and blacks was taken to imply subtle or overt job discrimination.

Several recent studies point to a decrease in the importance of religious effects on sex-role attitudes. Although all studies used probability samples, they were restricted in various ways. Mason et al. (1976) report data from five sample surveys of women conducted between 1964 and 1974. They found no consistent or strong relationships between cultural variables (including religion) and women's attitudes. On one item, Roman Catholic women were less egalitarian than others; Jewish women were more egalitarian. For other items the reverse occurred (Mason et al., 1976:583). Duncan and Duncan (1978) examined social change in the Detroit area using studies conducted 1953–1959 and a 1971 replication. They report religious effects on the responses to four questions. Differences between Protestants and Roman Catholics appeared to be modest, decreasing, or nonexistent (Duncan and Duncan, 1978:43, 69, 212, 233). Thornton and Freedman (1979:838), using data collected between 1962 and 1977 from a Detroit Standard Metropolitan Statistical Area sample of white women who either had just married or just had a first, second, or fourth birth, report that the most distinctive pattern was that of fundamentalist Protestants. Their attitudes resembled those of other women in 1962 but subsequently diverged so much that by 1977 they scored least liberal on feminist issues.

Empirical studies thus tend to support the hypotheses that Roman Catholic–Protestant behavior and attitude differences are declining. If adaptation to the secular culture tends to bureaucratize religious organizations in similar ways and if the credibility problem tends to erode individual faith, then one would also expect attendance at religious services to decline over time. An increase in attendance would throw our theoretical perspective into question. We now examine data on that topic.

TRENDS IN ATTENDANCE AT SERVICES

The most often used measure of religious observance is frequency of attendance at services (Argyle, 1968:422). It is a more useful variable than membership. It indicates more plausibly than membership the part that religious faith plays in a person's life because it reflects a commitment of time. Furthermore, attendance data are more accurate. The criteria for membership differ for various denominations and change over time. However, the disadvantage of using attendance at services as an independent variable is that one cannot speak of its effects on attitudes and behaviors that are concurrently measured. There is no way to untangle the causal pattern.

In western countries attendance at religious services has generally declined since the second half of the nineteenth century. Many observers saw a temporary recovery in the 1950s, especially in Great Britain and the United States. Argyle (1968:423), noting that there was no generally accepted explanation for this unexpected event, surmised that one factor might be the churches' greater emphasis on activities that appealed to teenagers. A better explanation is that the extent of the 1950s religious revival was greatly overestimated—as Lipset (1959) put it, "What religious revival?" Despite widespread belief in a major postwar religious revival in the United States, it is not clear that religious membership was actually increasing in the 1950s (Glock and Stark, 1965:68, 74). Membership statistics were not reliable on changes in church membership over time. Data on Sunday attendance at services, more reliable than membership data, showed neither as consistent nor as great an increase as did the membership data on which Herberg had relied. Attendance data confirmed a leveling of any upward trend by the late 1950s, as measured by the proportion of adults who had attended services the week before the interview.[5]

Recent evidence indicates that attendance at services in the United States has declined somewhat from 1964 to 1978. Using NORC and GSS data, Tom Smith (1980:14–15) reports an increase in the proportion of infrequent attenders and a decrease in the proportion of frequent attenders.[6] The proportion of respondents who attended religious services once a year or less (versus more than once a year) increased from 17% in 1964 to 38% in 1978, a significant linear trend. Conversely, the proportion attending once a week or more (versus less than once a week) decreased from 52% in 1964 to 35% in 1978, a significant but not simple linear change.

Since Tom Smith reported only aggregate changes by year, we then

---

[5]The decline in attendance in Sweden (Gustafsson, 1969:363), typically a bellwether of social change, also made a postwar membership increase in the United States seem improbable.

[6]A study based on the GSS, 1972–1978, reports that the best nonreligious predictor of attendance for whites is socioeconomic status (Beeghley et al., 1981:403). The best nonreligious predictors across all denominations and churches are socioeconomic status and age.

tested whether the attendance decreases reported in those years varied by major religious category and denomination. We used GSS data for 1972–1980. Unfortunately, we could not use Smith's computer program because it is not widely available. We therefore used Haberman's (1979:571–585) FREQ, which has an advantage over other commonly used log-linear programs. FREQ allows testing for linear trends when the categories are not equal interval, important in this instance because the GSS was not conducted in 1979. Our criteria for reporting linear trends are relaxed over Smith's in that we tested for linear trends even if the hypothesis of independence could not be rejected. To avoid overfitting the model, we did not accept linear models whose likelihood χ^2 ratio (or L^2) was smaller than the degrees of freedom. Otherwise our criteria resembled Smith's. The presence of a significant linear component means that the model that included a linear constraint on year was a significant improvement over the model of independence, but the linear model had to be rejected as an adequate description of the change—that is, the trend varied from a simple linear projection. The presence of a significant linear trend implies that change occurred at a constant rate along a straight line.

On theoretical grounds we expected Roman Catholic attendance rates to decline most, not because their rates are typically highest—in 1980, for example, 48% of Roman Catholics, 35% of Protestants, 9% of Jews, and 2% of persons of no religion attended services nearly weekly or more (see Table 8.1)—but rather because the Roman Catholic communion has adapted recently in unprecedented fashion to the secular culture.

Examining attendance changes from 1972–1980, we found a borderline significant linear component (at the .07 level) in the increased proportion of Roman Catholics who attended infrequently. The observed increase was from 17% to 23%. However, the increase in the proportion of infrequent attenders was more marked for Protestants. Those who attended religious services once a year or less (versus more than once or twice a year) increased from 28% to 32%, and this increase was both linear and significant. For Jews and persons of no religion, no significant change occurred (see Table 8.1). However, the decrease in the proportion of very frequent attenders occurred only for Roman Catholics. The proportion who attended services nearly weekly or oftener (versus those who attended less than weekly) declined from 61% in 1972 to 48% in 1980, a decline with a significant linear component (see Table 8.1).

Using the same GSS data, we then analyzed the response by Protestant denomination: Baptist, Episcopalian, Lutheran, Methodist, Pres-

Table 8.1
PROPORTION OF RELIGIOUSLY AFFILIATED PERSONS WHO ATTENDED SERVICES IN SELECTED YEARS

Year	Protestant	(N)	Catholic	(N)	Jewish	(N)	None	(N)
	Attended Once or Twice a Year or Less Versus More Than Once or Twice a Year							
1972	.28	(1,027)	.17	(410)	.46	(54)	.86	(79)
1973	.30	(933)	.27	(388)	.50	(42)	.90	(95)
1974	.33	(951)	.21	(376)	.55	(44)	.92	(101)
1975	.29	(974)	.30	(362)	.48	(23)	.88	(112)
1976	.31	(948)	.29	(390)	.48	(27)	.90	(110)
1977	.34	(1,002)	.25	(373)	.54	(35)	.88	(90)
1978	.34	(979)	.28	(384)	.62	(29)	.93	(116)
1980	.32	(934)	.23	(360)	.28	(32)	.93	(105)

Year	Protestant	(N)	Catholic	(N)	Jewish	(N)	None	(N)
	Attended Nearly Weekly or More Versus Less Than Weekly or More							
1972	.38	(1,027)	.61	(410)	.06	(54)	.03	(79)
1973	.36	(933)	.48	(388)	.07	(42)	.00	(95)
1974	.36	(951)	.50	(376)	.05	(44)	.02	(101)
1975	.37	(974)	.46	(362)	.13	(23)	.01	(112)
1976	.36	(948)	.43	(390)	.04	(27)	.03	(110)
1977	.34	(1,002)	.50	(373)	.14	(35)	.02	(90)
1978	.34	(979)	.48	(384)	.10	(29)	.03	(116)
1980	.35	(934)	.48	(360)	.09	(32)	.02	(105)

[*] We are grateful to Carolyn White and the Social Science Quantitative Laboratory of the University of Illinois at Urbana-Champaign for tabulation of these unpublished NORC data.

byterian, other Protestant, and no denomination. The "other Protestant" category, about one-fifth of all Protestants, is presumably comprised mainly of fundamentalists (see Bacheller, 1980:891). We saw no reason to expect one denomination to decline more rapidly than another. The proportion of infrequent attenders increased only for Baptists and Methodists. There was a significant linear trend in the increase of Baptist infrequent attenders, from 26% in 1972 to 32% in

Table 8.2
PROPORTION OF PROTESTANTS WHO ATTENDED SERVICES IN SELECTED YEARS (ROUNDED)*

Attended Once or Twice a Year or Less Versus More Than Once or Twice a Year

Year	Baptist	(N)	Methodist	(N)	Lutheran	(N)	Presbyterian	(N)	Episcopalian	(N)	Other	(N)	No Denomination	(N)
1972	.26	(323)	.29	(231)	.20	(137)	.27	(80)	.49	(33)	.30	(185)	.58	(36)
1973	.26	(310)	.32	(196)	.29	(123)	.32	(57)	.46	(41)	.24	(163)	.62	(43)
1974	.26	(321)	.41	(189)	.30	(113)	.35	(74)	.29	(38)	.31	(174)	.61	(41)
1975	.22	(309)	.34	(174)	.25	(139)	.39	(76)	.36	(44)	.24	(182)	.63	(49)
1976	.23	(302)	.40	(162)	.32	(104)	.44	(78)	.40	(48)	.23	(195)	.61	(59)
1977	.32	(323)	.35	(192)	.29	(136)	.49	(66)	.35	(37)	.29	(190)	.62	(58)
1978	.33	(318)	.39	(190)	.34	(115)	.37	(62)	.44	(39)	.25	(208)	.43	(46)
1980	.32	(306)	.33	(170)	.29	(92)	.39	(79)	.39	(41)	.22	(194)	.54	(52)

Attended Nearly Weekly or More Versus Less Than Weekly or More

Year	Baptist	(N)	Methodist	(N)	Lutheran	(N)	Presbyterian	(N)	Episcopalian	(N)	Other	(N)	No Denomination	(N)
1972	.43	(323)	.32	(231)	.38	(137)	.36	(80)	.24	(33)	.44	(185)	.22	(36)
1973	.39	(310)	.32	(196)	.33	(123)	.40	(57)	.19	(41)	.47	(163)	.14	(42)
1974	.40	(321)	.28	(189)	.30	(113)	.32	(74)	.34	(38)	.46	(174)	.22	(41)
1975	.39	(309)	.35	(174)	.36	(139)	.37	(76)	.25	(44)	.47	(182)	.08	(49)
1976	.39	(302)	.28	(162)	.33	(104)	.24	(78)	.25	(48)	.55	(195)	.12	(59)
1977	.34	(323)	.32	(192)	.29	(136)	.24	(66)	.27	(37)	.48	(190)	.19	(58)
1978	.35	(318)	.25	(190)	.24	(115)	.24	(62)	.18	(39)	.53	(208)	.33	(46)
1980	.36	(306)	.28	(170)	.29	(92)	.32	(79)	.15	(41)	.53	(194)	.29	(52)

* We are grateful to Carolyn White and the Social Science Quantitative Laboratory of the University of Illinois at Urbana-Champaign for tabulation of these unpublished NORC data.

179

1980. For Methodists, there was a significant linear component (borderline trend), from 29% in 1972 to 33% in 1980 (see Table 8.2). The proportion of frequent attenders changed only for respondents reporting no denomination. The proportion who attended nearly weekly or more (versus less than nearly weekly or more) increased from 22% in 1972 to 29% in 1980, a significant linear trend (see Table 8.2).

In sum, the proportion of infrequent attenders is increasing among both Protestants and Roman Catholics. The proportion of frequent attenders is declining, as predicted, only among Roman Catholics. Among Protestant denominations, the attendance decline seems to affect primarily Baptists and Methodists. These findings are consistent with a theory that implies decreasing effects of religion on attitudes and behavior.

To recapitulate, our two main hypotheses follow from the view that in the long run technologically induced trends tend to diminish the effect of religion on attitudes and behaviors. The problem of developing effective bureaucratic organizations in order to adapt to the environment tends to make all large religious groups more alike. The rise of science coupled with ever higher levels of public education give all major religions a serious credibility problem. How to modernize a theology without losing its essence is a problem that troubles most theologians. Only the sects, who choose to defy rather than adapt to the secular culture, can enjoy the luxury of adhering to time-hallowed beliefs. We therefore expect that the main effect of religion on sex-role attitudes will be to differentiate those of fundamentalist Protestants from those of all other persons, whatever their affiliation. Mainstream Protestant–Roman Catholic differences should therefore disappear.

DATA AND METHODS

The data used in this chapter come from several sources. Most of the data come from our national probability sample of United States adults (N = 2,002) interviewed by telephone late in 1978 (see Chapter 2), but data for two items replicated from other surveys to examine trends over time come from Gallup and the GSS. We have recoded our independent variables used for these two items to conform to the coding used in the several 1938–1969 Gallup surveys and to that of the GSS for 1972 and 1977. We replicated a third item, but we do not use it to analyze trends because Evers and McGee (1980) had recently done so. Before presenting the wording of the items and the coding of all variables, we discuss why only three items in this chapter replicate other survey items.

When we designed the study, we hoped to replicate as many items as possible that dealt with women's market and family work. The social indicators literature convinced us that greater use of replicated items would increase the usefulness of survey research. For three reasons our search for usable items proved unfruitful.

First, many current issues regarding the family surfaced only in the 1960s. The items on marriage and morals in the earlier years of sample surveys seem dated. We reproduce several typical items below to communicate their flavor, not to point with scorn but rather as a reminder that our concerns may seem equally quaint in 30 or 40 years. In 1937 and 1947 respondents were asked if they objected to teachers' smoking away from school (G. Gallup, 1972:608, 1511). In 1952 wives were asked if they sought their husbands' opinions before buying a new hat. Husbands and wives were asked if it was all right for one spouse to open the other's mail (G. Gallup, 1972:1063, 1051). In 1956 and 1957: "Do you object to women drinking in public places such as bars or restaurants or not?" (Southwick, 1975:219).

Second, questions on women's roles outside the home abounded in national surveys until 1950 but then fell off to zero by the late 1950s. They began a slow revival in the 1960s (Erskine, 1971:276). The number of possible items is therefore low for this period. The index to questions that were repeated in United States national surveys conducted by the Roper Public Opinion Research Center lists few questions on sex roles (Southwick, 1975:407–409), and most seem dated. Another compendium of questions that were repeated by certain major surveys from 1947 to 1978 (Converse et al., 1980) lists only six items in the chapter on women and only three concern attitudes. None seemed suited to our purposes: whether housekeeping is just a job for the wife or whether she enjoys it; the imputed reasons that women take jobs; and whether women should stay out of politics (Converse et al., 1980:102–123).

Third, replication involves technical problems. From a wealth of survey items—George Gallup (1972) lists all the items used from 1935 through 1971 in more than 7,000 reports—sampling variation, omission of important background variables, and wording changes reduce the pool of usable items. Before 1950, except for special surveys, the Gallup polls used a purposive design for selecting cities, towns, and rural areas, and used quota sampling for selecting individuals (G. Gallup, 1972:vi). Some earlier surveys omitted such background variables as education and religion.

Despite such problems, we chose two items (listed in G. Gallup, 1972; Southwick, 1975; T. Smith, 1980) to use in assessing trends. They are not without problems (as will be shown later). Both items appeared in a number of Gallup polls and the GSS. Each survey represents a national probability sample with numbers ranging from 1527 to 3559 and includes data on age, race, sex, education (except in 1938), community size, region, religion (except in 1938 and 1949—we include these two surveys in order to observe the effects of the other variables), and party affiliation. The item content stood the test of time well, but the increasingly favorable responses indicate that they may soon outlive their usefulness. There will be little variance to explain. Our analysis draws on Spitze and Huber (1980).

The first item asked whether the respondent would vote for a qualified woman for President of the United States (FEPRES, using the GSS mnemonic). The first wording, used in the mid-1930s, prejudged sex as a qualification: "Would you vote for a woman for President if she was qualified in every other respect?" Variant wordings appeared in 1945, 1949, 1955, and 1963. In 1949: "If the party whose candidate you most often support nominated a woman for President of the United States, would you vote for her if she seemed qualified for the job?" In 1955 the 1949 wording was used except that the word "best" preceded "qualified." In 1959: "If your party nominated a generally well-qualified woman for President, would you vote for her?" In 1969 and on: "If your party nominated a woman for President, would you vote for her if she were qualified for the job?" We used the 1969 wording. We can therefore replicate only studies from 1969 on, in a strict sense. Duncan and Duncan (1978:3–5) analyzed this item only by sex because they were concerned about the possible effects of wording changes. We compare our 1978 findings with those of the GSS and Gallup because the substantive interest outweighs the admitted risks of incomparability.

The most comprehensive analysis of the willingness to vote for a woman president is Ferree's (1974:394) report on 1958, 1967, and 1972 using sex, education, age, religion, region, size of place, and party affiliation as background variables. Roman Catholics and Protestants did not differ significantly on the item, but Jews differed from both. Jewish men consistently favored a woman for President more than did their counterparts. This was not true of Jewish women until 1972, when they became as liberal as Jewish men (Ferree, 1974:397).

The second item we replicated was worded as follows in the Gallup surveys: "Do you approve of a married woman's earning money in business or industry if she has a husband capable of supporting her?" (FEWORK, in the GSS mnemonic). In the GSS the words "or disapprove" followed "approve". This item was used in Gallup surveys in

1938, 1945, and 1970 and in the GSS in 1972, 1974, 1975, 1977, and 1978. We used the Gallup wording, which turned out to be a mistake. We could not obtain the 1945 survey and the 1938 survey used neither education nor religion as background variables. Duncan and Duncan (1978:91) analyzed differential change in response to the question by cohort and sex during the 1970s, when the item was included in the GSS. They did not report effects for religion.

Because the data from the Gallup polls, the GSS, and our survey were not collected in identical form, the variables were recoded as follows for the two replicated items. Age was coded in years. We collapsed it into dummy variables: under 30 (reference category), 30–39, 40–49, 50–59, 60 and over. Education was coded in years, collapsed into dummy variables: 8 or less (reference category), 9–11, 12, 13 or more. Race is coded 1 = black, 0 = other. Region is coded in four dummy variables: South (reference category), East, Central, and West. Party is coded 1 = Republican, 2 = Independent or other, 3 = Democrat. Religion is coded in dummy variables for Protestant (reference category), Roman Catholic, Jewish, other, or none. Size of place is coded 1 = farm; 2 = under 2500; 3 = 2500–9999; 4 = 10,000–99,999; 5 = 100,000–499,999; 6 = 500,000–999,999; 7 = 1 million or more. The two dependent variables were coded as dichotomies, 1 = yes, 0 = no. "Don't know" responses were coded as .5 in order to avoid losing these cases. This should not affect the findings much because the percentage of such responses ranged from 1 to 4.

Equations predicting each dependent variable were estimated by sex for each year for which data are available. For reasons of economy, we used OLS regressions for all predictions. Although the two dependent variables are dichotomies, in only 6 of the 24 equations do the dependent variable means fall outside the 25–75% range within which the results for OLS and other techniques are similar (Goodman, 1976).

The independent variables for the remaining equations (dependent variables 3–16) are coded as follows. Age is coded in years. Education is coded in number of years completed. Race is coded 1 = black, 0 = other. Family income is coded in categories from 1 = under $5000 to 7 = over $30,000. Ever-divorced status is coded as a dummy variable, 1 = yes, 0 = no. The presence of an employed wife (for men) and own employment status (for women) are coded 1 = full-time or part-time, 0 = not employed. Religion is coded first in dummy variables, Protestant (reference category), Roman Catholic, Jewish, other, or none. A further analysis compares Roman Catholics (reference category) and several Protestant denominations: Baptist, Episcopalian, Lutheran, Methodist, Presbyterian, and "other Protestant." Attendance at religious services is measured as the response to this question: "During the past year, did you usually attend religious services about . . ." and coded 1 = never, 2 = a few times a year, 3 = once a month, 4 = twice a month, 5 = once a week or more often.

We now turn to the 14 dependent variables used in the remainder of this chapter. For convenience they are divided into two broad categories connected by a bridging category. The first category concerns issues central to women's work outside the home, ending with an item on approval of affirmative action regulations for women. The bridging category begins with such an item for blacks, then focuses on issues dealing with black and white families. The last five issues concern the family. In the questionnaire the items were balanced as to direction (liberal versus illiberal response), but they have been recoded, as needed, so that the liberal response is always high. The mnemonics are given in capital letters.

The third, fourth, and fifth questions relate to women's employment. The third question (CONVENIENT) dealt with a woman's right to be employed even if it was not always convenient for her family. The lead-in: "For each of the following statements, please tell me whether you strongly agree, agree, disagree, or strongly disagree." The statement: "A married woman should be able to have a job even if it is not always convenient for her family." It was coded on a scale from 1 to 4 with the liberal response coded as 4. "Don't know" was coded as 2.5, the midpoint of the scale, as always in this chapter for questions using the "strongly agree . . ." format.

The fourth question (SHOULDWORK) concerned expectations as to whether women's being employed should depend on marital status and childrens' ages. The lead-in: "In our society most people think that an able-bodied man should have a job. Do you think that any able-bodied woman should be expected to work if she is (a) unmarried and has completed school; (b) married and has no children; (c) married and has no children under 18; (d) married and has no children under age 6?" "Yes" responses were summed to form a scale from 0 to 4.

The fifth question (BOSS) dealt with preference for a boss of particular sex. "Would you prefer to have a man as boss, a woman as boss, or don't you care either way?" It was coded 1 = don't care, 0 = prefer man. Preference for a woman as boss was coded as missing because so few people (1.7%) did. It is also unclear whether this response falls on the same continuum.

The next three questions dealt with policies concerning women's employment. The sixth question (EQJOBS) concerned women's chance to hold jobs equal to men's: "Which of the following statements comes closest to your opinion? (a) All women should have an equal chance with men for any job regardless of whether they have to support themselves or not; (b) only women who have to support themselves should have an equal chance with men for jobs; (c) a man should have preference over all women for any job." This item was coded on a scale of 1–3 with 1 = man should have preference, 2 = only women who support themselves, 3 = equal chance.

The seventh question (ERA) concerns the Equal Rights Amendment. ERA overlaps the employment and family categories because the central problems it addresses cover property rights, marriage and divorce, the right to engage in an occupation, and freedom from discrimination in occupation and education (Babcock et al., 1975:147). The screen question: "Have you heard or read about the Equal Rights Amendment to the Constitution which would give women equal rights and responsibilities?" Those who said yes were asked: "Do you favor or oppose the Equal Rights Amendment?" It was coded 1 = favor, 0 = oppose, .5 = don't know.

A 1970 national telephone survey reported that 66% of the men and 47% of the women, a total of 56%, favored the ERA (Chandler, 1972:39). A 1975 Gallup poll reported that 63% of the men and 54% of the women favored the ERA (Gallup Opinion Index, 1975). The GSS has never included an ERA item.

The eighth question (WOMAFF) asked respondents how they felt about Affirmative Action job rules for women. The question: "Equal opportunity regulations require employers to seek out qualified women for jobs. Do you favor or oppose this regulation?" It was coded 1 = favor, 0 = oppose.

The next three items concern racial minorities. They bridge labor market and family issues. The ninth item, MINAFF, applies the content of the eighth item to minorities: "These regulations also require employers to seek qualified members of minority groups for jobs. Do you favor or oppose this?" It was coded 1 = favor, 0 = oppose.

The tenth item (NEIGHBOR) is a family issue not specifically related to women. The question: "Some people think it would be better if everyone lived in neighborhoods where all people had the same kind of racial background while others think it would be better if each neighborhood included people from different racial backgrounds. What do you think?" It was coded 1 = different, 0 = same.

The eleventh item (KIDMONEY) tapped the opinion that women on welfare are sexually immoral. Although it is not explicitly related to race, it probably evokes racial images in the public mind because of the number of black women receiving Aid for Dependent Children funds.

The item was cast in the "strongly agree" format of the third item. The statement, "too many women on welfare have illegitimate babies in order to increase the amount of money they get," was coded on a scale of 1–4, with the liberal response as high. "Don't know" was coded as 2.5, the midpoint.

The next three questions tapped family issues. The twelfth item, ABORT, asked about the circumstances under which it is acceptable for a woman to have a legal abortion. It replicated the six items used by NORC in the 1965 Amalgam Survey and by the GSS in the 1970s, and it closely resembles item sets used in other surveys (see Evers and McGee, 1980:265–266). We analyzed the response to the three 'soft' reasons in Chapter 6. Here we analyze only the combined response (for the six items, see the Appendix, item 33). The "yes" responses were summed to form a scale ranging from 0 to 6.

Evers and McGee (1980) analyzed these items using surveys conducted by NORC in 1965 and the General Social Survey in 1972–1977. They reported patterns and trends in relation to certain background characteristics. Race and religion were trichotomized as white Roman Catholics, nonwhites, and white non-Catholics. For the 'hard' reasons white non-Catholics approved abortion most, followed by white Roman Catholics, then by nonwhites. For the 'soft' reasons, the race–religion relationship was weaker. The trend in approval tended to be consistent across the six items but was only weakly and inconsistently related to age, religion, or education. No single sociodemographic aggregate defined by age, religion, or education changed disproportionately in this time period (Evers and McGee, 1980:264).

The thirteenth item (DIVORCE) concerned ease of getting one. It was cast in the format of the third question. The statement, "it should be easier to get a divorce than it is now," was coded on a scale of 1–4 with the liberal response as high. NORC and the GSS used a similar item, but it had 23 syllables in contrast to the 15 in ours, hence we preferred ours for a telephone interview. For trends in response to the GSS item, see Tom Smith (1980:43).

The fourteenth item (NAME) asked whether a woman should keep her name after marriage in order for us to get a benchmark response on what may become a more salient issue. The question was phrased, "Some people think that a married woman should keep her maiden name all her life while others think she should take her husband's last name. What do you think?" It was coded 1 = keep own name or up to woman, 0 = take husband's name.

The last two items concerned homosexuality. The fifteenth question (HOMO) asked: "Do you think there should be some kind of restrictions on the kinds of jobs that homosexual men and women are allowed to have or do you feel that homosexuals should be free to take any kind of job?" This item was coded as 1 = free, 0 = restrictions. The sixteenth item (LESBIAN) asked: "Do you think women who are homosexuals can be just as good mothers as other women?" This was also coded 1 = yes, 0 = no. We found no other national sample surveys that dealt with lesbians and none that dealt with homosexuals as parents.[7] However, several items in national surveys have dealt with job restrictions on homosexuals.

In 1970 a poll conducted by the Institute for Social Research asked whether homosexual men should or should not be allowed to work in various professions. Up to a third of respondents approved homosexual men as court judges, school teachers, ministers, medical doctors, or government officials. About four-fifths would approve their being beauticians, artists, musicians, or florists (de Boer, 1978a:272). In 1975 a national sample survey in Great Britain asked respondents whether they agreed or disagreed that homosexuals should never be allowed to have certain occupations, such as teaching or medicine. About half the respondents agreed (de Boer, 1978a:271). In 1977 in the United States and Great Britain an American Institute of Public Opinion poll asked whether homosexuals should or should not have equal rights to job opportunities. In the United States 54% of the men and 58% of the women agreed that they should have equal rights; in Britain, 65% agreed (de Boer, 1978a:271).

In 1973, 1974, 1976, and 1977 the GSS asked a series of questions about approval of civil liberties for six groups: men and women atheists, fascists, racists, and socialists, and male communists and homosexuals. (The reason for the sex restriction is not obvious.) Respondents were asked whether a man who admits to being a homosexual should be allowed to teach in a university or not. In each year about half the respondents felt that an admitted male homosexual should be allowed to teach in colleges or universities (T. Smith, 1980:26). A little more than half would favor not removing a book written by a male homosexual from the library (T. Smith, 1980:95). About three-fifths would favor letting a male homosexual make a speech (T. Smith, 1980:206).

FINDINGS

Our strategy for analyzing dependent variables 3–16 is as follows. First, we will report regressions for each of these dependent variables

[7]Sociologists have neglected the study of homosexuality (Huber et al., 1982). For recent comparative work, see the references in Davies (1982).

using religious affiliation and other demographic variables. We will also report the increase in explained variance when the religious affiliation dummy variables are added to equations that have been run with only the other demographic variables.

Second, we will report the effect of attendance at religious services when it, too, is added to the equation. Since the causal ordering between attendance at services and some of our dependent variables is questionable, we report only its coefficient for equations in which it is included. Effects of other variables are reported from equations that excluded attendance at services.

Third, we will report comparisons between specific Protestant denominations and Roman Catholics, taken from equations estimated only for Roman Catholics (reference category) and Protestant denominations. For these equations, only the coefficients for these religion dummy variables are reported, although the same control variables are included as in the preceding set of equations.

We will run each of these sets of equations for each sex separately. Multiple regression analysis is used for all equations. Splits for dichotomous dependent variables are all within the 25–75% range.

Two Trends

The first two items were replications used to assess trends in the effect of religious affiliation on attitudes. The first question (FEPRES) concerned willingness to vote for a qualified woman for President. From 1949 to 1978 men's approval rose from 49% to 83% (see Table 8.3); women's, from 55% to 83% (see Table 8.4). Religious affiliation had few significant effects on men's attitudes. Compared to Protestant men, Roman Catholic men were more liberal in 1963 and 1978; Jewish men, in 1959 and 1972; men of no religion, in 1963. These findings support our expectation that, if religious effects appear, Roman Catholics will be more liberal than Protestants. However, these spotty effects hardly constitute a trend (see Table 8.3). Religious affiliation also had few significant effects on women's attitudes, with one exception. Compared to Protestant women, Jewish women were more liberal in 1972; women of other religion, in 1969; and women of no religion, in 1978. An interesting shift, however, appears from the earlier to the later period in the effect of being Roman Catholic. In 1955 no religious effects were significant, but in 1959 and 1963 Roman Catholic women were less liberal than Protestant women. This relationship reversed in 1969; Roman Catholic women remained more liberal in 1972 and 1978 (see Table 8.4).

Table 8.3

UNSTANDARDIZED REGRESSION COEFFICIENTS PREDICTING MEN'S WILLINGNESS TO VOTE FOR A WOMAN PRESIDENT BY YEAR (FEPRES)[a]

		Year							
		1949	1955	1959	1963	1969	1972	1977	1978
Age:	30-39	-.089	-.008	-.012	.029	.002	-.697	-.038	.003
	40-49	-.118*	.024	.029	.059	-.015	-.067	-.124*	-.026
	50-59	-.082	-.033	-.044	.141	.005	-.012	-.035	-.054
	60+	-.112	.007	.060	.077*	.065	-.104*	-.147*	-.112*
Ed:	9-11 yrs	-.008	-.015	.047	-.011	.177*	.000	.102*	-.012
	12 yrs	-.001	-.070	-.006	.088*	.023	.631	.093*	-.000
	13+ yrs	.035	.125*	.006	.163*	.092	.066	.191*	.050
Race		.016	-.091	.080	-.040	-.066	.094*	-.043	.011
Religion:	Cath	--	-.022	-.047	.108*	.022	.059	.046	.104*
	Jew	--	-.127	.207*	.336	.022	.284*	.145	.079
	Other	--	-.107	-.104	-.247	-.025	-.096	-.112	-.003
	None	--	-.057	.058	.316*	.014	.011	-.002	.047
City Size		.026*	.009	-.014	.000	.003	-.012	-.010	-.004
Region:	East	.058	.039	.009	.015*	-.007	.086	-.039	-.013
	Central	.093	.027	.046	.047	-.011	.061	.015	-.023
	West	.088	.120*	.022	.106*	-.029	.099	-.007	-.005
Party		-.001	-.006	-.004	.047*	-.024	-.004	.004	--
a		.413	.424	.661	.225	.467	.690	.791	.825
R^2 (adjusted)		.01	.01	.00	.04	.00	.02	.06	.03
N		676	773	755	1680	801	806	691	906
Mean FEPRES		.49	.49	.61	.60	.61	.72	.81	.83

* $P < .05$

[a] We are grateful to Sage Publishing Company for permission to publish the coefficients for age, education, and race which appeared in Glenna Spitze and Joan Huber "Changing Attitudes Toward Women's Nonfamily Roles," Sociology of Work and Occupations 3 (August, 1980:326).

We cannot adequately explain the Roman Catholic–Protestant reversal in women's opinion during this period. Yet we should note that it occurred in the period that witnessed a decrease in approval of a woman as President, a decrease for all female cohorts (and three male ones) born before 1940 (Spitze and Huber, 1980:328). The proportion of women who approved was a little lower in 1963 and 1969 than it had

Table 8.4
UNSTANDARDIZED REGRESSION COEFFICIENTS PREDICTING WOMEN'S
WILLINGNESS TO VOTE FOR A WOMAN PRESIDENT BY YEAR (FEPRES)[a]

		Year							
		1949	1955	1959	1963	1969	1972	1977	1978
Age:	30-39	-.020	-.097*	.045	-.090*	-.006	-.102*	-.029	-.025
	40-49	-.037	-.115*	.002	.010	-.052	-.100*	-.056	-.094*
	50-59	-.061	-.049	-.010	.057	-.050	-.130*	-.044	-.145*
	60+	-.099	-.096	-.040	-.001	-.122*	-.168*	-.308*	-.142*
Ed:	9-11 yrs	.020	.075	.013	.007*	.113*	.019	.071	.116*
	12 yrs	.061	.082	.010	.065*	.099	.071	.091*	.125*
	13+ yrs	.127*	.149*	-.034	.107*	.039	.069	.162*	.157*
Race:		.264*	.193*	-.015	.162*	.062	.158*	.033	.036
Religion:	Cath	--	.053	-.121*	-.064*	.129*	.082*	.030	.058*
	Jew	--	.208	.169	-.008	.064	.274*	.168	.028
	Other	--	.078	-.020	.031	.270*	-.022	-.150	.028
	None	--	-.335	.103	.066	.182	.109	.114	.097*
City Size		.006	.010	-.005	-.005	-.006	-.001	.004	.001
Region:	East	.113	-.041	.017	.051	.071	.044	.064	.081*
	Central	.067	-.044	.111*	.047	.001	.005	-.008	.034
	West	.110	-.013	.134*	.030	-.002	.051	-.026	.056
Party		.038	.022	.024	.009	-.005	-.008	.004	--
a		.337	.496	.558	.513	.304	.726	.717	.695
R^2 (adjusted)		.03	.03	.02	.02	.02	.05	.12	.05
N		726	766	753	1858	806	805	835	1086
Mean FEPRES		.55	.58	.58	.53	.54	.73	.76	.83

* $P < .05$

[a] We are grateful to Sage Publishing Company for permission to publish the coefficients for age, education, and race which appeared in Glenna Spitze and Joan Huber "Changing Attitudes Toward Women's Nonfamily Roles," Sociology of Work and Occupations 3 (August, 1980:326).

been in 1949 (see Table 8.4), suggesting that attitudes on this item may have shifted more in accord with broad period effects than in response to such individual attributes as age, race, education, and religion. What kinds of events occurred between 1955 and 1969 that would have made women (except the youngest ones) less liberal on this issue?

Impressionistic evidence suggests that the 1950s and 1960s were the era of family togetherness. The bulging baby boom cohorts occupied their mothers' attention. The mass media bombarded the public with the message that mothers were the social glue that stuck the family together. Possibly Roman Catholic women were socialized to lay more stress on the importance of the maternal role and were actually surrounded by more children to lay some stress on. Furthermore, by the early 1960s the baby boom cohorts began to enter adolescence. The peer group took over; a generation gap appeared. Perhaps the decrease in approval of a woman as President signified only the hope that things might quiet down again if only women would stay home and mind the children—and leave decision making to men.

Effects of other variables (see Tables 8.3 and 8.4) will be discussed briefly (for details, see Spitze and Huber, 1980) as we wish to focus on religion. They are largely as would be expected. Older men and women are generally less liberal than younger ones. More highly educated people are generally more liberal than others. Racial differences are not always significant. When they are, blacks are more liberal than whites, especially black women. The few significant differences between the South and other regions show it to be less liberal. Neither city size nor party affiliation merits discussion.

The second trend question (FEWORK) concerns approval of a married woman's working in business or industry even if her husband could support her. For men, approval rose from 20% in 1938 to 77% in 1978; for women, from 27% to 79% (see Table 8.5).

Because religion was not used as a background variable in 1938, we can examine religious effects only for the 1970s. Almost no consistent patterns or significant differences appear. Roman Catholic men were less liberal than Protestant men in 1977 and more liberal in 1978. This pattern seems so unlikely that we tend to ascribe it to compositional differences between the GSS and our sample. The only difference for women is that women of no religion were more liberal than Protestant women in 1977. The effects of other background variables on this item are consistent with those reported for the one regarding willingness to vote for a woman president. Younger and more educated respondents are more liberal than their counterparts. Unfortunately, we do not know whether approval of a woman's working in business or industry decreased in the 1950s and 1960s.

In sum, the effects of religious affiliation on these two items are minimal, with the sole exception of the Protestant–Roman Catholic reversal regarding voting for a woman president in women's opinion. We shall now examine how the religion variable affects other attitudes concerning women's employment.

Table 8.5
**UNSTANDARDIZED REGRESSION COEFFICIENTS PREDICTING APPROVAL OF A
WOMAN'S WORKING IN BUSINESS OR INDUSTRY BY YEAR (FEWORK)[a]**

	Men				Women			
	1938	1972	1977	1978	1938	1972	1977	1978
Age: 30-39	.042	-.053	-.035	.003	.001	.063	-.019	-.022
40-49	-.024	.005	-.149*	-.027	-.007	.008	-.088*	-.056
50-59	.005	-.006	-.039	-.054	-.082	-.033	-.080	-.130*
60+	-.046	-.088	-.265*	-.112*	-.175*	-.252*	-.262*	-.172*
Ed: 9-11 yrs.	--	.090	.067	-.012	--	.087	.063	.156*
12 yrs	--	.316*	.146*	-.000	--	.102*	.113*	.282*
13+ yrs	--	.363*	.256*	.050	--	.285*	.225*	.404*
Race	-.029	.104*	-.073	.011	.063	.104*	-.014	-.033
Religion: Cath	--	-.063	-.173*	.104*	--	.063	-.026	-.002
Jew	--	.080	-.009	.079	--	.022	.042	.047
Other	--	.029	-.160	-.003	--	-.142	.170	-.090
None	--	.121	.098	.047	--	-.050	.193*	.061
City Size	-.004	.018	.017	-.004	-.006	.013	.007	.008
Region: East	-.051	.049	.150*	-.013	-.107	-.019	.086	-.007
Central	-.071*	-.058	.059	-.023	-.168	-.093*	-.040	-.045
West	-.029	-.148	.124*	-.005	-.115	-.132	.019	.019
Party	.009	-.026	-.012	--	-.016	.008	-.017	--
a	.280	.460	.579	.825	.480	.604	.638	.523
R^2 (adjusted)	.01	.13	.14	.03	.02	.15	.10	.10
N	1586	806	692	906	735	806	836	1086
Mean FEWORK	.20	.62	.67	.77	.27	.68	.65	.79

* $P < .05$

[a] We are grateful to Sage Publishing Company for permission to publish the coefficients for age, education, and race which appeared in Glenna Spitze and Joan Huber "Changing Attitudes Toward Women's Nonfamily Roles," _Sociology of Work and Occupations_ 3 (August, 1980:328).

Women's Roles in Paid Work

Three dependent variables that reflect attitudes toward women's employment roles were tested (see Table 8.6). When asked whether a married woman should have a job even if it is not always convenient for her family (CONVENIENT), the proportion of respondents who

Table 8.6
UNSTANDARDIZED COEFFICIENTS PREDICTING OPINION ON CONVENIENT, SHOULDWORK, AND BOSS (STANDARDIZED COEFFICIENTS IN PARENTHESES)

Background variables High=liberal	CONVENIENT		SHOULDWORK		BOSS	
	Men Strongly agree	Women Strongly agree	Men Women should work	Women Women should work	Men No preference	Women No preference
Age	-.001(-.029)	-.008(-.137)*	.003(.027)	-.005(-.048)	-.001(-.026)	-.004(-.097)*
Education	.030(.142)*	.041(.132)*	-.020(-.049)	-.037(-.071)*	.009(.058)	.013(.068)*
Race	-.052(-.021)	-.097(-.035)	.580(.117)*	.744(.161)*	.068(.038)	.041(.024)
Family income	.028(.078)*	.032(.077)*	-.045(-.063)	-.083(-.119)*	-.021(-.081)*	-.010(-.036)
Ever-divorced	-.004(-.002)	.098(.054)	.018(.006)	-.129(-.043)	.028(.025)	-.126(-.110)*
Wife (own) employment	.113(.091)*	.201(.129)*	-.000(-.000)	.285(.109)*	.064(.072)*	-.034(-.036)
Catholic	-.031(-.020)	.002(.001)	.120(.039)	.070(.024)	.016(.014)	.047(.043)
Jew	.000(.000)	.048(.012)	.425(.070)*	.040(.006)	.030(.014)	-.041(-.017)
Other	.199(.035)	.122(.020)	1.112(.100)*	.147(.014)	-.028(.007)	.057(.015)
None	.075(.045)	.254(.079)*	.112(.034)	.116(.027)	.086(.070)*	.121(.075)*
a	2.8	2.13	1.53	.22	.68	.73
R² (total)	.05	.11	.04	.07	.02	.04
variance explained by religion	.004	.010*	.014*	.001	.005	.006
X̄ dependent variable	2.58	2.60	1.29	1.42	.73	.68
N	909	1092	910	1092	894	1062
Religious attendance	-.021(-.062)	-.061(-.150)*	-.036(-.054)	-.051(-.076)*	-.016(-.064)	.126(.049)

* P <.05

agreed was lower than that to the second question (FEWORK) regarding approval of a woman's working in business or industry; 56% strongly agreed or agreed.

We scaled responses to several questions asking whether an able-bodied woman should work if she were unmarried, married with no children, married with youngest child over 18, or married with youngest child over 6 (SHOULDWORK). Seventy-three percent of the men and 79% of the women thought that an unmarried woman should work, but the proportion who agreed dropped sharply for the other three questions, to 29%, 20%, and 12% for men, and to 31%, 23%, and 12% for women.

When asked whether the respondent preferred a man or woman as boss or had no preference (BOSS), 69% had no preference. Men's response was, somewhat unexpectedly, more liberal than women's. This question might be viewed as being similar to the willingness to vote for a woman president, reflecting attitudes toward women in expert or leadership roles.

There were almost no significant religious differences among these three job-related attitudes and no significant Roman Catholic– Protestant differences. The "no religion" category was significant for women for the right of a woman to work even if it were not convenient for her family and for both sexes for preference of a man or woman boss. Jewish and men of other religion were more liberal on circumstances under which a woman should work. The religion variables added little to the explained variance of these items. Effects of other independent variables are largely as expected. Liberal responses relate to education positively (except when a woman should work and boss preference for men) and to age for a woman's right to work (CONVENIENT) and boss preference for women. Men with employed wives are more liberal on these latter two issues. Employed women are more liberal on a woman's right to work (CONVENIENT) and when a woman should work. The lack of effect of employment status for women on boss preference is unexpected, given the finding that exposure to women in boss/professional roles decreases prejudice against them (Ferber et al., 1979). Also unexpected is the negative impact for women of ever-divorced status on boss preference. Finally, the effects of family income might appear inconsistent, increasing the liberal response on a woman's right to work and decreasing it on boss preference (for men) and when a woman should work. However, it may make sense that people with more money would favor women's working at their own pleasure (CONVENIENT) but not just because they were expected to (SHOULD-WORK).

Employment Policy

The next set of variables concerns policies related to women's employment. The question, EQJOBS, asks whether all women should have an equal chance for jobs regardless of whether they must support themselves; if only women who must support themselves should have an equal chance; or if a man should always have preference. Of the respondents 65% chose the first statement; 28%, the second; and 5%, the third. The question on ERA concerns women's general rights, but it clearly has employment-related implications. The screener question showed that 93% of both women and men had heard or read of it. Of these, men were more likely than women, to approve it, 59% versus 50%. Asked whether respondents favored equal opportunity regulations for women, 66% of men and 71% of women favored such regulations (see Table 8.7).

The pattern of religious effects varies on these three questions. They probably tap different hopes and fears. Religious affiliation has no effect on equal opportunity for women (EQJOBS). Roman Catholics respond more favorably than do Protestants to equal opportunity regulations for women (WOMAFF), perhaps because they are usually more likely to favor government intervention in labor issues. Finally, there are large differences on ERA, with Roman Catholics, Jews, and persons of no religion more favorable than Protestants. Comparing these effects to those on other employment-related issues, we suspect that the sharper differences are due to the perception of the ERA as threatening to the family rather than as improving women's labor market opportunities. We shall soon see the extent to which the ERA response resembles the response to family-related items.

Effects of other variables are as expected, although it is interesting to note that the effects of age and education on equal opportunity regulations for women and ERA appear only for women, perhaps because of women's differential long-term labor force experience (although we do control for current labor force status). Family income positively affects only equal opportunity (both sexes). Being ever-divorced increases favorability to equal opportunity (as does current employment) for women; and to the ERA, for men. Blacks favor the ERA more than whites do (see Table 8.7).

Minorities: Employment and Family Issues

The next set of items focuses on minority groups but in effect it bridges employment and family issues. Parallel to the earlier question

Table 8.7
UNSTANDARDIZED COEFFICIENTS PREDICTING OPINION ON EQJOBS, ERA, WOMAFF (STANDARDIZED COEFFICIENTS IN PARENTHESES)

Background variables High=liberal	EQJOBS Men All women equal chance	EQJOBS Women	ERA Men favor	ERA Women	WOMAFF Men favor	WOMAFF Women
Age	-.007(-.145)*	-.010(-.220)*	-.002(-.048)	-.003(-.092)*	.000(.014)	-.004(-.119)*
Education	.037(.183)*	.051(.206)*	-.002(-.014)	.021(.116)*	.001(.007)	.013(.070)*
Race	-.033(-.014)	-.038(-.017)	.243(.147)*	.186(.117)*	.120(.064)	.090(.056)
Family income	.049(.140)*	.026(.079)*	-.000(-.001)	.003(.011)	-.004(-.015)	-.001(-.004)
Ever-divorced	.032(.020)	.092(.064)*	.076(.073)*	.029(.028)	.053(.045)	.059(.056)
Wife (own) employment	.049(.041)	.106(.065)*	.042(.052)	.049(.058)	.062(.067)	-.016(-.018)
Catholic	.030(.020)	.051(.037)	.124(.121)*	.069(.069)*	.096(.083)*	.082(.082)*
Jew	-.082(-.027)	.074(.024)	.270(.132)*	.196(.088)*	.057(.025)	.022(.010)
Other	-.103(-.019)	-.003(-.000)	.097(.026)	-.100(-.028)	-.087(-.021)	.112(.032)
None	.062(.040)	.021(.011)	.110(.099)*	.171(.118)*	.052(.042)	-.019(-.013)
a	2.15	2.18	.64	.36	.58	.71
R² (total)	.11	.16	.05	.07	.02	.03
variance explained by religion	.002	.002	.028*	.021*	.007	.007
X̄ dependent variable	2.60	2.61	.66	.59	.67	.73
N	902	1088	885	1066	907	1090
Religious attendance	-.027(-.083)	-.039(-.122)*	-.049(-.218)*	-.032(-.139)*	-.012(-.049)	-.017(-.072)

* P <.05

on equal opportunity regulations for women (WOMAFF), when asked whether respondents favored equal opportunity regulations for minority groups (MINAFF), women favored such regulations more than men did, 70% vs. 62% (see Table 8.8). Regarding racially mixed neighborhoods (NEIGHBOR), 68% of the men and 71% of the women approved. Although the item asking whether respondents felt that women on welfare have babies in order to increase their incomes (KIDMONEY) does not explicitly refer to race, it may tend to evoke racial images. To our surprise, 62% of the men and 67% of the women agreed that women on welfare so behaved. The majority of the respondents attributed an amazingly low level of common sense to welfare mothers, considering the size of payments per person and the costs of rearing a child (see Table 8.8).[8]

There were few religious effects on these race-related attitudes. What few there were showed Protestants to be less liberal than other categories. Men with no religion were more likely than Protestant men to favor mixed neighborhoods. Roman Catholic women and women with no religion were more likely than Protestant women to disagree that women on welfare had babies to increase their incomes (see Table 8.8). Not surprisingly, the strongest effects for these items were for race for both sexes (but only for women on WELFARE) and education (on racially mixed neighborhoods for both sexes and equal opportunity regulations for minorities for women). We also found that women with higher family income and the ever-divorced of both sexes were less liberal on the welfare question; ever-divorced men were less favorable to mixed neighborhoods; and older women were less favorable to affirmative action for minorities. The effect of ever-divorced status for women is surprising. Presumably the experience of divorce includes a measure of financial insecurity that might make them somewhat sympathetic to welfare mothers; apparently the reverse occurs (see Table 8.8).

Family Issues

The next three items mark the transition to family issues. Concerning the circumstances under which it should be possible for a woman to obtain a legal abortion (ABORTION), approval is high for the so-called hard reasons—the woman's health (92%), pregnancy resulting from

---

[8]Becker (1981:252), like the respondents, holds that AFDC increases a woman's financial well-being. This would be true only if the grant more than covered the cost of the child, a question that Becker does not address.

rape (86%), and defect in the baby (85%). For the soft reasons, approval represents solid majorities, but it is lower. For low income, it is 57%; for being unmarried and not wanting to marry, 52%; for not wanting any more children, 52%. Here we analyze only the combined scores (see Chapter 6 for analysis of the soft reasons). When asked whether a woman should continue to use her birth name after she marries (NAME), only 25% of men and 24% of women thought she should keep her own name or would leave the choice to the woman (see Table 8.9). When asked whether divorce should be easier to obtain than it is now (DIVORCE), 31% of the men and 29% of the women agreed (see Table 8.9).

In contrast to the employment-related issues, these family-related items elicit rather strong religious effects. Roman Catholic men are less favorable than Protestant men to abortion, the only item on which they have been least liberal. In contrast, Roman Catholic women do not differ from Protestant women on this issue, perhaps because some women have had to face the difficult dilemma of an unwanted pregnancy and may be less sympathetic than men to an abstract party line. Roman Catholic women are more liberal than Protestant women on divorce. Roman Catholic men are more liberal than Protestant men on a woman's retaining her maiden name. Jewish men and women are more liberal on both divorce and abortion than Protestants. Men and women with no religious affiliation are more liberal on all three issues (see Table 8.9). Not only do family-oriented issues elicit more religious differences than do the more abstract political or social issues, the differences (with the exception of Roman Catholic men on abortion) follow the pattern that we expected. Thus far, for variables other than abortion, Roman Catholics, Jews, and persons with no religion are all more liberal than are Protestants.

For other independent variables, we find the usual liberalizing effects of education (on maiden name and abortion) and of family income on abortion. Perhaps, again, persons with higher incomes are used to doing as they wish and therefore favor a policy that increases their options, just as they favored a woman's right to work and opposed issues necessitating that a woman work. Blacks are more favorable to divorce, perhaps because their typically lower incomes make getting a divorce more difficult than it is for nonblacks. Not surprisingly, ever-divorced men and women favor divorce and such women also favor abortion and retension of maiden name more than do their counterparts. Employed women tend to favor divorce and abortion but, inexplicably, their husbands tend to oppose abortion. At first we thought that this puzzling outcome might reflect the way the wife-employment

Table 8.8
UNSTANDARDIZED COEFFICIENTS PREDICTING OPINION ON MINAFF, NEIGHBOR, KIDMONEY (STANDARDIZED COEFFICIENTS IN PARENTHESES)

Background variables High=Liberal	MINAFF		NEIGHBOR		KIDMONEY	
	Men favor	Women favor	Men mixed	Women mixed	Men Strongly disagree	Women Strongly disagree
Age	.001(.028)	-.002(-.064)*	-.001(-.022)	-.002(-.060)	-.001(-.000)	-.001(-.014)
Education	.005(.033)	.015(.080)*	.022(.160)*	.030(.174)*	.003(.012)	.021(.056)
Race	.194(.099)*	.187(.112)*	.200(.121)*	.178(.114)*	-.004(-.001)	.219(.066)*
Family income	-.006(-.021)	-.010(-.039)	-.001(-.006)	-.013(-.056)	-.013(-.028)	-.047(-.093)*
Ever-divorced	-.007(-.005)	.037(.034)	-.077(-.074)*	.009(.009)	-.162(-.075)*	-.158(-.073)*
Wife (own) employment	.041(.043)	-.009(-.010)	.011(.013)	-.024(-.027)	.027(.016)	-.048(-.025)
Catholic	.041(.034)	.066(.063)	.031(.030)	.052(.054)	.095(.045)	.164(.079)*
Jew	.086(.036)	.006(.003)	-.046(-.023)	.042(.020)	.037(.008)	.246(.054)
Other	-.145(-.033)	.115(.031)	-.161(.043)	-.016(-.005)	.095(.015)	.146(.020)
None	.014(.011)	-.006(-.004)	.096(.087)*	.034(.024)	.115(.050)	.283(.093)*
a	.48	.60	.46	.47	2.22	2.02
R^2 (total)	.01	.03	.05	.05	.01	.03
variance explained by religion	.003	.005	.010	.003	.003	.013*
$\bar{X}$ dependent variable	.62	.70	.74	.75	2.22	2.10
N	908	1090	887	1079	909	1091
religious attendance	-.012(-.034)	-.012(-.048)	.004(.019)	.002(.010)	.028(.060)	.008(.016)

* $P < .05$

199

Table 8.9

UNSTANDARDIZED COEFFICIENTS PREDICTING OPINION ON ABORTION, NAME, AND DIVORCE (STANDARDIZED COEFFICIENTS IN PARENTHESES)

Background variables High=liberal	ABORTION yes Men	ABORTION yes Women	NAME own or up to woman Men	NAME own or up to woman Women	DIVORCE strongly agree Men	DIVORCE strongly agree Women
Age	-.004(-.030)	-.013(-.080)	-.002(-.049)	-.003(-.085)*	-.002(-.032)	-.007(-.104)*
Education	.090(.141)*	.058(.070)*	.022(.149)*	.040(.219)*	-.005(-.019)	-.006(-.016)
Race	.262(.034)	.140(.019)	.079(.045)	.177(.109)*	.520(.161)*	.484(.157)*
Family income	.186(.170)*	.122(.107)*	.009(.034)	.044(.016)	-.002(-.005)	-.008(-.017)
Ever-divorced	.233(.049)	.662(.136)*	.003(.003)	.069(.065)*	.191(.092)*	.137(.068)*
Wife (own) employment	-.301(-.080)*	.364(.086)*	-.025(-.029)	-.041(-.016)	.028(.017)	.135(.077)*
Catholic	-.366(-.078)*	-.180(-.038)	.076(.069)*	.044(.043)	.074(.037)	.245(.127)*
Jew	.832(.089)*	1.294(.124)*	.057(.026)	.003(.001)	.557(.140)*	.580(.135)*
Other	.570(.033)	-.312(-.019)	-.064(-.016)	-.113(-.032)	.316(.043)	-.168(-.025)
None	.663(.130)*	1.183(.173)*	.184(.155)*	.295(.198)*	.306(.141)*	.247(.088)*
a	2.40	2.94	-.27	-.20	2.23	2.32
R² (total)	.12	.13	.06	.12	.07	.08
variance explained by religion	.034*	.049*	.017*	.039*	.032*	.032*
X̄ dependent variable	4.17	4.09	.27	.26	2.25	2.19
N	910	1092	891	1066	907	1090
religious attendance	-.404(-.392)*	-.393(-.360)*	-.042(-.175)*	-.025(-.107)*	-.122(-.278)*	-.098(-.218)*

* P <.05

variable was constructed. It is coded 0 for men with no wife present and 0 for husbands of nonemployed wives. If young single men were quite liberal on this issue, it might cause the men with employed wives to appear to be less liberal. However, the zero-order correlation for men between having an employed wife and age is only −.06 and that between age and abortion is only −.01. Hence this explanation seems doubtful.

Homosexual Exployees and Lesbian Mothers

Finally, we examine two variables that in a sense are family-related. Many persons see homosexuality as a threat to traditional family values. When asked whether there should be any restrictions on the kinds of jobs homosexual men and women are allowed to have (HOMO), 47% of men and 53% of women agreed there should be no restrictions (see Table 8.10).[9] Of the respondents 44% of the men and 42% of the women agreed that lesbians could be as good mothers as other women (LESBIAN)—see table 8.10.

We find the expected pattern of religious effects. Roman Catholics are more liberal than Protestants on both items (women only on job restrictions for homosexuals), as are Jews (women only on LESBIAN), and persons of no religion. The amount of variance explained by religion for these items is relatively high, as it is for all items that appear to relate to the family. In fact, the mean percent of variance explained by religion for the family items is 3.1%, compared with .6% for the other items examined here, excluding the ERA, which is hard to classify (see Table 8.10). These two issues (HOMO and LESBIAN) relate to few variables other than religion. Older women are less liberal on both issues. Ever-divorced women are more liberal on lesbian mothers, whereas men with employed wives are more liberal on job restrictions for homosexuals.

To summarize thus far: When religious differences occur, Roman Catholics are almost always more liberal than Protestants, as are Jews and persons of no religion. These differences appear much more often on family-related issues than on employment and policy issues. Of 30 possible comparisons between Protestants and the other three categories (we exclude the "other religion" category because it is so tiny),

[9]Respondents were asked to list up to three jobs that should be restricted. "Teacher" and "occupation dealing with the young" were mentioned most often by far.

Table 8.10
UNSTANDARDIZED COEFFICIENTS PREDICTING OPINION ON HOMO AND LESBIAN (STANDARDIZED COEFFICIENTS IN PARENTHESES)

Background variables High=liberal	HOMO no restrictions		LESBIAN yes	
	Men	Women	Men	Women
Age	-.019(-.050)	-.006(-.159)*	-.000(-.009)	.003(-.097)*
Education	-.002(-.014)	.002(.009)	.009(.067)	.007(.040)
Race	.109(.056)	.093(.052)	.073(.044)	.078(.049)
Family income	-.003(-.011)	.002(.009)	.006(-.026)	-.000(-.000)
Ever-divorced	-.012(-.010)	.070(.061)	.035(.033)	.099(.096)*
Wife (own) employment	.066(.068)*	.039(.038)	.014(.017)	.001(.001)
Catholic	.063(.052)	.147(.132)*	.090(.087)*	.102(.102)*
Jew	.257(.107)*	.290(.117)*	.138(.067)	.279(.126)*
Other	.302(.069)*	-.126(-.032)	.096(.025)	-.216(-.062)*
None	.119(.091)*	.195(.120)*	.134(.120)*	.184(.127)*
a	.55	.67	.43	.52
R^2 (total)	.03	.08	.03	.06
variance explained by religion	.020*	.035*	.017*	.037*
X̄ dependent variable	.51	.57	.58	.56
N	909	1091	909	1091
religious attendance	-.045(-.171)*	-.060(-.230)*	-.044(-.197)*	-.052(-.224)*

* $P < .05$

there are 22 positive significant coefficients on family-related issues. If ERA is considered as being family-related, this adds 6 to the 22, for a total of 28 of a possible 36 comparisons. Of the comparisons between Protestants and the other three groups on other issues, only 9 of 48 comparisons produce significant coefficients (see Table 8.11). Most of these patterns are similiar for men and women.

Attendance at Services

We next examine the effects of attendance at religious services on these 14 items. Since the causal ordering between concurrently measured behavior and attitudes is questionable, we did not include atten-

Table 8.11

PATTERN OF RELIGIOUS AFFILIATION AND ATTENDANCE AT SERVICES ON SELECTED ATTITUDES BY SEX

Dependent Variables	More Liberal Than Protestant[a]			Low Attenders More Liberal[b]	
	Roman Catholic	Jew	No Religion	Men	Women
CONVENIENT			F		-
SHOULDWORK		M			-
BOSS			M F		
EQJOBS					-
WOMAFF	M F				
MINAFF					
NEIGHBOR			M		
KIDMONEY	F		F		
ERA	M F	M F	M F	-	-
ABORTION	c	M F	M F	-	-
NAME	M		M F	-	-
DIVORCE	F	M F	M F	-	-
HOMO	F	M F	M F	-	-
LESBIAN	M F	F	M F	-	-

[a] Significant positive coefficient.

[b] Significant negative coefficient.

[c] The coefficient for men is negative and significant, the sole exception.

dance at services in the equations reported thus far. However, we do report in Tables 8.6–8.10 the effects of attendance at services on each attitude as it is added to the previous equations. The pattern of association (summarized in Table 8.11) is striking. It resembles those reported in the previous section. For both men and women, attendance at services relates strongly to holding less liberal attitudes on all family-related items and on ERA. For the other 8 items, there are only 3 (of 16 possible) negative effects, all for women on job-related issues (CONVENIENT, SHOULDWORK, AND EQJOBS). Thus the effect of attendance at services, like the effect of religious affiliation, falls primarily on the family-related variables. We now turn to the question of denominational differences in liberalism in sex-role issues.

Which Protestants Are Least Liberal?

Since Protestants tend to be less liberal than the other three major religious categories, our final question is whether these differences relate to membership in specific Protestant denominations. We therefore reestimated all of the equations, including only Protestants and Roman Catholics, and creating dummy variables for all Protestant denominations, using Roman Catholics as the reference category. The coefficients are therefore interpretable as comparisons between Roman Catholics and a specific Protestant denomination. Of the Protestant category in this sample, these specific denominations comprise the following percentages of men (and women, in parentheses): Baptist, 33% (29%); Methodist, 19% (21%); Lutheran, 9% (11%); Presbyterian, 8% (7%); Episcopalian, 4% (4%); other or nondenominational Protestant, 27% (29%).

Our findings can be summarized quite simply. First, Baptists and "other Protestants" are the only religious groups to be consistently less liberal than Roman Catholics. Twelve of 28 Baptist–Roman Catholic comparisons and 14 of 28 "other Protestant"–Roman Catholic comparisons yield significant coefficients. Only a very few other coefficients are significant. For example, Methodist and Presbyterian men and Episcopalian women are more liberal than their Roman Catholic counterparts on abortion (see Tables 8.12, 8.13). Second, again we find that most of these differences occur for issues that seem related to the family. Attitudes of Baptists and "other Protestants" apparently explain religious differences between Protestants and Roman Catholics, Jews, and persons of no religion.

Table 8.12
UNSTANDARDIZED COEFFICIENTS COMPARING MEN IN PROTESTANT DENOMINATIONS TO ROMAN CATHOLIC MEN (STANDARDIZED COEFFICIENTS IN PARENTHESES)

Protestant denominations	CONVENIENT	SHOULDWORK	BOSS	EQJOBS	ERA	WOMAFF	MINAFF
Baptist	.029(.021)	-.184(-.066)	-.151(-.145)*	-.071(-.051)	-.130(-.136)*	-.129(-.121)*	-.046(-.041)
Methodist	.078(.044)	-.074(-.022)	.031(.024)	-.007(-.004)	-.068(-.058)	-.045(-.035)	-.057(-.042)
Lutheran	.066(.028)	-.207(-.045)	.061(.036)	-.113(-.050)	-.080(-.051)	-.051(-.029)	.056(.031)
Presbyterian	.081(.031)	-.076(-.015)	.024(.012)	.043(.017)	-.102(-.057)	-.044(-.022)	.077(.037)
Episcopal	.126(.033)	-.118(-.016)	.164(.059)	.253(.069)	.030(.012)	-.246(-.086)*	-.209(-.070)
Other	-.044(-.029)	-.077(-.026)	.059(.052)	-.016(-.011)	-.175(-.169)*	-.103(-.089)*	-.052(-.044)
N	711	712	702	708	699	710	711

Protestant denominations	NEIGHBOR	KIDMONEY	ABORTION	NAME	DIVORCE	HOMO	LESBIAN
Baptist	-.116(-.121)*	-.169(-.087)	.257(.059)	-.107(-.111)*	-.031(-.018)	-.107(-.097)*	-.129(-.136)*
Methodist	.035(.030)	-.065(-.027)	.578(.107)*	-.066(-.056)	-.081(-.037)	.054(.040)	-.033(-.028)
Lutheran	.009(.006)	.016(.005)	-.040(-.005)	-.022(-.014)	.016(.006)	-.036(-.019)	-.014(-.009)
Presbyterian	.024(.013)	-.177(-.048)	.960(.117)*	-.014(-.008)	.097(.030)	.101(.049)	-.053(-.030)
Episcopal	-.001(-.000)	.077(.015)	.719(.061)	-.109(-.042)	.035(.007)	.044(.015)	.095(.037)
Other	-.017(-.017)	-.129(-.061)	.283(.060)	-.086(-.083)	-.183(-.097)*	-.169(-.141)*	-.163(-.159)*
N	692	712	712	698	711	711	711

Dependent variables

CONTROL variables=age, education, race, income, wife employment, ever-divorced.

205

Table 8.13
UNSTANDARDIZED COEFFICIENTS COMPARING WOMEN IN PROTESTANT DENOMINATIONS TO ROMAN CATHOLIC WOMEN (STANDARDIZED COEFFICIENTS IN PARENTHESES)

Protestant denominations			Dependent variables				
	CONVENIENT	SHOULDWORK	BOSS	EQJOBS	ERA	WOMAFF	MINAFF
Baptist	-.055(-.031)	.026(.009)	-.061(-.053)	-.042(-.029)	-.061(-.059)	-.061(-.058)	-.034(-.032)
Methodist	.021(.010)	-.102(-.030)	-.038(-.029)	.005(.003)	-.035(-.029)	-.086(-.072)	-.099(-.079)*
Lutheran	-.056(-.021)	-.017(-.004)	.039(.023)	.000(.000)	-.008(-.005)	-.093(-.060)	-.106(-.066)
Presbyterian	.093(.028)	-.229(-.042)	.070(.033)	-.019(-.007)	-.061(-.031)	-.020(-.010)	-.013(-.007)
Episcopal	.258(.057)	-.097(-.013)	-.032(-.108)*	.146(.039)	.051(.019)	-.101(-.004)	.122(.044)
Other	-.015(-.009)	-.105(-.036)	-.072(-.063)	-.149(-.104)*	-.015(-.146)*	-.113(-.109)*	-.074(-.069)
N	929	921	905	926	905	929	928

	NEIGHBOR	KIDMONEY	ABORTION	NAME	DIVORCE	HOMO	LESBIAN
Baptist	-.099(-.098)*	-.157(-.073)	-.019(-.004)	-.086(-.084)*	-.302(-.152)*	-.198(-.170)*	-.150(-.146)*
Methodist	-.006(-.005)	-.128(-.052)	.054(.095)*	.004(.003)	-.274(-.120)*	-.071(-.053)	-.033(-.028)
Lutheran	.048(.032)	-.108(-.034)	.339(.047)	-.023(-.015)	-.157(-.053)	-.069(-.040)	-.040(-.026)
Presbyterian	-.019(-.010)	-.246(-.061)	.537(.059)	-.045(-.024)	-.087(-.024)	-.101(-.047)	.017(.009)
Episcopal	-.047(-.018)	.046(-.008)	1.454(.116)*	.156(.061)	-.012(-.002)	-.028(-.009)	.077(.029)
Other	-.089(-.088)*	-.236(-.111)*	-.161(-.033)	-.078(-.078)*	-.308(-.157)*	-.203(-.176)*	-.180(-.177)*
N	929	928	929	910	929	928	928

CONTROL variables=age, education, race, income, wife employment, ever-divorced

DISCUSSION

Using national sample data collected in 1978, supplemented by Gallup, NORC, and GSS data collected earlier, we hypothesized that (a) Roman Catholic opinion would be more liberal than Protestant opinion on sex-role issues and that (b) the opinion of Baptists and "other Protestants" would be less liberal than that of Roman Catholics and members of major Protestant denominations. In brief, we expected that the major effect of religious affiliation on United States public opinion would be to differentiate fundamentalist Protestants from all other respondents. Of all religious groups, fundamentalist Protestants most vigorously resist the currents of secular change.

Social change in the past 200 years has undermined the central tenets of the Judeo–Christian tradition. Whatever else religion does, it relates ideas about ultimate reality to ideas of how humans should live. Metaphysical beliefs and moral norms confirm and support one another (Geertz, 1968:406). New ways of doing things that undermine established norms also undermine religious beliefs. People have lost an overall social agreement as to the right ways in which to live together. They therefore cannot find intelligible the claim to moral authority advanced by religious organizations (MacIntyre, 1967:54). Yet when religious organizations revise their definitions of moral behavior, they lose their distinctive attributes, becoming more like one another and like secular bureaucracies. The sects refuse to adapt. By adhering literally to fundamental religious precepts concerning appropriate roles for women and men, they separate themselves from mainstream culture.

In the main our two major hypotheses received support. When Roman Catholic and Protestant beliefs differed, Roman Catholics were always more liberal—with one exception: Roman Catholic men's view of legal abortion. When we divided the Protestant category into Baptists, Episcopalians, Lutherans, Methodists, Presbyterians, and "other Protestants," then only the Baptists and "other Protestants" were less liberal than were Roman Catholics. Religious affiliation affected mainly the items pertaining to the family: divorce, married woman's name, abortion, jobs for homosexuals, the adequacy of lesbians as mothers. It rarely affected views of women's labor market behavior. Attendance at religious services was also associated with holding less liberal views on family issues.

What do these findings imply for the effect of religion on United States politics? First, that religion will play little part when political issues concern women and the labor market. Second, that religious effects may be more important on issues concerning the family, especially on moral issues related to sexual behavior. Predictably, the next controversial issue will probably be legal abortion. The battle is certain to be hard fought. The opponents of legal abortion perceive, correctly, we think, that they must act now. Opposition to abortion will likely decrease over time. The opponents include the Roman Catholic hierarchy, fundamentalist Protestants, and Far Right groups. The alliance is unstable. Roman Catholic stands on social issues typically lean toward liberalism. Some Roman Catholics also question whether the moral rules of the Church should become the law of the state.

We predict that the opponents of legal abortion will not prevail. Even if we are wrong, abortion will not be eliminated. It will only be driven underground. As the history of the demographic transition attests, when people want to limit the number of children they have, then they do so. In the long run, however, technological improvement of contraceptive devices may make the abortion controversy less relevant. Other issues of sexual morality may not readily be outdated by technological change. The effect of religious affiliation on such issues will probably be quite noticeable, but the Roman Catholics will be standing with their more secularized Protestant colleagues. The fundamentalist Protestants and the Far Right will stand alone.

CHAPTER NINE

Conclusions

The primary data for this research come from a telephone survey of a national probability sample of United States residents interviewed late in 1978 by the Survey Research Laboratory of the University of Illinois. Whenever possible, both husbands and wives were interviewed. Almost all respondents were aged 18–65. The total sample (N = 2002) included 682 couples—that is, 1364 husbands and wives married to each other.

The study investigates how people respond to issues related to the costs and benefits of rearing children and working for pay. We asked respondents about the division of labor and household decision making, how they felt about a variety of topics concerning marriage, children, and work as well as other issues related to sex roles. The major explanatory variable that integrates this study is the wife's labor force status.

To understand how people behave and what they think, one must know what kind of daily work they do. In Chapter 1 we therefore examined various subsistence technologies because the way that food production meshes with childrearing tends to determine who produces, who consumes, and who controls distribution beyond the family. It therefore shapes patterns of sex stratification because those who produce have more power and prestige than those who consume and, in all societies, those who control distribution beyond the family have the most power and prestige (Friedl, 1975:8). The simpler the technology, the more easily can one see how it interacts with replacement needs to determine women's status relative to men's.

In foraging societies, hunters have more power and prestige than gatherers because a large animal can be distributed beyond the family. Gatherers collect only enough to feed their own families. Because of high death rates, women had to be pregnant or lactating for most of their reproductive years lest the society die. Since nursing a child is incompatible with hunting large animals because of the unpredictable number of days that hunters must be away from camp, only men could be spared for hunting (Friedl, 1975:17).

In contrast, use of the hoe in a garden-size plot meshed well with the functional requirements of pregnancy and lactation. Hence both women and men produced food in horticultural societies (Friedl, 1975:98). Men monopolized the clearing of new land, but this failed to give them the advantage that hunters had in controlling the distribution of food beyond the family. Since divorce interfered little with maintaining the subsistence of either spouse or their children, divorce rates were high in comparison with United States rates (Friedl, 1975:93). At least until quite recently, women's status relative to men's was probably higher than in any other societal type.

In agricultural societies, women's status hit a historical low. Men monopolized the plow, in part because their size and strength gave them an advantage in managing large draft animals and in part because the distance of the fields from home made it hard for women to combine breastfeeding and plowing. What depressed women's status most, however, was the effect of plow technology on the value of land. It became the chief form of wealth. Unlike the hoe, the plow brings enough nutrients to the surface to enable people to make continuous use of a given piece of land. Since a given acreage feeds a limited number of persons, the number of heirs must be controlled. Monogamous marriage therefore predominates in plow cultures (Goody, 1976). Husbands could take mistresses or concubines because their children had no inheritance rights. Since men prefer to pass wealth only to their own children, however, wives' premarital and marital sexual behavior were controlled by a variety of customs ranging from the relatively benign double standard of sexual behavior to such painful measures as footbinding and clitoral excision.

The transition from agricultural to industrial technology began about 1800. As the United States developed over the nineteenth century, men's productive activities increasingly took place in the market; women's home production decreased over the century until, finally, their main relation to the market was as buyers of goods for their families. Men monopolized access to education and skill-training as well as the use of the most productive machinery. Employed women were typically young or very poor. The tiny minority of women who aspired to positions of power and prestige in the professions were excluded from training or permitted to enter only marginal positions. Legally, women tended to be nonentities, a holdover from agricultural societies. The admission of women into colleges and the completion of the demographic transition at the end of the nineteenth century helped to improve women's status, but change came slowly in the first half of the twentieth century. In popular and scholarly thought, only men did real work.[1]

This pattern of sex stratification began to change more rapidly after 1950 as a result of several interacting trends. Demand rose sharply for workers in typical women's jobs, owing to the baby boom (which increased demand for teachers and nurses) and to corporate expansion (which increased demand for clerical workers). Young and unmarried women were in short supply because birthrates during the Depression had been low, because more 18–19-year-old women were staying in school, and because the age of marriage decreased during the 1940s. The demand for paid workers tended to be filled by women born 1910–1920, the mothers of older school children. Women in this cohort were educationally advantaged over women born before 1910 because high school completion rates had jumped from 29% to 49% during the 1930s. During the 1950s the rates of married women's labor-force participation continued to climb despite a negative view of maternal employment—some years would pass before research showed that fears about the effects of maternal employment on the child were groundless (Hoffman, 1974) or that nonparental child care outside the home was not harmful (Cochran and Bronfenbrenner, 1979:145). As women became producers for more of their adult lives, they became socially more powerful, a little more akin to a political group.

Women are still far from being socially equal to men. Their underrepresentation in top jobs is changing slowly.[2] Direct discrimination seems less common now than a few decades ago, but women's responsibility for housework still hobbles them as competitors for top jobs. A

[1]Even after World War II a huge research literature investigating the development of "modern" attitudes in less developed countries ignored women (Form, 1979).

[2]Moreover, the differences in size and types of their organizations expose men to many more resources than they do women, even though men and women have about the same number of memberships, on average (McPherson and Smith-Lovin, 1982:883).

prime question for the future of sex stratification is whether or to what extent the division of household labor will change. We speculate on this question after reviewing our findings.

This brief review of sex stratification during industrialization showed that our foreparents reacted to the changes they confronted by adapting their behavior to their interests as best they could. In turn, their behavioral response to economic forces motivated appropriate attitude changes. The theory of the demographic transition, for example, makes intuitive sense because it connects individual perceptions of self interest to aggregate economic change. A theory that aims to explain individual attitudes and behavior at a given time (that is, a theory suited for micro-cross-sectional data) must be related to a macrotheory that makes historical sense. It should show how trends in mortality, education, earnings, employment, marriage, divorce, and fertility interacted over time in order to predict how contemporary problems of meshing work and childrearing will affect the traditionality of sex-role behaviors and attitudes.

Our macrotheory has four major variables: mortality, education, fertility, and women's labor-force participation. Although trends in all these variables interact, they can be ordered sequentially over time to show the direction of the causal forces. Early in industrialization, after death rates had begun to fall and the level of education had begun to rise, fertility began to decrease. Only after most women were relatively well-educated and were having relatively few children could favorable economic conditions induce their labor force entry in large number. In the United States, these conditions prevailed simultaneously for a brief period during World War I, a longer period during World War II, and for an extended period after 1950. The causal forces therefore lead from decreased mortality and increased education to decreased fertility then, finally, to a massive increase in women's labor-force participation. How does this theory relate to a microtheory?

We reasoned that the variable that best differentiates traditional and nontraditional sex-role behaviors and attitudes at the individual level should be the one that has most recently changed at the macrolevel (see Chapter 1). Its ripple effects are recent. In contrast, people have had plenty of time to adjust individually and collectively to the effects of variables that experienced major change some time ago. Americans take low infant mortality and grade school completion for granted. Low fertility became a norm by 1900 when the demographic transition was completed. In contrast, the rise in married women's employment is recent enough that its repercussions continue. We therefore expected women's labor-force participation to be the most important single variable affecting traditional sex-role attitudes and behaviors.

In Chapter 1 we contrasted our choice of women's labor-force participation as the current microforce of change with economist Gary Becker's (1976, 1981) emphasis on the importance of the wife/husband earnings ratio in determining household economic decisions. The purpose of the comparison is to give readers alternative frameworks for organizing ideas about the direction of change in household organization rather than to provide precise comparisons in each chapter. Any comparison of sociological and economic theories must be rough and suggestive at best. Economists take attitudes (preferences) as a given since they do not want to use inexact variables. Their main variables are therefore behavioral. Since aggregate levels of attitudes change over time, however, taking attitudes as given makes for problems in developing realistic microtheories for cross-sectional data. Sociologists use both attitudes and behavior as variables. Their theories thus include more of the real world but at the cost of less precision. Yet comparing our major hypothesis with Becker's can be suggestive because our most fundamental assumptions are similar. Our approach is materialist. Human attitudes and behaviors develop in response to what men and women must do to solve the problems associated with making a living and rearing children. This is akin to Becker's assumption that behavior tends to be the result of rational economic calculation.

Our review of Becker's theory of the New Home Economics in Chapter 1 indicated that the wife/husband earnings ratio was the major independent variable for studies relating the household to the market because, assuming that nearly everyone wants children, it explains why women do housework and men do market work. Women invest less in their market capital than men do. They have less use for it since they will be out of the labor force for many of their most productive years. A low wife/husband wage ratio implies household gain from a complementary division of labor: husband in the market, wife at home. The higher the wife/husband wage ratio, the less stable the marriage and the fewer the children.

The New Home Economists' key assumption is that nearly everyone wants children. Since children require caretakers, their presence implies complementary marital roles. We suggested, instead, that preference for children may be variable rather than constant. The economic costs and benefits of rearing them can be measured (although with difficulty). Indeed, the cost/benefit ratio can hardly fail to attract the attention even of people who think that the use of quantitative procedures detracts from the quality of life. However, if preference for children is variable rather than constant, then why do people get married? One suspects that desire for children is one reason. Yet some couples marry even though they plan no children. Companionship perhaps? One cannot know if the preference for companionship is bred into the human race, but one can observe that most humans prefer it to isolation. However, if companionship were a major reason for marriage, then a low wife/husband wage ratio would not be relevant, and neither would a low husband/wife ratio. Households would gain most if both spouses maximized their marketability. Assuming that the desire for children is a measurable variable rather than an unmeasured constant opens the door to new theories about the economics of housekeeping and raises suspicions that the wife/husband wage ratio may be only a minor factor of change at the microlevel.

Our argument, then, for expecting women's labor-force participation rather than wife/husband wage ratio to be the most important single factor differentiating traditional sex-role attitudes and behaviors is that, first, on logical grounds, it makes sense to assume that the macrovariable that last experienced substantial change will have the most effect in studies that use micro-cross-sectional data. Women's labor-force participation clearly fits this description better than any other household variable. In contrast, wife/husband wage ratio has proved to be remarkably resistant to change. Second, it is women's labor-force participation that makes wives economically independent. A woman may not live well on her own earnings, but she can live alone if she must. Third, women's labor-force participation should have social effects, as did men's entry into wage work more than a century ago. Doing paid work puts women in contact with other women and men on a daily basis, unlike housework, which tends to have isolating effects (Lopata, 1970). The kind of bonding that elicits collective action comes from working together. Fourth, doing paid work, especially if it is full-time, year round, reminds women more of their responsibility for housework. It is easier for a housewife to see her responsibility as fair than for an employed wife.

In Chapter 3 we investigated the extent and sources of husband/wife reporting discrepancies about decision making and about performing major household tasks in order to assess whether such data can be gathered from one spouse or must be collected from both. We tested the effect of wife/husband age and education differences but not the effect of their wage ratio. We found that aggregate response patterns were similar, although for the division of household labor, respondents tended to overestimate their own relative contribution. However, aggregate agreement masked a moderate degree of individual-level disagreement. Although husband/wife education differences had no effect, the degree of inconsistent reporting did relate to a number of background characteristics: having a lower level of education, being older, greater spouse age differences, having less liberal sex-role attitudes, and being black. These attributes may imply lower levels of communication on these issues because they are less salient for such persons or perhaps because couples with these attributes have lower levels of communication on all issues.

In multivariate analysis, only the age and education effects remained. When the direction of inconsistency was examined, however, the only significant effect was for members of wife-employed couples to disagree more on housework than others do, in the direction of overestimating their own contribution. We interpreted this to mean that the issue was more salient for such couples, perhaps implying greater guilt for those husbands, given their presumably small contribution to housework. We conclude that, with this one exception, husband/wife reporting differences are random rather than systematic. We suggest that collecting data from both spouses on such topics would needlessly increase the expense of research designed to determine aggregate levels of behavior or to relate those behaviors to household or individual characteristics.

In Chapter 4 we tested four hypotheses about the division of household labor as perceived by each spouse: The effect of time availability (measured as employment status); of relative power (measured by wife/husband earnings and education ratios, spouses' perceptions of household decision making, and frequency of thought of divorce); of sex-role attitudes; and of husband's and wife's preference for house- or market work. We found that the wife's employment was especially influential. In contrast, the wife/husband education and earnings ratios had no significant effects. The husband's thought of divorce decreased his household contribution. Nontraditional sex-role attitudes of both spouses, especially of husbands, increased equality of household input. Finally, the wife's taste for housework increased her share. This effect disappeared, however, with controls for wife's employment. Both the sex-role attitude and taste variables must be interpreted cautiously due to problems of causal ordering. The wife's employment status strongly affected the division of household labor, but the wife/husband wage and education ratios had no effects. The use of cross-sectional data may explain the lack of even moderate effects for education and wage ratios as well as the consistency of behavior with attitudes and tastes. Presumably we measured an equilibrium situation that had been negotiated over time rather than a current battleground in which relative resources might play a part. The degree of pragmatism that we observed led us to preduct that the division of household labor will become more equal only over the long run, as women's increased labor-force participation necessarily reduces their time input to housework.

In Chapter 5 we extended the Becker et al. (1977) economic theory of marital stability by testing variables Becker suggested as well as sociological predictors that were related to household and market work. Our independent variable was not divorce, however; instead it was the respondent's thought of divorce, allowing us to separate motivations of both husbands and wives. We found no effects for several variables that, according to Becker, effectively predict divorce.[3] The level of the husband's earnings and the ratio of the wife's earnings to family income had no effects. The presence of young children affected husbands but not wives.[4] Spouse differences in religion affected husbands strongly, but age differences, weakly. Neither difference affected wives. As the Becker theory predicted, however, age at marriage negatively affected wives, and marital duration negatively affected both spouses. However, our findings underscored the importance of wives' market work and husbands' housework. The longer a wife was employed, the more both spouses thought about divorce.[5] For each of the five daily tasks that husbands share equally in two-earner families, the wife is 3% less likely to have thought of divorce. Thus, in thinking about divorce, women's employment history affects thought of divorce, whereas the wife/family income ratio has no effects.

In Chapter 6 we examined subgroup differences in attitudes toward fertility and pronatalist government policies in order to assess whether the United States climate of opinion on this topic is best described as being pro- or antinatalist. We had argued earlier that the structure of United States society had become antinatalist and we expected that United States attitudes could also be described as anti-natalist. We found that the views of the more powerful subcategories (in general,

---

[3]A recent study similarly reports no relation between the timing of remarriage and many of the readily quantifiable socioeconomic and demographic factors (Mott and Moore, 1982:139). Becker's theory predicts that economic factors affect the timing of remarriage.

[4]Becker (1981:224) thought divorce was much less likely if there were children, especially young ones, in the United States and other wealthy countries.

[5]Because of multicollinearity, we could not include wife's employment history and current employment status in the same equation. We omitted current employment because it could be a response to as well as a cause of thinking about divorce.

whites, the highly educated, and the higher income respondents) are least pronatalist. They tend to be more concerned about world over-population than are other groups. They also tend to favor availability of legal abortion, and they do not tend to think that women belong at home nor that voluntarily childless couples are being self-centered. These attitudes are hardly pronatalist, and they are consistent with the lack of support for free child care typically expressed by respondents in these subcategories. Free child care is favored more by women than by men, and the men who favor it tend to be black, Roman Catholic, to have an employed wife and a low income. The women who favor it tend to be young, black, Jewish or of no religion, and not currently married. These do not tend to be the attributes of the powerful. The effect of children on parental happiness or life satisfaction can hardly be called pronatalist. Children of any age or number had no effects on such feelings of well-being. Altogether the climate of opinion on issues to do with rearing children seems rather far from being pronatalist. At the least, these findings cast doubt on the usefulness of Becker's as-sumption that the desire for children is a constant.

In Chapter 7 we assessed the extent to which the increase in wives' labor-force participation has affected husbands' and wives' perception of household decision making, the division of household labor, and their sex-role attitudes. We questioned whether the effects of wives' market work were cumulative or immediate and whether the wife's current employment status, 10-year work history, or absolute level of earnings would have the strongest effects. We found that wives' current employment status, work history, and level of earnings affected hus-bands' but not wives' perceptions of household decision making. Hus-bands of employed wives see them as making more decisions than do husbands of nonemployed wives. All three employment variables had about the same effects, indicating that the effects are not cumulative. For both husbands and wives, the wife's current employment status affects the division of household labor more than do her earnings or her past employment.[6] This may reflect wives' decreased input into house-

---

[6]At first glance, the significant effect of wife's earnings on husband's housework con-tribution reported in Chapter 7 seems inconsistent with the lack of effect of wife's propor-tionate contribution to family income on the division of labor reported in Chapter 4. We have several possible explanations for this pair of findings. First, equations in Chapter 4 include wife's employment status, which is correlated .45 with earnings ratio and would thus detract from its potential effect. However, when we run separate regressions for employed and nonemployed wives (Tables 4.4 and 7.5), the effect of the wife's earnings but not earnings ratio remains. Thus we seem to have a real difference in the way the wife's earnings and the earnings ratio operate. Second, perhaps a high level of earnings is

work—too few hours in the day—rather than husbands' increased input. The noncumulative effect of the three employment variables and the lesser effects for earnings and work history imply that the total effect of wives' employment on housework occurs more as a pragmatic response to her decreased number of hours at home rather than as a more systematic response to her earnings and the length of time she has been employed. Wives' employment status, work history, and earnings similarly affected both husbands' and wives' sex-role attitudes about married women's employment. Attitudes less obviously related to employment were less affected. Thus the effects of wives' employment status, work history, and earnings are not cumulative for decision making, household labor, or sex-role attitudes.

Finally, in Chapter 8 we consider religious effects on sex-role attitudes. A major function of religion is to legitimate marriage and fertility patterns that affect collective survival. The major United States religions stem from traditions that subordinated women, but religious beliefs have been attenuated by the impact of the secular culture. We therefore expected that respondents who adhere most strongly to a literal interpretation of the Bible would tend to have the least liberal sex-role attitudes. Such fundamentalists were operationally defined as Baptists and persons in the large "other Protestant" category. In the main, Roman Catholics tend to be no less liberal than Protestants on sex-role attitudes. With the sole exception of the attitudes of Roman Catholic men on abortion, Roman Catholics were equally or more liberal than were Protestants. The lesser liberality of Protestants was explained by the response of the Baptist and "other Protestant" categories. The main relationship of both religious affiliation and attendance at services was to family-related items: divorce, abortion, jobs for homosexuals, and issues concerning lesbian mothers. Religion rarely affected labor market or race issues.

These findings suggest support for our meta-theory concerning the relationship of macro- and microvariables. Women's labor-force participation, whose level has increased dramatically in the last several decades, often affected household behaviors and attitudes. In contrast, the wife/husband wage ratio has been quite stable. We reported its effects on the division of household labor and on thoughts of divorce. We found no effects just where Becker's theory would have predicted them.

---

the crucial factor that allows women either to demand more participation by their husbands in housework or to buy more goods and services to replace their own housework time. A high earnings ratio may make little difference when total family income is small; and equal earners tend to be low-income receivers (Model, 1981:234).

Substantively, the effect of women's labor-force participation on household attitudes and behaviors implies more equality between women and men, although it does not imply full equality (Kahn-Hut, 1982:11). Equal time spent in work outside the household is only a necessary rather than a sufficient condition for equality, as women's status in the Soviet Union attests (H. Scott, 1974; Lapidus, 1978:43). Full equality would require men to take over half of household labor. Yet so resistant is the division of household labor to change that studies of variation in it have been called much ado about nothing (Miller and Garrison, 1982:242). Women's proportion of total working time may even be increasing. By 1976 women accounted for 55% of all market and housework hours expended in Canada (Meissner, 1981).

Despite these indicators of resistance to change and despite the fact that our data show that change occurs more on pragmatic than ideological grounds, we are inclined to predict, on the basis of two logical possibilities, that the division of household labor will tend to experience substantial change in the next few decades. First, the division of household labor could be made more equal by decreasing the amount of work performed in the household—that is, by such measures as building dwellings that required less maintenance work and by shifting some activities (such as laundry and cooking) to facilities outside the household. In effect, this would reduce the wife's contribution, thereby raising the husband's relative contribution. Second, the division could be made equal by raising the husband's absolute contribution to half. It would also be possible to combine the reduction of work performed by household members with the increase of the husband's total contribution to half.

Proposals to change the household division of labor are rare. One common approach to the problem of household drudgery is to suggest that it be transferred to agencies outside the household. Probably the most famous proponents of this approach are Engels and Marx. They recommended that housework be taken over in part by the state, specifically by agents of the state who, like angels, were of unspecified sex. In the first workers' state, however, experiments in communal living and dining were short-lived (H. Scott, 1982:144) and it would take an army of workers to provide individual household services on a wide scale.[7]

A much less common approach to the division of household labor is to suggest that men's absolute share be increased. As the Swedes recognized, women's social position cannot be changed without changing

---

[7]And who would clean for the cleaners? Hardly anyone addresses the problem of domestic help as a moral issue. Lewis Mumford (1938), an exception, once observed that all healthy humans should care for their own daily needs.

men's (H. Scott, 1982:x). This option is typically couched in utopian language: Work should be restructured to make it less oppressive and alienating. Flexible and reduced work schedules would enable men and women to share a more humane family life. However, it is not clear why businesses would want to adopt such plans nor what effect reduced hours of work would have on the economic stagnation and decreasing productivity that plagues all industrialized countries. Nor is it clear that male wage and salary workers would like their hours of market work shortened in order to spend more time doing things for and with their families.

Both of these proposals have possibilities for the long run, and both would probably be involved in any change in the division of household labor. Currently, however, the introduction of measures to transfer household tasks to agencies of the state seems quite unlikely because the size of the United States budget is a source of nearly universal concern. Nevertheless, we think this possibility may become much more important by the end of the century if concern about declining fertility increases substantially, as we think it will.

An increased level of concern about declining fertility would give the taxpayers an incentive to make the burden of parenting and nonparenting couples more equal.[8] Today most of the cost of rearing a child—including the opportunity cost of the mother's time—falls on the child's parent(s). If the taxpayers want to ensure the production of another generation, they may have to see to it that the costs are distributed more widely than they now are. Because women's level of education is now so high, it would be prohibitively expensive to provide maternal grants large enough to induce women to stay home and have babies. It would cost the taxpayers less to make it easier for mothers to remain in the labor force, and this alternative would probably be more attractive to women than being paid to stay home. The most obvious source of support is the provision of child care. Other measures would include the design and construction of dwellings that are easier to keep clean and that are located close to where the jobs are. The list of possibilities is long.

However, the main reason that we expect substantial change in the

---

[8]It would probably also give the Far Right fringe an increased but misplaced concern about legal abortion. In a population in which contraceptive knowledge is widespread, abortion has relatively little effect on total fertility. Historically, abortion became common when a population had a relatively strong inducement to decrease its fertility but lacked a convenient and effective contraceptive technique. Approval of legal abortion is now sufficiently well-established in the United States that it seems unlikely that more than minor and temporary reversals can occur.

division of household labor in the next few decades is because women are now in a position to take advantage of the ideology of equal opportunity. This ideology holds that rewards are fair because everyone has an equal chance to attain them. Everyone knows that this belief represents an ideal goal with a problematic relation to reality. Yet it prevails in all industrial societies because it so well serves the ends of political stability. It makes people feel they deserve the rewards they get.

However, the ideology also provides leverage to those who feel they are playing by the rules but not getting a fair share of the rewards (Rytina and Spitze, 1981). Women are in this situation today.[9] Among the married couples in our sample, 78% think housework should be shared equally if both spouses are fully employed—even though their own behavior fails to reflect this ideal. Although some married men still look on housework as if it were a terrible accident in which they do not want to get involved (Cheuse, 1982:60), American culture by and large makes people sympathetic to claims for fair play, at least at that point in time when the claim becomes obvious.

In turn, men may be induced to change their ways by a preference for living with a housemate rather than living alone owing to a desire for children, the need for companionship, or a simple preference for economy of scale in housing.[10] Men, especially if they are the rational creatures Becker supposes them to be, may come to take more interest in a housemate's wages. Other things equal, employed wives will probably prefer men who carry their fair share of the load at home. Nonemployed women probably would prefer such men too, but there is little they can do about it. Economic independence gives women clout they lacked in the days when housemates played complementary roles that cemented them for life. The extent to which employed women will use their clout remains to be seen. Doing market work gives women choices. Perhaps the most important choice is the ability to leave a man who will not do his share.

Equalizing the division of household labor will not happen overnight. Yet the pace of change seems remarkably swift if one takes a long view of human history. The word "feminist" appeared in print for the first time not quite 90 years ago (A. Rossi, 1973:xiii), and already it is beginning to appear that social equality is possible for women.

[9]For example, a recent survey reports that about three-fifths of Italian women feel there is no security for the future in being a housewife; about three-fourths think that housewives do a lot of work for society but society does not recognize this work (Russo, 1980:98). We are grateful to Elke Ammassari for bringing this important sample survey to our attention.

[10]These preferences could result as easily in same-sex as cross-sex choice of partner.

APPENDIX

University of Illinois Survey Research Laboratory: Attitudes Toward Women and Work Main Questionnaire

(Interviewer: Record but do not ask sex of respondent.)

Male *(SKIP to Q.6, p.6)* 1   9

Female *(ASK Q.1a below)* 2

Time interview began _____ ☐ AM
　　　　　　　　　　　　　　　　☐ PM

(Ask Q. 1a - 5 of WOMEN only:)

1a.　Have you ever been employed either full-time or part-time?

Yes 1   10

No *(SKIP to Q. 5, p. 5)* . . . 2

b.　Since you were 18 years old, in how many years have you been employed for at least six months of the year?

_____years   11⁻12

(If "0", SKIP to Q. 2a)

c.　Have you been employed either full-time or part-time at any time during the past 10 years?

Yes 1   13

No *(SKIP to Q. 2a)* 2

d.　In the past 10 years, how many years have you worked?

_____years   14⁻15

e.　For how many of these _____ years did you work for six months or more?

_____years   16⁻17

(If 0, SKIP TO Q.2c)

f.　Of these _____ years, how many years did you usually work full-time, that is, at least 35 hours a week?

_____years   18⁻19

(If 10, SKIP to Q. 2g and use 1977)

| SKIP TO Q.2c |

222

2a. <u>Not including the present year</u> (1978), in what year were you last employed?

_____   20-21

Only worked in 1978
(SKIP to Q.3a, p.3) *97*

b. During _____ did you work mostly . . .

Part-time or 1   22

Full-time? 2

SKIP TO Q.2f

2c. Were you employed in 1977?

Yes *(SKIP to Q.2e)* 1   23

No 2

d. In what year were you last employed?   _____

Only worked in 1978
(SKIP to Q.3a, p.3) . . . *97*   24-25

e. During _____ did you work mostly . . .

Part-time or 1   26

Full-time? 2

f. Did you work for more than six months of _____?

Yes 1   27

No 2

g. During _____ was your yearly income from your job, before
taxes, . . .

	(Weekly)	*(Monthly)*		
Less than	*$ 96*	*$ 416*	Less than $5,000? Yes *(SKIP to Q.2i)* 1	28
Less than	*$192*	*$ 833*	Less than $10,000? Yes *(SKIP to Q.2i)* 2	
Less than	*$288*	*$1,250*	Less than $15,000? Yes *(SKIP to Q.2i)* 3	
Less than	*$385*	*$1,667*	Less than $20,000? Yes *(SKIP to Q.2i)* 4	
Less than	*$481*	*$2,083*	Less than $25,00? Yes *(SKIP to Q.2i)* 5	
Less than	*$577*	*$2,500*	Less than $30,000? Yes *(SKIP to Q.2i)* . . . . 6 No *(SKIP to Q.2i)* 7	

Don't know (Ask Q. 2h) . . . *8*

Refused (Ask Q. 2h) *9*

(If "Don't Know" or "Refused" to Q.2g:)

2h. Can you tell me if it was . . .

                                More than \$5,000, or 1   29

                                  Less than \$5,000? 2

                                  Don't know.. . . . . *8*

                                  Refused *9*

2i. Some easy jobs pay too much and some hard jobs pay too little. What about your type of work? Is the pay that most people get for your type of work . . .

                                  About right, ... 1   30

                                  Too low, or 2

                                  Too high? 3

                                  Don't know (SKIP to Q.3a) . . 8

j. What do you think would be a fair yearly pay for your type of work?

                       \$ _____   \$ _____   31-36

                        (Monthly)   (Yearly)

                       Don't know *999998*

3a. Are you currently . . .

                                  Employed full-time, ... 1   37

                                  Employed part-time, ... 2

                                  Retired, ... 3

                                  Temporarily unemployed, or
                                    (SKIP to Q.5, p.5) 4

                                  Not employed and not looking
                                    for work? *(SKIP to Q.5,p.5)*. . . 5

b. What (is/was) your main occupation or job title?

_____   38-40

c. What kind of work (do/did) you do; that is, what (are/were) your main duties on this job?

_____

_____

_____

-4- DK 2

3d. In what kind of business or industry (is/was) this; that is, what product (is/was) made or what service (is/was) given?

41-43

_____

_____

e. Is/Was this mainly . . .

Manufacturing, ... 1
Wholesale trade, ... 2
Retail trade, ... 3
A service, or 4
Something else? *(Specify)*____

_____ 5

| *If R is retired, SKIP to Q. 9a, p. 9* |

4a. Do you have any children under 12 currently living with you?

Yes 1 44
No *(SKIP to Q.5)* 2

b. Who usually takes care of your children while you are working?
(Circle all that apply.)

Husband 1 45
Mother/mother-in-law 2 46
Older child(ren) 3 47
Other relatives 4 48
Friend 5 49
Babysitter 1 50
Daycare center 2 51
Nursery school 3 52
Children care for
    themselves 4 53
Other *(Specify)* _____ 1 54

-5-   DK 2

4c. How difficult is it to arrange for this childcare? Is it . . .

Very difficult, ... 1 [55]
Somewhat difficult, ... 2
Not very difficult, or . . . 3
Not at all difficult? 4

d. Has it <u>always</u> been_____to arrange for childcare while you were
working?

Yes . . . . 1 [56]
No 2

5. I'd like to ask about your employment plans, if any. Do you plan to . . .

Work continuously until retirement, . . 1 [57]
Work most of the time, ... 2
Work some of the time, or 3
Not work at all? 4
Don't know 8

SKIP to Q. 9a, p.9

-6-

DK 2

6. Have you <u>ever</u> been employed either full-time or part-time?

Yes . . . . 1 ⁵⁸

No *(SKIP to Q.9a, p9)* . . . 2

7a. Were you employed in 1977?

Yes *(SKIP to Q.7c)*. . . . . . 1 ⁵⁹

No 2

   b. In what year were you last employed? . . . . _____ ⁶⁰⁻⁶¹

Only worked in 1978
(SKIP to Q.8a, p.7) 97

   c. During _____ did you work mostly . . .

Part-time, or . . . . 1 ⁶²

Full-time? 2

   d. Did you work for more than six months of _____ ?

Yes . . . . 1 ⁶³

No 2

   e. During _____ was your yearly income from your job, before taxes, . . .

(Weekly)	*(Monthly)*	
Less *than* $ 96	$ 416	Less than $5,000? Yes *(SKIP to Q. 7g)* . . . . 1 ⁶⁴
Less *than* $192	$ 833	Less than $10,000? Yes *(SKIP to Q. 7g)* 2
Less *than* $288	$1,250	Less than $15,000? Yes *(SKIP to Q. 7g)* 3
Less *than* $385	$1,667	Less than $20,000? Yes *(SKIP to Q. 7g)* 4
Less *than* $481	$2,083	Less than $25,000? Yes *(SKIP to Q. 7g)* 5
Less *than* $577	$2,500	Less than $30,000? Yes *(SKIP to Q. 7g)* . . . . 6 No *(SKIP to Q. 7g)* 7
		Don't know (Ask Q. 7f) . . . 8
		Refused (Ask Q. 7f) 9

(If "Don't Know" or "Refused" to Q. 7e:)

7f. Can you tell me if it was . . .

More than $10,000, or . . . . 1 [65]

Less than $10,000? 2

Don't know 8

Refused 9

7g. Some easy jobs pay too much and some hard jobs pay too little. What about your type of work? Is the pay that most people get for your type of work . . .

About right, ... 1 [66]

Too low, or 2

Too high? 3

Don't know (SKIP to Q.8a) . . 8

h. What do you think would be a fair yearly pay for your type of work?

$_____ $_____   [67-72]
(*Monthly*)   (Yearly)

Don't know 999998

8a. Are you currently . . .

Employed full-time, ... 1 [73]

Employed part-time, ... 2

Retired, ... 3

Temporarily unemployed, or
(*SKIP to Q. 9a, p.9*) 4

Not employed and not looking for
work? (*SKIP to Q.9a, p.9*) 5

b. What (is/was) your main occupation or job title?

[74-76]

_____

c. What kind of work (do/did) you do; that is, what (are/were) your main duties on this job?

_____

_____

_____

d. In what sort of business or industry (is/was) this; that is, what product (is/was) made, or what service (is/was) given?

[77-79]

_____

[80/2]

-8-

8e. Is/Was this mainly . . .

Manufacturing, ... 1

Wholesale trade, ... 2

Retail trade, ... 3

A service, or 4

Something else? *(Specify)*____

_____5

(Go to Q. 9a, p. 9)

-9- $\frac{DK}{1-5}\frac{3}{}$DUP

(Ask EVERYONE:)

9a. Are you currently . . .

Married, ... 1 [6]

Separated, *(SKIP to Q.16a,p.12)* . . 2

Divorced, *(SKIP to Q.14b,p.11)* . . 3

Widowed, or *(SKIP to Q.14a,p.11)* . 4

Never married? *(SKIP to Q.20,p.14)* . 5

b. In what year were you married?   _____ [7-8]

10. We'd like to know who makes the following decisions in your family.

Who decides . . .	Wife always	Wife usually	Both equally	Husband usually	Husband always	*Other*	*Not app.*	
a. Where to go on vacation? Is it the	1	2	3	4	5	6	7	[9]
b. What job the husband should take? Is it the	1	2	3	4	5	6	7	[10]
c. What house or apartment to live in?	1	2	3	4	5	6	7	[11]
d. Whether the wife should have a job?	1	2	3	4	5	6	7	[12]
e. Whether to move if the husband gets a job offer in another city? . .	1	2	3	4	5	6	7	[13]

(Ask Q. 11a & b of MEN only:)

11a. Is your wife currently employed full-time or part-time?

Yes . . . . 1 [14]

No 2

b. Overall, how (do/would) you feel about your wife's working? (Are you/Would you be) . . .

Strongly in favor, ... 1 [15]

Somewhat in favor, ... 2

Somewhat opposed, or 3

Strongly opposed? 4

(Does not care) 5

SKIP to Q. 12

-10-

BK 3

(Ask Q. 11c of WOMEN only:)

11c. Overall, how (does/would) your husband feel about your
working? (Is he/Would he be) . . .

Strongly in favor, ... 1	[16]
Somewhat in favor, ... 2	
Somewhat opposed, or 3	
Strongly opposed? 4	
(Does not care) 5	

(Ask EVERYONE :)

12. Certain things have to be done in every household. Please
tell me who does the following tasks in your family.

Who . . .	Wife always	Wife usually	Both equally	Husband usually	Husband always	Other	*Not app.*	
a. Prepares regular meals for your household? Is it the	1	2	3	4	5	*6*	*7*	[17]
b. Shops for the food for your household? Is it the	1	2	3	4	5	*6*	*7*	[18]
c. Takes care of the children or old people in your household?	1	2	3	4	5	*6*	*7*	[19]
d. Does the daily housework?	1	2	3	4	5	*6*	*7*	[20]
e. Cleans up after meals?	1	2	3	4	5	*6*	*7*	[21]

13a. Has the thought of getting a divorce from your (husband/wife)
ever crossed your mind?

Yes 1	[22]
No *(SKIP to Q.14a)* 2	

b. In the past year, would you say that you have thought
about getting a divorce . . .

Often, ... 1	[23]
Sometimes, ... 2	
Once in a while, or 3	
Hardly ever? 4	

-11-   DK 3

14a. Have you <u>ever</u> been divorced?

                                    Yes . . . . 1 ²⁴

                                    No *(SKIP to Q.16a,p.12)* . . . 2

                                                                        25-26
    b. In what year did you get the divorce?   _____

                                    (If R is male, SKIP to Q. 15a)

(Ask Q. 11c - e of WOMEN only:)

    c. Were alimony payments ordered by the court?

                                    Yes . . . . 1 ²⁷

                                    No *(SKIP to Q.15a)* 2

    d. In 1977 did any of your family income come from
        alimony payments?
                                    Yes . . . . 1 ²⁸

                                    No *(SKIP to Q.15a)* 2

    e. About what percentage of your family income
        in 1977 came from alimony payments?
                                    ($_____)   _____% 29-31
                                          week/month

(Ask EVERYONE:)

15a. At the time of the divorce, did you have any children under 18
      living at home?
                                    Yes *(If R is male,*
                                      SKIP to Q.16a,p.12) . . . . 1 ³²

(Ask Q. 15b - g of WOMEN only:)   No *(SKIP to Q.16a,p.12)* . . . 2

    b. Were child support payments ordered by the court?

                                    Yes . . . . 1 ³³

                                    No *(SKIP to Q.16a,p.12)* . . . 2

    c. Overall, how regularly did your former husband make these
        payments? Would you say the payments were . . .

                                    Very regular, ... 1 ³⁴

                                    Somewhat regular, ... 2

                                    Somewhat irregular, or . . . 3

                                    Very irregular? 4

    d. Of the amount ordered by the court, would you say his
        payments were usually for the . . .

                                    Full amount, ... 1 ³⁵

                                    More than three quarters, . . 2

                                    More than half, ... 3

                                    More than one quarter, or . . 4

                                    Less than one quarter? . . . 5

-12-   DK 3

15e. Did you usually receive the payments, . . .

> On time, ... 1 [36]
>
> One to three days late, . . . 2
>
> Four to six days late, or . . 3
>
> One week or more after
> they were due? 4

f. In 1977, did any of your household income come
    from child support payments?

> Yes . . . . 1 [37]
>
> No *(SKIP to Q.16a)* 2

g. About what percentage of your household income in
    1977 came from child support payments?

> ($_____)   _____ % [38-40]
>   *week/month*

(Ask EVERYONE:)

16a. Are there any children under 12 currently living in your household?

> Yes . . . . 1 [41]
>
> No *(SKIP to Q. 16d)* 2

b. How many children under 12 live with you now?   _____ [42]

c. What is the age of the youngest child living in your household?

> _____years [43-44]

d. How many children have you had in total, including adopted children?

> [45-46]
> _____
>
> *(If "0" SKIP to Q.19a, p. 13)*

e. Is this the number you wanted, more than you wanted, or fewer than
    you wanted?

> Number wanted . . . . 1 [47]
>
> More 2
>
> Fewer 3

17. During the last seven days, about how many hours have
     you spent just doing things with your children, like
     helping them with schoolwork, reading to them, or
     playing with them?

> _____hours [48-50]

-13-   DK 3

18. Compared to the way your own (mother/father) felt, have
     you enjoyed being around your child(ren) more, about the
     same, or less than (she/he) did?

                                              More 1 51
                                              Same 2
                                              Less 3
                                              Don't know 8

19a. In what year were you born?   _____ 52-54
                                              (If 1937 or earlier, SKIP to Q.21,p.14)

   b. Do you expect to have any (more) children?

                                              Yes 1 55
                                              No *(SKIP to Q.19d)* 2
                                              Uncertain *(SKIP to Q. 21,p14)* 3

   c. How many (more) children do you expect to have? _____children 56
                                              (SKIP to Q. 21, p. 14)

   d. Is this because you are unable to have children, because
       you have decided not to have any (more), or because of
       something else? *(Circle only one.)*

                                    Unable to have children *(SKIP to Q. 21,* 1 57
                                    p. 14)
                                        R. sterilized 2
                                        R's. spouse sterilized 3
                                    R. decided not to 4
                                    Something else 5
                                    Don't know (SKIP to Q. 21, p.14) . . . 8
                                    Refused (SKIP to Q. 21, p. 14) 9

   e. What were the reasons for this decision? *(Record up to 3)*

                                                                        58-59
_____
                                                                        60-61
_____
                                                                        62-63
_____

                          +---------------+
                          | *SKIP TO Q. 21* |
                          +---------------+

-14-   DK 3

20. In what year were you born?   64-66
                                                                         _____

21. Taking all things together, how would you say things are these days?
     Would you say you are very happy, pretty happy, or not too happy?

                                   Very happy 1   67

                                   Pretty happy 2

                                   Not too happy 3

22. In general, would you rather do the kind of work that people do on jobs or
     the kind of work that is done around the house?

                                   Jobs 1   68

                                   House 2

                                   Both *3*

                                   Neither *4*

23a. Have you heard or read about the Equal Rights Amendment to the Constitution
     which would give women equal rights and equal responsibilities?

                                   Yes 1   69

                                   No *(SKIP to Q. 24)* 2

  b. Do you favor or oppose the Equal Rights Amendment?

                                   Favor 1   70

                                   Oppose 2

                                   Don't know 8

  c. Please tell me whether you think each of the following would be very
     likely, somewhat likely, somewhat unlikely, or very unlikely to happen
     if the Equal Rights Amendment were passed.

         If the E.R.A. were passed . . .

	Very likely	Somewhat likely	Somewhat Unlikely	Very unlikely	*Don't Know*
(1) It would be harder for men to get good jobs. Would this be	1	2	3	4	*8* 71
(2) It would increase women's job opportunities. Would this be	1	2	3	4	*8* 72
(3) It would be easier for men to divorce their wives	1	2	3	4	*8* 73
(4) It would be harder for women to get child support	1	2	3	4	*8* 74

24. In general, do you feel labor unions have kept women out of higher paying jobs or do you feel that labor unions have given women an equal chance for higher paying jobs?

Kept women out 1   75
Given equal chance 2
Neither 3
Don't know 8

25. Population experts predict that the world population will double in 40 years. Are you very worried, somewhat worried, not very worried, or not at all worried about this population increase?

Very worried 1   76
Somewhat worried 2
Not very worried 3
Not at all worried 4
Don't know 8   77-79|BK
                                   80|3
                                  1-5|DUP

26. For each of the following statements, please tell me whether you strongly agree, agree, disagree, or strongly disagree.

		Strongly Agree	Agree	Disagree	Strongly disagree	*Don't know*	
a.	Women on welfare who become pregnant should be able to get an abortion at no cost to themselves. Do you	1	2	3	4	*8*	6
b.	Too many women getting welfare have illegitimate babies in order to increase the amount of money they get. Do you	1	2	3	4	*8*	7
c.	It should be easier to get a divorce than it is now. . . .	1	2	3	4	*8*	8
d.	Any woman who is raped is at least partially to blame.	1	2	3	4	*8*	9
e.	Married couples who do not want children are being too self-centered. . . .	1	2	3	4	*8*	10
f.	It would be better for American society if fewer women worked.	1	2	3	4	*8*	11
g.	A woman who works can be just as good a mother as one who does not.	1	2	3	4	*8*	12

-16-   DK 4

	Strongly Agree	Agree	Disagree	Strongly disagree	Don't know
26h. A married woman should be able to have a job even if it is not always convenient for her family. 1		2	3	4	8 13
i. It is more important for a husband to have a good job than for a wife to have a good job. 1		2	3	4	8 14
j. There should be free child-care centers so that women can take jobs. 1		2	3	4	8 15
k. Men are born with more drive to be ambitious and successful than women. 1		2	3	4	8 16
l. By nature women are happiest when they are making a home and caring for children. . . . 1		2	3	4	8 17
m. Women have just as much chance to get big and important jobs; they just aren't interested. 1		2	3	4	8 18
n. A preschool child is likely to suffer if his or her mother works. 1		2	3	4	8 19
o. It is much better for everyone involved if the man is the achiever outside the home and the woman takes care of the home and family. 1		2	3	4	8 20

27a. Equal opportunity regulations require employers to seek out qualified women for jobs. Do you favor or oppose this regulation?

Favor 1   21

Oppose 2

Don't know 8

b. These regulations also require employers to seek qualified members of minority groups for jobs. Do you favor or oppose this?

Favor 1   22

Oppose 2

Don't know 8

28. Do you approve of a married woman earning money in business or industry if she has a husband capable of supporting her?

> Yes . . . . 1 [23]
>
> No 2
>
> *Don't know* 8

29. <u>If there is a limited number of jobs</u>, do you approve or disapprove of a married woman holding a job in business or industry when her husband is able to support her?

> Approve . . . . 1 [24]
>
> Disapprove 2
>
> *Don't know* 8

30. If a husband and wife both work full-time, do you think the wife should be responsible for the daily housework, that the husband should help her, or that the husband and wife should share daily housework equally?

> Wife responsible . . . . . . 1 [25]
>
> Husband help 2
>
> Both equally 3
>
> *Don't know* 8

31. Which one of the following three statements comes closest to your opinion?

a. All woman should have an equal chance with men for any job regardless of whether they have to support themselves or not. . . . . 1 [26]

b. Only women who have to support themselves should have an equal chance with men for jobs. 2

c. A man should have preference over all women for any job. 3

32. If your party nominated a woman for President, would you vote for her if she were qualified for the job?

> Yes . . . . 1 [27]
>
> No 2
>
> *Don't know* 8

33. Please tell me whether or not you think it should be possible for a pregnant woman to obtain a legal abortion . . .

		Yes	No	Don't know	
a.	If there is a strong chance of serious defect in the baby	1	2	8	28
b.	If she is married and does not want any more children	1	2	8	29
c.	If the woman's own health is seriously endangered by the pregnancy	1	2	8	30
d.	If the family has a very low income and cannot afford more children	1	2	8	31
e.	If she became pregnant as a result of rape	1	2	8	32
f.	If she is not married and does not want to marry the man	1	2	8	33

34. Some people think it is all right for a husband to hit his wife under certain conditions. Do you think it would be all right for a husband to hit his wife . . .

		Yes	No	Don't know	
a.	If she is always nagging and complaining?	1	2	8	34
b.	If the wife struck the husband first?	3	4	8	35
c.	If the wife is seeing other men?	1	2	8	36

35a. Did your father ever hit your mother?

Yes 1 37
No *(SKIP to Q.35c)* 2
Don't know (SKIP to Q.35c). . 8

b. Would you say this happened . . .

Often, ... 1
Sometimes, or 2 38
Rarely? 3
Don't know 8

c. Did your mother ever hit your father?

Yes 1
No *(SKIP to Q.36a)* 2 39
Don't know (SKIP to Q.36a). . 8

d. Would you say this happened . . .

Often, ... 1 40
Sometimes, or 2
Rarely? 3
Don't know 8

36a. Do you think there should be some restrictions on the kinds of jobs that homosexual men and women are allowed to have, or do you feel that homosexuals should be free to have any kind of job?

                                    Some restrictions 1   41
                                    Free *(SKIP to Q.37)* 2
                                    Don't know (SKIP to Q.37) . . 8

b. What kinds of jobs should <u>not</u> be open to homosexuals?

                                                                          42-43

_____

                                                                          44-45

_____

                                                                          46-47

_____

37. Do you think women who are homosexuals can be just as good mothers as other women?

                                    Yes 1   48
                                    No 2
                                    Don't know 8

(Ask WOMEN only:)

38. In some job situations women sometimes experience unwanted sexual advances. Have you ever experienced unwanted sexual advances on the job?

                                    Yes 1   49
                                    No 2
                                    Never worked 7

(Ask EVERYONE:)

39. I'd like to ask you some questions about what people should be paid for their work.

    a. What do you think should be the lowest yearly income any person should be able to make for working full-time?

                        $_____ *(SKIP to Q. 39c)*   50-55

                        Don't know *999998*

    b. Would you say . . .

                                    More than $3,000? No 1   56
                                    More than $5,000? No 2
                                    More than $7,000? No 3
                                    More than $9,000? No 4
                                                      Yes 5

39c. What do you think should be the highest yearly income any person should
be able to make for working full-time?

$_____ *(SKIP to Q. 40)*   57—63

Don't know *9999998*

d. Would you say . . .

More than $50,000? No 1   64

More than $100,000? No 2

More than $500,000? No 3

More than $1,000,000? No 4

Yes 5

40. Would you prefer to have a man as boss, a woman as boss, or don't you care
either way?

Man 1   65

Woman 2

Don't care 3

41. Some people think that a married woman should keep her maiden name all
her life, while others think she should take her husband's last name.
What do you think?

Keep maiden name 1   66

Take husband's name 2

Up to the woman 3

Don't know 8

42. Do you think that elderly people who can no longer fully care for themselves
would be better off living in a good nursing home or living with their own
children?

Nursing home 1   67

Their children 2

Don't know 8

43. Some people think it would be better if everyone lived in neighborhoods
where all people had the same kind of racial background while others think
it would be better if each neighborhood included people from different
racial backgrounds. What do you think?

Same racial background 1   68

Different racial backgrounds . . . 2

Don't know 8

-21-   DK 4-5

44. In our society most people think that an able-bodied man should have a job.

Do you think that an able-bodied woman should be
expected to work if she is . . .   Yes   No   *Don't know*

a. Unmarried and has completed school? 1   2   *8*   69

b. Married and has no children? 1   2   *8*   70

c. Married and has no children under age 18? . . 1   2   *8*   71

d. Married and has no children under age 6? . . . 1   2   *8*   72

                                                                     73-79|BK

45. Now I'm going to read a list of the ways you might have felt or behaved   80|4
during the past week. Please tell me how many days you have felt this
way.

On how many days during the past week . . .

                                                               Days   1-5|DUP

a. were you bothered by things that usually don't
   bother you? . . . . _____   6

b. did you not feel like eating; your appetite
   was poor? . . . . _____   7

c. did you feel that you could not shake off the
   blues even with help from your family or friends? . . . . _____   8

d. did you feel that you were just as good as
   other people? . . . . _____   9

e. did you have trouble keeping your mind on what
   you were doing? . . . . _____   10

f. did you feel depressed? . . . . _____   11

g. did you feel that everything you did was
   an effort? . . . . _____   12

h. did you feel hopeful about the future? . . . . _____   13

i. did you think your life had been a failure? . . . . . . _____   14

j. did you feel fearful? . . . . _____   15

k. was your sleep restless? . . . . _____   16

l. were you happy? . . . . _____   17

m. did you talk less than usual? . . . . _____   18

n. did you feel lonely? . . . . _____   19

o. were people unfriendly? . . . . _____   20

p. did you enjoy life? . . . . _____   21

q. did you have crying spells? . . . . _____   22

r. did you feel sad? . . . . _____   23

s. did you feel that people disliked you? . . . . _____   24

t. did you feel you could not get "going"? . . . . _____   25

-22-

46. During the past 12 months, how often did it happen that you did not have enough money to afford the kind of . . .

		Very often	Fairly often	Not very often	Never	
a)	Food you thought your household should have? Did this happen	1	2	3	4	26
b)	Clothes you thought your household should have? Did this happen	1	2	3	4	27
c)	Medical care you thought your household should have? Did this happen	1	2	3	4	28

47. We have talked about various parts of your life. I would like to ask you about your life as a whole. How satisfied are you with your life as a whole these days? If you had to pick a number from 1 to 7, with 1 being very dissatisfied and 7 being very satisfied, which number would come closest to how satisfied or dissatisfied you feel? *(Define scale again when necessary.)*

```
                              Very dissatisfied . . . . . . 1  29

                                                            2

                                                            3

                                                            4

                                                            5

                                                            6

                              Very satisfied  . . . . . . . 7

                              Don't know . . . . . . . . . 8
```

48a. What is your religious preference?

```
                              Protestant . . . . . . . . . 1  30

                              Catholic (SKIP to Q.48c). . . 2

                              Jewish (SKIP to Q.48c)  . . . 3

                              Other
                                 (Specify and SKIP to Q.48c)

                              _____ 4

                              None (SKIP to Q.49) . . . . . 5
```

   b. What specific denomination is that, if any?

```
                              Baptist . . . . . . . . . . . 1  31

                              Methodist . . . . . . . . . . 2

                              Lutheran  . . . . . . . . . . 3

                              Presbyterian  . . . . . . . . 4

                              Episcopalian  . . . . . . . . 5

                              Other (Specify)_____

                              _____ 6

                              No denomination given or
                                 nondenominational church. . 7
```

-23-   DK 5

48c. During the past year, did you usually attend religious services about . . .

Once a week or more often,. . 1
32
Twice a month, ... 2

Once a month, ... 3

A few times a year, or . . . 4

Never? 5

49. Do you belong to a labor union?   Yes 1 33

No 2

50a. What is the highest grade or year of school you have completed?
   (Circle highest grade or year.)

None *(SKIP to Q.51)* 00 34-35

Elementary . . . 01 02 03 04 05 06 07 08

High school 09 10 11 12

College 13 14 15 16

Some graduate school 17

Graduate or professional degree 18

   b. In what year did you last attend school?

36-37
_____ _____

(Still in school) . . . 97

51. What is your racial background?

White 1
38
Black 2

Spanish-American 3

American Indian 4

Oriental 5

Other *(Specify)* 6

___ _____

-24-   DK 5

52a. Was you total family income before taxes last year, 1977, . . .

                                    Less than $5,000? Yes *(End interview)* . . 1   39
                                    Less than $10,000? Yes *(End interview)*. . 2

                                    Less than $15,000? Yes *(End interview)*. . 3

                                    Less than $20,000? Yes *(End interview)*. . 4

                                    Less than $25,000? Yes *(End interview)*. . 5

                                    Less than $30,000? Yes *(End interview)*. . 6

                                                No *(End interview)* . . 7

                                    Don't know 8

                                    Refused 9

(If "Don't know" or "Refused" to Q. 52a:)
52b. Can you tell me if it was . . .

                            More than $11,000, or 1   40
                            Less than $11,000? 2

                            Don't know 8

                            Refused 9

THANK YOU FOR YOUR COOPERATION

Time interview ended _____ ☐ AM
                                  ☐ PM

    (Interviewer: If R is married, ask to speak with R's spouse:)

Now I'd like to speak with your (husband/wife) to find out how he/she feels about these issues.

                                  Int. I.D. # _____   41-43
                                            44-70 | BK

                                  Coder #   _____   71-73

                                  Check Coder # _____   74-76

                                  Keypunch # _____   77-79

                                            80/5

References

Abbott, Edith
  1919   Women in Industry. New York: Appleton.
Adams, Francis
  1875   The Free School System of the United States. London: Chapman & Hall.
Adorno, Theodore
  1950   The Authoritarian Personality. New York: Harper & Row.
Aldous, Joan
  1977   "Family interaction patterns." Pp. 105–135 in Alex Inkeles (ed.), Annual Review of Sociology. Palo Alto: Annual Reviews.
Ambert, Anne-Marie
  1980   Divorce in Canada. Don Mills, Ontario: Academic Press Canada.
Araji, Sharon
  1977   "Husbands' and wives' attitude–behavior congruence on family roles." Journal of Marriage and the Family 39:309–320.
Argyle, Michael
  1968   "Religious observance." Pp. 421–428 in David Sills (ed.), International Encyclopedia of the Social Sciences 13. New York: Macmillan & The Free Press.
Armytage, W. H. G.
  1970   Four Hundred Years of English Education. Cambridge: Cambridge University Press.
Babcock, Barbara Allen, Ann Freedman, Eleanor Holmes Norton, and Susan Ross
  1975   Sex Discrimination and the Law. Boston: Little Brown.
Bacheller, Martin (ed.)
    1980   The 1980 Hammond Almanac. Maplewood, N. J.: Hammond Almanac.

Bahr, Stephen
   1974 "Effects on power and the division of labor in the family." Pp. 167–185 in Lois Wladis Hoffman and Ivan Nye (eds.), Working Mothers. San Francisco: Jossey–Bass.
Baker, Elizabeth Faulkner
   1925 Protective Labor Legislation. New York: Columbia University Press.
Baker, Susan
   1980 "Biological influence on human sex and gender." Signs 6:80–96.
Ballweg, John
   1969 "Husband–wife response similarities of evaluative and nonevaluative survey questions." Public Opinion Quarterly 33:249–254.
Banks, J. A., and Olive Banks
   1964 Feminism and Family Planning in Victorian England. New York: Schocken.
Barker, Ernest
   1944 The Development of Public Services in Western Europe, 1660–1930. London: Oxford University Press.
Bayo, Francisco, and Milton Glanz
   1955 "Mortality experiences of workers entitled to old-age benefits under OASDI, 1941–1961." Social Security Administration, Actuarial Study 60. Washington: United States Government Printing Office.
Becker, Gary
   1973 "A theory of marriage. Part I." Journal of Political Economy 81:813–846.
   1974 "A theory of marriage. Part II." Journal of Political Economy 82:S11–S26.
   1976 The Economic Approach to Human Behavior. Chicago: University of Chicago Press.
   1981 A Treatise on the Family. Cambridge, Mass.: Harvard University Press.
Becker, Gary, Elisabeth Landes, and Robert Michael
   1977 "An economic analysis of marital instability." Journal of Political Economy 85:1141–1187.
Beeghley, Leonard, Ellen Van Velsor, and Wilbur Bock
   1981 "The correlates of religiousity among black and white Americans." Sociological Quarterly 22:403–412.
Bellah, Robert
   1968 "The sociology of religion." Pp. 406–414 in David Sills (ed.), International Encyclopedia of the Social Sciences 13. New York: Macmillan & The Free Press.
Ben Porath, Yoram
   1973 "Labor force participation rates and the supply of labor." Journal of Political Economy 81:697–704.
Berelson, Bernard
   1969 "National family planning programs: Where we stand." Pp. 341–387 in S. J. Behrman, Leslie Corsa, Jr., and Ronald Freedman (eds.), Fertility and Family Planning. Ann Arbor: University of Michigan Press.
Berger, Peter
   1969 The Sacred Canopy. New York: Doubleday.
   1980 The Heretical Imperative. New York: Doubleday.
Berger, Suzanne, and Michael Piore
   1980 Dualism and Discontinuity in Industrial Societies. Cambridge: Cambridge University Press.

Bergmann, Barbara
   1978   "Improving post-divorce payment mechanisms." WEAL National Newsletter
          4:2.
Berheide, Catherine White, Sarah Fenstermaker Berk, and Richard Berk
   1976   "Household work in the suburbs: The job and its participants." Pacific So-
          ciological Review 19:491–504.
Berk, Richard
   1980   "The new home economics: An agenda for sociological research." Pp. 113–148.
          in Sarah Fenstermaker Berk (ed.), Women and Household Labor. Beverly Hills:
          Sage.
Berk, Richard, and Sarah Fenstermaker Berk
   1978   "A simultaneous equation model for the division of household labor." So-
          ciological Methods and Research 6:431–468.
   1979   Labor and Leisure at Home. Beverly Hills: Sage.
Berk, Sarah Fenstermaker, and Anthony Shih
   1980   "Contribution to household labor: Comparing wives' and husbands' reports."
          Pp. 191–228, in Sarah Fenstermaker Berk (ed.), Women and Household Labor.
          Beverly Hills: Sage.
Berkner, Lutz, and Franklin Mendels
   1978   "Inheritance systems, family structure, and demographic patterns in western
          Europe, 1700–1900." Pp. 209–223, in Charles Tilly (ed.), Historical Studies of
          Changing Fertility. Princeton: Princeton University Press.
Biryukova, A. P.
   1980   "Special protective legislation and equality of opportunity for women workers
          in the USSR." International Labour Review 119:51–65.
Blake, Judith
   1965   "Demographic science and the redirection of population policy." Pp. 41–69. in
          M. C. Sheps and J. C. Ridley (eds.), Public Health and Population Change.
          Pittsburgh: University of Pittsburgh Press.
   1969   "Population policy for Americans: Is the government being misled?" Science
          164:522–529.
   1971a "Reproduction motivation and population policy." Bioscience 21:215–220.
   1971b "Abortion and public opinion: The 1960–70 decade." Science 171:540–549.
   1972   "Coercive pronatalism and American population policy." Pp. 59–84, in Robert
          Parke, Jr. and Charles Westoff (eds.), Aspects of Population Growth Policy. U. S.
          Commission on Population Growth and the American Future 6. Washington
          D. C.: United States Government Printing Office.
   1973a "The teenage birth control dilemma and public opinion." Science 180:708–
          712.
   1973b "Elective abortion and our reluctant citizenry: Research on public opinion in
          the United States." Pp. 447–467 in Howard Osofsky and Joy Osofsky (eds.), The
          Abortion Experience. New York: Harper & Row.
   1979   "Is zero preferred? American attitudes toward childlessness in the 1970s." Jour-
          nal of Marriage and the Family 79:245–257.
Blau, Francine
   1978   "The data on women workers, past, present, and future." Pp. 29–62, in Ann
          Stromberg and Shirley Harkess (eds.), Women Working. Palo Alto, Calif.:
          Mayfield.
   Forthcoming   "Discrimination against women: Theory and evidence." In William
          Darity (ed.), Labor Economics. Boston: Martinus Nijhoff.

Blaug, Mark
  1976   "The empirical status of human capital theory: A slightly jaundiced view."
          Journal of Economic Literature 14:827–855.
Blood, Robert
  1963   "The husband–wife relationship." PP. 282–305, in Ivan Nye and Lois Wladis
          Hoffman (eds.), The Employed Mother in America. Chicago: Rand McNally.
Blood, Robert, and Robert Hamblin
  1958   "The effect of the wife's employment on the family power structure." Social
          Forces 36:347–354.
Blood, Robert, and Donald Wolfe
  1960   Husbands and Wives. New York: The Free Press.
Blumberg, Rae Lesser
  1978   Stratification: Socioeconomic and Sexual Inequality. Dubuque, Iowa: Wm. C.
          Brown.
Bogue, Donald
  1980   "Which way will fertility go in the 1980s?" Paper presented at the Population
          Association of America. Denver.
Boles, Janet
  1979   The Politics of the Equal Rights Amendment. New York: Longman.
Bolt, Merry, Anne Wilson, and Wendy Larsen
  1979   "Women's biology—Mankind's destiny: The population explosion and wom-
          en's changing roles. Pp. 3–17, in Jo Freeman (ed.), Women: A Feminist Perspec-
          tive. Palo Alto, Calif.: Mayfield.
Booth, Alan, and Susan Welch
  1978   "Spousal consensus and its correlates: A reassessment." Journal of Marriage
          and the Family 40:23–32.
Booth, Alan, and Lynn White
  1980   "Thinking about divorce." Journal of Marriage and the Family 42:605–616.
Borker, Susan, and Julia Loughlin
  1980   "Female labor force participation and divorce: A longitudinal study of mature
          women." Paper presented at the Annual Meeting of the American Sociological
          Association. New York.
Boserup, Ester
  1970   Women's Role in Economic Development. London: George Allen & Unwin.
Boulding, Elise
  1976   The Underside of History. Boulder: Westview Press.
Bowen, William, and T. Aldrich Finegan
  1969   The Economics of Labor Force Participation. Princeton: Princeton University
          Press.
Bowles, Samuel
  1972   "Unequal education and the reproduction of the social division of labor." Pp.
          36–64 in Martin Carnoy (ed.), Schooling in a Corporate Society. New York:
          David McKay.
Bradburn, Norman
  1969   The Structure of Psychological Well-being. Chicago: Aldine.
Bradshaw, Jan
  1981   "Guest editor." Women's Studies International Quarterly 4:v.
Brandeis, Elizabeth
  1935   "Labor legislation." Pp. 399–697 in John R. Commons (ed.), History of Labor in
          the United States, 1896–1932, Vol. 3. New York: Macmillan.

Braun, Rudolf
    1978 "Early industrialization and demographic change in the canton of Zürich." Pp.
          289–334 in Charles Tilly (ed.), Historical Studies in Changing Fertility. Prince-
          ton: Princeton University Press.
Breckinridge, Sophonisba
    1906 "Legislative control of women's work." Journal of Political Economy
          14:107–109.
Bronfenbrenner, Urie
    1979 The Ecology of Human Development. Cambridge, Mass.: Harvard University
          Press.
Bumpass, Larry, and Ronald Rindfuss
    1979 "Children's experience of marital disruption." American Journal of Sociology
          85:49–65.
Bumpass, Larry, and James Sweet
    1972 "Differentials in marital stability: 1970." American Sociological Review
          37:754–766.
Buric, Olivera, and Andjelka Zecevic
    1967 "Family authority, marital satisfaction, and the social network in Yugoslavia."
          Journal of Marriage and the Family 29:325–336.
Burr, Wesley, Louis Ahern, and Elmer Knowles
    1977 "An empirical test of Rodman's theory of resources in cultural context." Journal
          of Marriage and the Family 39:505–514.
Butts, Freeman, and Lawrence Cremin
    1953 A History of Education in American Culture. New York: Henry Holt.
Butz, William, and Michael Ward
    1979a "The emergence of countercyclical U. S. fertility." American Economic Review
          69:318–328.
Butz, William, and Michael Ward
    1979b "Will U. S. fertility remain low? A new economic interpretation." Population
          and Development Review 5:663–688.
Cain, Glen
    1966 Married Women in the Labor Force. Chicago: University of Chicago Press.
Campbell, Angus, Philip Converse, and Willard Rodgers
    1976 The Quality of American Life. New York: Russell Sage Foundation.
Caplow, Theodore
    1954 The Sociology of Work. Minneapolis: University of Minnesota Press.
Carlton, Frank [1908]
    1965 Economic Influences upon Educational Progress in the United States,
          1820–1850. Classics in Education 27. New York: New York Teachers College,
          Columbia.
Carroll, Berenice
    1980 "Review essay: Political science, part II. International politics, comparative
          politics, and feminist radicals." Signs 5:449–458.
Cates, Willard, Jr.
    1977 "Abortion attitudes of black women." Women & Health 2:3–8.
Centers, Richard, Bertram Raven, and Arnoldo Rodrigues
    1971 "Conjugal power structure." American Sociological Review 36:264–278.
Chafe, William

1972   The American Woman: Her Changing Social, Economic, and Political Roles, 1920–1970. New York: Oxford University Press.
Chandler, Robert
1972   Public Opinion. New York: R. R. Bowker.
Cherlin, Andrew
1976   "Social and Economic Determinants of Marital Separation." Unpublished Ph. D. Dissertation. University of California at Los Angeles.
1977   "The effect of children on marital dissolution." Demography 14:265–272.
1978   "Remarriage as an incomplete institution." American Journal of Sociology 84:634–650.
Cheuse, Alan
1982   "How I learned to accept helping around the house." Ladies Home Journal (January):56–65.
Childe, Gordon
1951   Man Makes Himself. New York: Mentor.
Chilman, Catherine
1979a Adolescent Sexuality in a Changing American Society. Washington, D. C.: United States Department of Health, Education, and Welfare.
1979b "Illegitimate births to adolescents: An overview of social and psychological research." Marriage & Family Review 2:1–11.
Clark, Alice
1919   Working Life of Women in the Seventeenth Century. London: George Routledge.
Clark, Robert, Ivan Nye, and Viktor Gecas
1978   "Husband's work involvement and marital role performance." Journal of Marriage and the Family 40:9–21.
Cochran, Moncrieff, and Urie Bronfenbrenner
1979   "Child rearing, parenthood, and the world of work." Pp. 138–154 in Clark Kerr and Jerome Rosow (eds.), Work in America. New York: Van Nostrand.
Cohen, Lawrence, and Marcus Felson
1979   "Social change and crime rate trends: A routine activities approach." American Sociological Review 44:588–607.
Cohen, Sarah, and James Sweet
1974   "The impact of marital disruption and remarriage on fertility." Journal of Marriage and the Family 36:87–96.
Converse, Phillip
1964   "The nature of belief systems in mass publics." Pp. in David Apter (ed.), Ideology and Discontent. New York: The Free Press.
Converse, Philip, Jean Dotson, Wendy Hoag, and William McGee
1980   American Social Attitudes Data Sourcebook, 1947–1978. Cited on p. 249. Cambridge, Mass.: Harvard University Press.
Coombs, Lolagene, and Dorothy Fernandez
1978   "Husband–wife agreement about reproductive goals." Demography 15:57–73.
Coser, Rose Laub, and Gerald Rokoff
1971   "Women in the occupational world." Social Problems 18:535–554.
Cott, Nancy
1979   Passionlessness: An interpretation of Victorian sexual ideology, 1790–1850." Pp. 162–181 in Nancy Cott and Elizabeth Pleck (eds.), A Heritage of Her Own. New York: Simon & Schuster.

Counts, George
  1937 "Education: History." Pp. 403–414 in E. R. A. Seligman (ed.), Encyclopedia of
         the Social Sciences 5. New York: Macmillan.
Cremin, Lawrence
  1968 The Transformation of the School: Progressivism in American Education,
         1876–1957. New York: Knopf.
  1970 American Education: The Colonial Experience, 1607–1783. New York: Harper
         & Row.
Cromwell, Ronald, and Stephen Wieting
  1975 "Multidimensionality of conjugal decision-making indices: Comparative analy-
         ses of five samples." Journal of Comparative Family Studies 6:139–152.
Cromwell, Vicky, and Ronald Cromwell
  1978 "Perceived dominance in decision making and conflict resolution among An-
         glo, Black, and Chicano couples." Journal of Marriage and the Family
         40:749–759.
Cutright, Phillips
  1971 "Income and family events: Marital stability." Journal of Marriage and the Fam-
         ily 33:291–306.
Cutright, Phillips
  1972 "Illegitimacy in the United States." Pp. 377–438 in Charles Westoff and Robert
         Parke, Jr. (eds.), Commission on Population Growth and the American Future,
         Research Reports 1. Washington, D. C.: United States Government Printing
         Office.
Daly, Mary
  1975 The Church and the Second Sex. New York: Harper & Row.
D'Antonio, William
  1980 "The family and religion: Exploring a changing relationship." Journal for the
         Scientific Study of Religion 19:89–104.
David, Henry
  1982 "Eastern Europe: Pronatalist policies and private behavior." Population Bul-
         letin 36:1–47.
Davies, Christie
  1982 "Sexual taboos and social boundaries." American Journal of Sociology
         87:1032–1063.
Davis, Kingsley
  1949 Human Society. New York: Macmillan.
  1963 "The theory of change and response in modern demographic history." Popula-
         tion Index 29:345–366.
  1967 "Population policy: Will current programs succeed?" Science 158:730–739.
de Boer, Connie
  1978a "The polls: Attitudes toward homosexuality." Public Opinion Quarterly
         42:265–276.
  1978b "The polls: Abortion." Public Opinion Quarterly 41:553–564.
Deckard, Barbara Sinclair
  1975 The Women's Movement. New York: Harper & Row.
DeTray, Dennis
  1973 "Child quality and demand for children." Journal of Political Economy 81 (part
         2): S70–S95.

DeVaney, Barbara
 1980 "The future of fertility." Paper presented at the Annual Meeting of the Population Association of America. Denver.
Dobbs, A. E. [1919]
 1969 Education and Social Movements, 1700–1850. New York: Kelley.
Douglas, Susan, and Yoram Wind
 1978 "Examining family role and authority patterns: Methodological issues." Journal of Marriage and the Family 40:35–47.
Dowdall, Jean
 1974 "Factors associated with female labor force participation." Social Science Quarterly 55:121–130.
Draper, Elinor
 1974 "Birth Control." Pp. 1065–1073 in Macropaedia 2. Chicago: Encyclopedia Britannica.
Driver, Ann Barstow
 1976 "Religion." Signs 2:434–442.
Duncan, Beverly, and Otis Dudley Duncan
 1978 Sex Typing and Social Roles. New York: Academic Press.
Easterlin, Richard
 1968 Population, Labor Force, and Long Swings in Economic Growth. New York: National Bureau of Economic Research.
 1969 "Towards a socioeconomic theory of fertility: Survey of recent research on factors in American fertility." Pp. 127–156 in S. J. Behrman, Leslie Corsa, Jr., and Ronald Freedman (eds.), Fertility and Family Planning. Ann Arbor: University of Michigan Press.
 1978 "What will 1984 be like? Socioeconomic implications of recent twists in age structure." Demography 15:397–432.
 1980 Birth and Fortune. New York: Basic Books.
Ebaugh, Helen Fuchs, and Allen Haney
 1980 "Shifts in abortion attitudes: 1972–1978." Journal of Marriage and the Family 42:491–499.
Ehrenreich, Barbara, and Deirdre English
 1979 For Her Own Good: 150 Years of the Experts' Advice to Women. Garden City, N. Y.: Doubleday.
El Saadawi, Nawal
 1982 The Hidden Face of Eve: Women in the Arab World. Boston: Beacon Press.
Epstein, Cynthia
 1970a "Encountering the male establishment: Sex-status limits on women's careers in the professions." American Journal of Sociology 75:965–982.
 1970b Woman's Place. Berkeley: University of California Press.
Ericksen, Julia, William Yancey, and Eugene Ericksen
 1979 The division of family roles." Journal of Marriage and the Family 41:301–314.
Erskine, Hazel
 1966 "The polls: The population explosion, birth control, and sex education." Public Opinion Quarterly 30:490–501.
Espenshade, Thomas
 1980 "Raising a child can now cost $85,000." Intercom 8:1–2.

Evers, Mark, and Jeanne McGee
  1980 "The trend and pattern in attitudes toward abortion: 1965–1976." Social Indi-
         cators Research 7:251–267.
Farkas, George
  1976 "Education, wage rates, and the division of labor between husband and wife."
         Journal of Marriage and the Family 38:473–483.
Ferber, Marianne
  1982 "Labor market participation of young married women: Causes and effects."
         Journal of Marriage and the Family 44:457–468.
Ferber, Marianne, and Bonnie Birnbaum
  1977 "The 'new home economics': Retrospects and prospects." Journal of Consumer
         Research 4:19–28.
  1980 "One job or two jobs: The implications for young wives." Journal of Consumer
         Research 7:263–271.
Ferber, Marianne, Joan Huber, and Glenna Spitze
  1979 "Preference for men as bosses and professionals." Social Forces 58:466–476.
Ferree, Myra Marx
  1974 "A woman for president? Changing responses: 1958–1972." Public Opinion
         Quarterly 38:390–399.
  1980 "Satisfaction with housework: The social context." Pp. 89–112 in Sarah
         Fenstermaker Berk (ed.), Women and Household Labor. Beverly Hills: Sage.
Fishbein, Martin
  1978 "Attitudes and behavioral predictions: An overview." Pp. 377–389 in Milton
         Yinger and Stephen Cutler (eds.), Major Social Issues: An Interdisciplinary
         View. New York: The Free Press.
Form, William
  1979 "Comparative industrial sociology and the convergence hypothesis." Annual
         Review of Sociology 5:1–25.
  1982a "Self-employed manual workers: Petty bourgeois or working class?" Social
         Forces 60:1050–1069.
  1982b "Economic segmentation of the American working class." Department of So-
         ciology, University of Illinois at Urbana-Champaign. Mimeo.
Form, William, and David McMillen
  In press "Women, men, and machines." Work and Occupations.
Freeman, Richard
  1979 "The work force of the future: An overview." Pp. 58–79 In Clark Kerr and
         Jerome Rosow (eds.), Work in America. New York: Van Nostrand.
Fried, Ellen Shapiro, and Richard Udry
  1980 "Normative pressures on fertility planning." Population and Environment
         5:199–209.
Friedl, Ernestine
  1975 Women and Men: An Anthropologists's View. New York: Holt, Rinehart &
         Winston.
Frisch, Rose
  1978 "Population, food intake, and fertility." Science 199:22–29.
Furstenberg, Frank
  1976 Unplanned Parenthood. New York: The Free Press.
Gallup, George
  1972 The Gallup Poll: Public Opinion 1935–1971. New York: Random House.

1977 "Human needs and satisfactions: A global survey." Public Opinion Quarterly 40:459–467.

Gallup Opinion Index
1975 Report 118. Princeton, N. J.

Gamble, Sidney
1943 "The disappearance of footbinding in Tinghsien." American Journal of Sociology 49:181–183.

Garden, Maurice
1975 Lyon et les Lyonnais au XVIIIᵉ Siècle. Paris: Flammarion.

Garrett, Clarke
1977 "Women and witches: Patterns of analysis." Signs 3:461–470.

Gauger, William, and Kathryn Walker
1980 "The dollar value of housework." Information Bulletin 60. Ithaca: Cornell University New York State College of Human Ecology.

Geertz, Clifford
1968 "Religion: Anthropological study." Pp. 398–406 in David Sills (ed.), International Encyclopedia of the Social Sciences 13. New York: Macmillan & The Free Press.

Gillespie, Dair
1971 "Who has the power? The marital struggle." Journal of Marriage and the Family 33:445–458.

Gillespie, Michael
1977 "Loglinear techniques and the regression analysis of dummy dependent variables." Sociological Methods and Research 6:3–22.

Glenn, Evelyn Nakano, and Roslyn Feldberg
1982 "Degraded and deskilled: The proletarianization of clerical work." Pp. 202–217 in Rachel Kahn-Hut, Arlene Kaplan Daniels, and Richard Colvard (eds.), Women and Work. New York: Oxford University Press.

Glenn, Norval, and Charles Weaver
1978 "A multivariate, multisurvey study of marital happiness." Journal of Marriage and the Family 40:269–282.

Glick, Paul
1979 "The future of the American family." Current Population Reports Special Studies. Series P-23 No. 78. Washington, D. C.: United States Bureau of the Census.

Glock, Charles, and Rodney Stark
1965 Religion and Society in Tension. Chicago: Rand McNally.

Goldmark, Josephine
1905 "The necessary sequel of child labor laws." American Journal of Sociology 11:312–325.

Goldschmidt, Walter
1959 Man's Way: A Preface to the Understanding of Human Society. New York: Holt, Rinehart & Winston.

Gömöri, Edith
1980 "Special protective legislation and equality of employment opportunity for women in Hungary." International Labour Review 119:66–77.

Goodman, Leo
1976 "The relationship between modified and usual multiple regression approaches to the analyses of dichotomous variables." Pp. 83–110 in David Heise (ed.), Sociological Methodology. San Francisco: Jossey–Bass.

Goody, Jack
  1976   Production and Reproduction. Cambridge: Cambridge University Press.
Gordon, Linda
  1977   Woman's Body, Woman's Right: Birth Control. New York: Penguin.
Gorecki, Jan
  1966   "Recrimination in Eastern Europe: An empirical study of Polish divorce law."
         American Journal of Comparative Law 14:603–629.
Gove, Walter, and Michael Geerken
  1977   "The effect of children and employment on the mental health of married men
         and women." Social Forces 56:66–76.
Gove, Walter, and Jeannette Tudor
  1973   "Adult sex roles and mental illness." Pp. 50–73 in Joan Huber (ed.), Changing
         Women in a Changing Society. Chicago: University of Chicago Press.
Graham, Patricia Albjerg
  1973   "Status transitions of women students, faculty and administrators." Pp.
         163–186 in Alice Rossi and Ann Calderwood (eds.), Academic Women on the
         Move. New York: Columbia University Press.
Granbois, Donald, and Ronald Willett
  1970   "Equivalence of family role measures based on husband and wife data. Journal
         of Marriage and the Family 32:68–72.
Greeley, Andrew
  1973   "The 'religious' factor and academic careers: Another communication." Ameri-
         can Journal of Sociology 78:1247–1255.
  1979   "The sociology of American Catholics." Annual Review of Sociology 5:91–111.
Greeley, Andrew, and Peter Rossi
  1966   The Education of Catholic Americans. Chicago: Aldine.
Griffith, Janet
  1973   "Social pressure on family size intentions." Family Planning Perspectives
         5:237–242.
Griliches, Zvi
  1974   "Comment." Journal of Political Economy 82, Part II: S219–S221.
Gunter, B. G.
  1977   "Notes on divorce filing as role behavior." Journal of Marriage and the Family
         39:95–97.
Gurin, Gerald, J. Veroff, and Sheila Feld
  1960   Americans View Their Mental Health. New York: Basic Books.
Gustafsson, Berndt
  1969   "The established church and the decline of church attendance in Sweden." Pp.
         360–365 in Norman Birnbaum and Gertrud Lenzer (eds.), Sociology and Re-
         ligion. Englewood Cliffs, N. J.: Prentice–Hall.
Alan Guttmacher Institute
  1980a "Digest." Family Planning Perspectives 12:50.
  1980b "Digest." Family Planning Perspectives 12:158–162.
Haberman, Shelby
  1979   Analysis of Qualitative Data. New York: Academic Press.
Hajnal, John
  1965   "European marriage patterns in perspective." Pp. 101–143 in D. V. Glass and D.
         E. C. Eversley (eds.), Population in History. London: Edward Arnold.

Hall, Bruce
 1981 "The cost of raising a child—update." Consumer Close-ups #8. Ithaca: Cornell
       University Cooperative Extension.
Harris, Marvin
 1964 Patterns of Race in the Americas. New York: Walker.
 1980 Cultural Materialism. New York: Random House.
Hart, Hornell
 1933 "Changing social attitudes and interests." Pp. 382–442 in President's Commit-
       tee on Social Trends, Recent Social Trends. New York: McGraw–Hill.
Haynes, Suzanne, and Manning Feinleib
 1980 "Women, work, and coronary heart disease: Prospective findings from the Fra-
       mingham Heart Study." American Journal of Public Health 70:133–141.
Hedges, Janice Neipert, and Jeanne Barnett
 1972 "Working women and the division of household tasks." Monthly Labor Review
       95:9–14.
Heer, David
 1962 "Husband and wife perceptions of family power structure." Marriage and Fami-
       ly Living 24:65–67.
 1963 "Dominance and the working wife." Pp. 251–262 in Ivan Nye and Lois Wladis
       Hoffman (eds.), The Employed Mother in America. Chicago: Rand McNally.
Heidenheimer, Arnold, Hugh Heclo, and Carolyn Teich Adams
 1975 Comparative Public Policy: The Politics of Social Choice in Europe and Amer-
       ica. New York: St. Martin's Press.
Herberg, Will
 1956 Protestant–Catholic–Jew. Garden City, N. Y.: Doubleday.
Hill, Russell, and Frank Stafford
 1980 "Parental care of children: Time diary estimates of quantity, predictability, and
       variety." Journal of Human Resources 15:219–239.
Hiller, Dana Vannoy
 1980 "Determinants of household and child care task-sharing." Paper presented at
       the Annual Meeting of the American Sociological Association. New York.
Himes, Norman [1936]
 1970 Medical History of Contraception. New York: Schockenpaperback.
Hirschman, Charles, and Marilyn Butler
 1981 "Trends and differentials in breastfeeding: An update." Demography 18:39–54.
Hoffman, Lois Wladis
 1963 "Parental power relations and the division of household tasks." Pp. 126–160 in
       Ivan Nye and Lois Wladis Hoffman (eds.), The Employed Mother in America.
       Chicago: Rand McNally.
 1974 "The effect of maternal employment on the child: A review of evidence." Devel-
       opmental Psychology 10:204–228.
Horsley, Richard
 1979 "Who were the witches? The social roles of the accused in European witch
       trials." Journal of Interdisciplinary History 9:689–715.
Hosken, Fran
 1979 The Hosken Report: Genital and Sexual Mutilation of Females. Lexington,
       Mass.: Women's International Network News.

Huber, Joan
   1976 "Toward a sociotechnological theory of the women's movement." Social Problems 23:371–388.
   1978 "Comparative poverty programs in industrialized countries." Pp. 109–125 in Milton Yinger and Stephen Cutler (eds.), Problems and Prospects in Sociology: An Interdisciplinary View. New York: The Free Press.
   1980 "Will U. S. Fertility Decline toward Zero?" Sociological Quarterly 21:481–492.
Huber, Joan, and William Form
   1973 Income and Ideology: An Analysis of the American Political Formula. New York: The Free Press.
Huber, Joan, Cynthia Rexroat, and Glenna Spitze
   1978 "ERA in Illinois: A crucible of opinion on women's status." Social Forces 57:549–565.
Huber, Joan, John Gagnon, Suzanne Keller, Ronald Lawson, Patricia Miller, and William Simon
   1982 Final Report: American Sociological Association Task Group on Homosexuality. The American Sociologist 17:164–180.
Huber, Joan, and Glenna Spitze
   1980 "Considering divorce: An expansion of Becker's theory of marital instability." American Journal of Sociology 86:75–89.
   1981 "Wives' employment, household behaviors, and sex-role attitudes." Social Forces 60:150–169.
Jaco, Daniel, and Jon Shepard
   1975 "Demographic homogeneity and spousal consensus: A methodological perspective." Journal of Marriage and the Family 37:161–169.
Johnson, Allan Griswold
   1977 "Sex differentials in coronary heart disease: The explanatory role of primary risk factors." Journal of Health and Social Behavior 18:46–54.
Jones, Elise, and Charles Westoff
   1973 "Changes in attitudes toward abortion." Pp. 468–481 in Howard Osofsky and Joy Osofsky (eds.), The Abortion Experience. New York: Harper & Row.
Jones, Robert Alun
   1982 Personal communication.
Kahn-Hut, Rachel, Arlene Daniels, and Richard Colvard
   1982 Women and Work. New York: Oxford University Press.
Kamerman, Sheila, and Alfred Kahn
   1979 "The day-care debate: A wider view." The Public Interest 54:76–93.
Kanoy, Korrel, and Brent Miller
   1980 "Children's impact on the parental decision to divorce." Family Relations 29:309–315.
Kanter, Rosabeth Moss
   1977 Men and Women of the Corporation. New York: Basic Books.
Kantner, John, and Melvin Zelnik
   1972 "Sexual experiences of young unmarried women in the U. S." Family Planning Perspectives 4:9–17.
Kasarda, John
   1971 "Economic structure and fertility: A comparative analysis." Demography

8:307–317.

1979 "How female education reduces fertility: Models and needed research." Mid-American Review of Sociology 4:1–22.

Katz, Michael (ed.)
1971 School Reform. Boston: Little Brown.

Keeley, Michael
1975 "Comment on 'An interpretation of the economic theory of fertility'." Journal of Economic LIterature 13:461–468.

Kessler, Ronald, and James McRae
1981 "Trends in the relationship between sex and psychological distress: 1957–1976." American Sociological Review 46:443–452.

Kirk, Dudley
1968 "Population I. The field of demography." Pp. 342–349 in David Sills (ed.), International Encyclopedia of the Social Sciences 12. New York: Macmillan & The Free Press.

Kirkpatrick, Clifford
1968 "Family II: Disorganization and dissolution." Pp. 313–322 in David Sills (ed.), International Encyclopedia of the Social Sciences 5. New York: Macmillan & The Free Press.

Komarovsky, Mirra
1973 "Cultural contradictions and sex roles." Pp. 111–122 in Joan Huber (ed.), Changing Women in a Changing Society. Chicago: University of Chicago Press.

Kreps, Juanita
1977 "Intergenerational transfers and the bureaucracy." Pp. 21–34 in Ethel Shanas and Marvin Sussman (eds.), Family, Bureaucracy, and the Elderly. Durham, N. C.: Duke University Press.

Lambert, Helen
1978 "Biology and equality: A perspective on sex differences." Signs 4:97–117.

Land, Kenneth, and Fred Pampel
1980 "Aggregate male and female labor force participation functions: An analysis of structural differences, 1947–77." Social Science Research 9:37–54.

Lapidus, Gail Worshofsky
1978 Women in Soviet Society. Berkeley: University of California Press.

Leibenstein, Harvey
1974 "An interpretation of the economic theory of fertility." Journal of Economic Literature 12:457–479.

Leibowitz, Arlene
1975 "Women's work in the home." Pp. 223–243 in Cynthia Lloyd (ed.), Sex, Discrimination, and the Division of Labor. New York: Columbia University Press.

Lenski, Gerhard
1961 The Religious Factor. Garden City, N. Y.: Doubleday.
1966 Power and Privilege. New York: McGraw–Hill.
1971 "The religious factor in Detroit revisited." American Sociological Review 36:48–50.
1976 "History and social change." American Journal of Sociology 82:548–564.

Lenski, Gerhard, and Jean Lenski
1978 Human Societies. New York: McGraw–Hill.

Levinger, George
1979 "Marital cohesiveness at the brink: The fate of application for divorce." Pp.

137–150 in George Levinger and Oliver Moles (eds.), Divorce and Separation. New York: Basic Books.

Levitan, Sar, and Robert Taggart
1976   The Promise of Greatness. Cambridge, Mass.: Harvard University Press.

Levy, Howard
1966   Chinese Footbinding: The History of a Curious Erotic Custom. New York: Walton Rawls.

Levy, Richard
1975   "New light on Mao: His views on the Soviet Union's Political Economy." China Quarterly 61:95–117.

Lipset, Seymour Martin
1959   "Religion in America: What religious revival?" Columbia University Forum 2:2. Cited on p. 68 in Charles Glock and Rodney Stark. 1965. Religion and Society in Tension, Chicago: Rand McNally.

Long, Clarence
1960   Wages and Earnings in the United States 1860–1890. Princeton: Princeton University Press.

Long, Larry
1974   "Women's labor force participation and the residential mobility of families." Social Forces 52:342–348.

Lopata, Helen Znaniecki
1970   Occupation: Housewife. New York: Oxford University Press.

Lorber, Judith
1975   "Beyond equality of the sexes: The question of the children." The Family Coordinator 24:465–472.

Lydall, Harold
1968   The Structure of Earnings. London: Oxford at the Clarendon Press.

Maccoby, Eleanor, and Carol Jacklin
1974   The Psychology of Sex Differences. Stanford, Calif.: Stanford University Press.

MacIntyre, Alasdair
1967   Secularization and Moral Change. London: Oxford University Press.

Macke, Ann Statham, Paula Hudis, and Don Larrick
1977   "Sex-role attitudes and employment among women." Paper presented at the United States Department of Labor Conference on the National Longitudinal Survey of Mature Women. Washington, D. C.

Madigan, Francis
1957   " Are sex mortality differentials biologically caused?" Milbank Memorial Fund Quarterly 35:203–223.

Mahoney, Thomas
1961   "Factors determining the labor force participation of married women." Industrial and Labor Relations Review 40:563–577.

Maret-Havens, Elizabeth
1977   "Developing an index to measure female labor force attachment." Monthly Labor Review 100:35–38.

Martin, Kay, and Barbara Voorhies
1975   Female of the Species. New York: Columbia University Press.

Mason, Karen Oppenheim
1974   Women's Labor Force Participation and Fertility. Research Triangle Park, N. C.: Research Triangle Institute.

1975 "Sex-role attitude items and scales from U. S. sample surveys." Ann Arbor: Population Studies Center, University of Michigan. (Mimeo.)

Mason, Karen Oppenheim, and Larry Bumpass
1975 "U. S. women's sex-role ideology, 1970." American Journal of Sociology 80:1212–1219.

Mason, Karen Oppenheim, John Czajka, and Sara Arber
1976 "Change in U. S. women's sex-role attitudes, 1964–1974." American Sociological Review 41:573–596.

Maynes, Scott
1978 "Attitudes, behavior, and economics." Pp. 390–411 in Milton Yinger and Stephen Cutler (eds.), Major Social Issues: An Interdisciplinary View. New York: The Free Press.

Mazumdar, Vina
1978 "Comment on suttee." Signs 4:269–273.

McCarthy, James
1978 "A comparison of the probability of the dissolution of first and second marriages." Demography 15:345–359.
1979 "Religious commitment, affiliation, and marriage dissolution." Pp. 179–197 in Robert Wuthnow (ed.), The Religious Dimension. New York: Academic Press.

McCormack, Thelma
1981 "Good theory or just theory? Toward a feminist philosophy of social science." Women's Studies International Quarterly 4:1–12.

McDonald, Gerald
1980 "Family power: The assessment of a decade of theory and research, 1970–1979." Journal of Marriage and the Family 42:841–854.

McNeill, William
1976 Plagues and Peoples. Garden City, N. Y.: Anchor Books.

McPherson, Miller, and Lynn Smith-Lovin
1982 "Women and weak ties: Differences by sex in the size of voluntary organizations." American Journal of Sociology 87:883–904.

Meissner, Martin
1981 "The domestic economy-half of Canada's work: Contemporary hours of work and changes 1911–76." Victoria: University of British Columbia. (Mimeo.)

Meissner, Martin, E. W. Humphreys, S. M. Meiss, and W. J. Scheu
1975 "No exit for wives: Sexual division of labour and the cumulation of household demands." Canadian Review of Sociology and Anthropology 12:424–459.

Michael, Robert
1977 "Why has the U. S. divorce rate doubled within the decade?" New York: National Bureau of Economic Research Working Paper 202.

Michael, Robert, and Gary Becker
1976 "On the new theory of consumer behavior." Pp. 131–149 in Gary Becker (ed.), The Economic Approach to Human Behavior. Chicago: University of Chicago Press.

Michael, Robert, Victor Fuchs, and Sharon Scott
1980 "Changes in the propensity to live alone, 1950–1976." Demography 17:39–56.

Micropaedia VIII
1974 "Sati." Encyclopaedia Britannica, 15th edition. Chicago: Encyclopaedia Britannica.

Miller, Joanne, and Howard Garrison
   1982   "Sex roles: The division of labor at home and in the work place." Annual
          Review of Sociology 8:237–262.
Mincer, Jacob, and Solomon Polachek
   1974   "Family investments in human capital: Earnings of women." Journal of Politi-
          cal Economy 82:76–108.
Model, Suzanne
   1981   "Housework by husbands." Journal of Family Issues 2:225–237.
Moffatt, Linda
   1976   "Housework and housewives: A review essay." Canadian Newsletter of Re-
          search on Women 5:90–93.
Mohr, James
   1978   Abortion in America. New York: Oxford University Press.
Moia, Nelly
   1979   "Comment on Garrett's 'Women and witches'." Signs 4:798–802.
Molm, Linda
   1978   "Sex-role attitudes and the employment of married women: The direction of
          causality." Sociological Quarterly 19:522–533.
Monahan, Thomas
   1955   "Is childlessness related to family stability?" American Sociological Review
          20:446–456.
Moore, Kristin, and Steven Caldwell
   1977   Out-of-wedlock Childbearing. Washington, D. C.: Urban Institute.
Moore, Kristin, and Sandra Hofferth
   1979   "Women and their children." Pp. 125–158 in Ralph Smith (ed.), The Subtle
          Revolution: Women at Work. Washington, D. C.: Urban Institute.
Moore, Kristin, and Isabel Sawhill
   1976   "Implications of women's employment for home and family life." Pp. 102–122
          in Juanita Kreps (ed.), Women and the American Economy. Englewood Cliffs,
          N. J.: Prentice–Hall.
Moore, Kristin, and Linda Waite
   1981   "Marital dissolution, early motherhood, and early marriage." Social Forces
          60:20–40.
Morgan, James, Ismail Sirageldin, and Nancy Baerwaldt
   1966   Productive Americans. Monograph 43. Ann Arbor: University of Michigan Sur-
          vey Research Center.
Moseley, K. P., and Immanuel Wallerstein
   1978   "Precapitalist social structures." Annual Review of Sociology 4:259–290.
Mott, Frank, and Sylvia Moore
   1982   "Marital transitions and employment." Pp. 120–145 in Frank Mott (ed.), The
          Employment Revolution: Young American Women of the 1970s. Cambridge,
          Mass.: MIT Press.
Mumford, Lewis
   1938   The Culture of Cities. New York: Harcourt Brace.
Musgrave, R. A.
   1955   "Incidence of the tax structure and its effects on consumption." Pp. 96–113 in
          Joint Economic Committee, Federal Tax Policy for Economic Growth. Wash-
          ington, D. C.: United States Government Printing Office.

Myers, George
  1979 "Foreword." Pp. vi–x in Joseph Spengler, France Faces Depopulation: Postlude Edition, 1937–1976. Durham, N. C.: Duke University Press.
Myrdal, Gunnar
  1968 Asian Drama. New York: Pantheon.
National Alliance for Optional Parenthood
  1979 17 December Newsletter.
National Council on Aging
  1976 The Myth and Reality of Aging in America. Washington, D. C.: National Council on Aging.
Newland, Kathleen
  1980 "Women, Men, and the Division of Labor." Worldwatch Paper 37. Washington, D. C.: Worldwatch Institute.
Nickols, Sharon, and Karen Fox
  1980 "The time crunch—what gives?" Paper presented at the American Home Economics Association. Dallas.
Niebuhr, Richard [1929]
  1957 The Social Sources of Denominationalism. New York: Meridian Books.
Noonan, John, and Cynthia Dunlap
  1972 "Unintended consequences: Laws indirectly affecting population growth in the United States." Pp. 115–156 in Robert Parke, Jr. and Charles Westoff (eds.), Aspects of Population Growth Policy, U. S. Commission on Population Growth and the American Future, Volume 6. Washington, D. C.: United States Government Printing Office.
Oakley, Ann
  1974 The Sociology of Housework. New York: Random House.
Ogburn, William, and Clark Tibbits
  1933 "The family and its functions." Pp. 661–708 in President's Commission on Social Trends, Social Trends I. New York: McGraw–Hill.
Oppenheimer, Valerie Kincade
  1970 The Female Labor Force in the United States. Berkeley: University of California Press.
  1973 "Demographic influence on female employment and the status of women." Pp. 184–199 in Joan Huber (ed.), Changing Women in a Changing Society. Chicago: University of Chicago Press.
Organisation for Economic Co-operation and Development
  1976 Expenditure on Income Maintenance Programs. Studies in Resource Allocation 3. Paris: Organisation for Economic Co-operation and Development.
Ossowski, Stanislaus
  1963 Class Structure and the Social Consciousness. Sheila Patterson, (trans.). New York: The Free Press.
Pagels, Elaine
  1976 "What became of god the mother? Conflicting images of god in early Christianity." Signs 2:293–303.
Paige, Karen Ericksen
  1982 "Patterns of excision and excision rationales in Egypt." Department of Psychology, University of California at Davis. Mimeo.

Parkin, Frank
   1979   Marxism and Class Theory: A Bourgeois Critique. New York: Columbia University Press.
Patterson, Michelle, and Laurie Engelberg
   1978   "Women in male-dominated professions." Pp. 266–292 in Ann Stromberg and Shirley Harkess (eds.), Women Working. Palo Alto, Calif.: Mayfield.
Peck, Ellen, and Judith Senderowitz
   1974   Pronatalism: The Myth of Man and Apple Pie. New York: Crowell.
Pechman, Joseph
   1971   Federal Tax Policy, Revisted Edition. Washington, D. C.: The Brookings Institution.
Peel, John, and Malcolm Potts
   1969   Textbook of Contraceptive Practice. Cambridge: Cambridge University Press.
Pimentel, David, and Marcia Pimentel
   1979   Food, Energy, and Society. New York: Wiley.
Placek, Paul, and Gerry Hendershot
   1974   "Public welfare and family planning: An empirical study of the 'brood sow' myth." Social Problems 21:658–673.
Pleck, Joseph
   1977   "The work-family role system." Social Problems 24:417–427.
Polachek, Solomon
   1975a "Potential biases in measuring male–female discrimination." Journal of Human Resources 10:205–229.
   1975b "Discontinuous labor force participation and its effect on women's market earnings." Pp. 90–122 in Cynthia Lloyd (ed.), Sex, Discrimination, and the Division of Labor. New York: Columbia University Press.
   1981   "Occupational self-selection: A human capital approach to sex differences in the occupational structure." Review of Economics and Statistics 63:60–69.
Polit, Denise
   1978   "Stereotypes relating to family size status." Journal of Marriage and the Family 40:105–119.
Powell, Katheryn
   1963   "Family variables." Pp. 231–240 in Ivan Nye and Lois Hoffman (eds.), The Employed Mother in America. Chicago: Rand McNally.
Presser, Harriet
   1974   "Early motherhood: Ignorance or bliss?" Family Planning Perspectives 6:8–14.
   1977   "Female employment and the division of labor within the home: A longitudinal perspective." Paper presented at the Annual Meeting of the Population Association of America. St. Louis.
Presser, Harriet, and Wendy Baldwin
   1980   "Child care as a constraint on employment. Prevalence, correlates, and bearing on the work and fertility nexus." American Journal of Sociology 85:1202–1213.
Price-Bonham, Sharon
   1976   "A comparison of weighted and unweighted decision-making scores." Journal of Marriage and the Family 38:629–640.
Rainwater, Lee
   1965   Family Design, Marital Sexuality, Family Size, and Contraception. Chicago: Aldine.

Rao, S. L. N., and L. F. Bouvier
1974 "Socioeconomic correlates of attitudes toward abortion in Rhode Island: 1971." American Journal of Public Health 64:765–774.
Reid, Margaret
1934 Economics of Household Production. New York: Wiley.
Riccio, James
1979 "Religious affiliation and socioeconomic achievement." Pp. 199–228 in Robert Wuthnow (ed.), The Religious Dimension. New York: Academic Press.
Rich, Eric
1970 The Education Act of 1970: A Study of Public Opinion. London: Longman Green.
Riley, Matilda White
1976 "Age strata in social systems." Pp. 189–217 in Robert Binstock and Ethel Shanas (eds.), Handbook of Aging and the Social Sciences. New York: Van Nostrand Reinhold.
1980 "Implications for the middle and later years." Pp. 31–40 in Women: A developmental perspective. Conference Report. Washington, D. C.: National Institute of Child Health and Development.
Rimlinger, Gaston
1971 Welfare Policy and Industrialization in Europe, America, and Russia. New York: Wiley.
Rindfuss, Ronald
1982 Personal communication.
Rindfuss, Ronald, Larry Bumpass, and Craig St. John
1980 "Education and fertility: Implications for the roles women occupy." American Sociological Review 45:431–447.
Rindfuss, Ronald, and Maurice MacDonald
1981 "Earnings, relative income, and fertility." Chapel Hill, N. C.: Carolina Population Center.
Robinson, John
1977 How Americans Use Time. New York: Praeger.
Rogers, Theresa
1976 "Interviews by telephone and in person: Quality of response and field performance." Public Opinion Quarterly 40:51–65.
Rollins, Boyd, and Stephen Bahr
1976 "A theory of power relationships in marriage." Journal of Marriage and the Family:619–627.
Rolph, Earl
1968 "Taxation. 1. General." Pp. 521–529 in David Sills (ed.), International Encyclopedia of the Social Sciences 15. New York: Macmillan & The Free Press.
Rosen, R. A. Hudson, H. H. Werley, J. W. Ager, and F. P. Shaw
1974 "Health professionals' attitudes to abortion." Public Opinion Quarterly 38:159–173.
Rosenfeld, Rachel
1978 "Women's intergenerational occupational mobility." American Sociological Review 43:36–46.
Rosenfield, Sarah
1980 "Sex differences in depression: Do women always have higher rates." Journal of Health and Social Behavior 21:33–42.

Rosenthal, Evelyn
  1978   "Working in midlife." Pp. 239–254 in Ann Stromberg and Shirley Harkess
          (eds.), Women Working. Palo Alto, Calif.: Mayfield.
Ross, Heather, and Isabel Sawhill
  1975   Time of Transition: The Growth of Families Headed by Women. Washington, D.
          C.: Urban Institute.
Rossi, Alice
  1964   "Equality between the sexes: An immodest proposal." Daedalus 93:607–652.
  1968   "Transition to parenthood." Journal of Marriage and the Family 30:26–39.
Rossi, Alice (ed.)
  1973   The Feminist Papers. New York: Columbia University Press.
Rossi, Alice
  1980   "Life-span theories and women's lives." Signs 6:4–32.
Rossi, Alice, and Ann Calderwood
  1973   Academic Women on the Move. New York: Russell Sage Foundation.
Rossi, Peter
  1981   "The presidential address: The challenge and opportunities of applied social
          research." American Sociological Review 45:889–904.
Rossi, Peter, and Katherine Lyall
  1977   Reforming Public Welfare: A Critique of the Negative Income Tax Experiment.
          New York: Russell Sage Foundation.
Russo, Gaetana Cazora
  1980   Essere Donna: Inchiesta sullo Status Sociale della Donna in Italia. Milano:
          Rizzoli Editore.
Ryder, Norman
  1978   "Components of temporal variations in American fertility." Paper presented to
          a Symposium on Recent Changes in Demographic Patterns in Developed So-
          cieties. London: Society for the Study of Human Biology.
  1979   "The future of American fertility." Social Problems 26:359–370.
  1981   "Where do babies come from?" Pp. 189–202 in T. Blalock (ed.), Sociological
          Theory and Methods. New York: The Free Press.
Rytina, Nancy
  1981   "Occupational segregation and earnings differences by sex." Monthly Labor
          Review 104:49–53.
  1982   "Tenure as a factor in the male–female earnings gap." Monthly Labor Review
          105:32–34.
Rytina, Steven, and Glenna Spitze
  1981   "Equity norms and household labor." Paper presented to the Annual Meetings
          of the American Sociological Association. Toronto.
Safilios-Rothschild, Constantina
  1969   "Family sociology or wives' sociology? A cross-cultural study of decision mak-
          ing." Journal of Marriage and the Family 31:290–301.
  1970   "The study of family power structure: A review, 1960–69." Journal of Marriage
          and the Family 32:539–532.
Samuelsson, Kurt
  1957   Religion and Economic Action: A Critique of Max Weber. New York: Harper &
          Row.
Sauvy, Alfred
  1961   Fertility and Survival: Population from Malthus to Mao Tse-Tung. London:
          Chatto & Windus.

Scanzoni, John
  1965   "A note on the sufficiency of wife responses in family research." Pacific Sociological Review 8:112–124.
  1970   Opportunity and the Family. New York: The Free Press.
  1978   Sex Roles, Women's Work, and Marital Conflict. Lexington, Mass.: Lexington Books.
Scarr, Sandra, and Richard Weinberg
  1978   "The influence of 'family background' on intellectual attainment." American Sociological Review 43:674–692.
Schoen, Robert, William Urton, Karen Woodrow, and John Baj
  1982   "Family formation and dissolution in 20th century America: A cohort analysis." Working Paper. Program for Population Research. Champaign–Urbana: University of Illinois.
Schuman, Howard
  1971   "The religious factor in Detroit: Review, replication, and reanalysis." American Sociological Review 36:30–47.
  1978   "Introduction: Ambiguities in the attitude–behavior relation." Pp. 373–376 in J. Milton Yinger and Stephen Cutler (eds.), Major Social Issues: An Interdisciplinary View. New York: The Free Press.
Scott, Hilda
  1974   Does Socialism Liberate Women? Experiences from Eastern Europe. Boston: Beacon.
  1978   "Eastern European women in theory and practice." Women's Studies Interational Quarterly 1:180–199.
  1982   Sweden's 'Right to be Human' Sex Role Equality: The Goal and the Reality. Armonk, N. Y.: Sharpe.
Shaw, Lois
  1980   "Changes in the work attachment of married women, 1966–1976." Paper presented to the Pacific Sociological Association. Anaheim, Cal.
Shaw, Lois, and Anne Statham
  1982   "Fertility expectations and the changing roles of women." Pp. 45–65 in Frank Mott (ed.), The Employment Revolution: Young American Women of the 1970s. Cambridge, Mass.: MIT Press.
Silka, Linda, and Sara Kiesler
  1977   "Couples who choose to remain childless." Family Planning Perspectives 9:16–25.
Silverman, W., and R. Hill
  1967   "Task allocation in marriage in the United States and Belgium." Journal of Marriage and the Family 29:353–359.
Simon, Julian
  1977   The Economics of Population Growth. Princeton, N. J.: Princeton University Press.
Sklar, June, and Beth Berkov
  1975   The American birthrate: Evidences of a coming rise." Science 189:693–700.
Smart, Ninian
  1974   "Religion, study of." Pp. 613–628 in Macropaedia 15. Chicago: Encyclopaedia Britannica.
Smelser, Neil
  1959   Social Change in the Industrial Revolution. Chicago: University of Chicago Press.

Smith, Tom W.
  1979   "Happiness: Time trends, seasonal variations, inter-survey differences, and other mysteries." Social Psychology Quarterly 42:18–30.
  1980   A Compendium of Trends on General Social Survey Questions. Report No. 129. Chicago: National Opinion Research Center
Smith-Lovin, Lynn, and Ann Tickamyer
  1978   "Non-recursive models of labor force participation, fertility behavior, and sex-role attitudes." American Sociological Review 43:541–557.
Sokoloff, Natalie
  1980   Between Money and Love: The Dialectics of Women's Home and Market Work. New York: Praeger.
Soltow, Martha, Carolyn Forché, and Murray Massre
  1972   Women in American Labor History, 1825–1935: An Annotated Bibliography. East Lansing: Michigan State University School of Labor and Industrial Relations and The Libraries.
Southwick, Jessie (ed.)
  1975   Survey Data for Trend Analysis: An Index to Repeated Questions in U. S. National Surveys Held by the Roper Public Opinion Research Center. Williamstown, Mass.: Roper Public Opinion Research Center.
Spengler, Joseph
  1979   France Faces Depopulation: Postlude Edition, 1936–1976. Durham, N. C.: Duke University Press.
Spitze, Glenna
  1979   "Work commitment among young women." Unpublished Ph.D. dissertation, University of Illinois at Urbana–Champaign.
Spitze, Glenna, and Joan Huber
  1980   "Changing attitudes toward women's non-family roles: 1938 to 1978." Sociology of Work and Occupations 7:317–335.
  1982   "Effects of anticipated consequences on ERA opinion." Social Science Quarterly 63:323–332.
Spitze, Glenna, and Joe L. Spaeth
  1978   "Employment among married female college graduates." Social Science Research 8:184–199.
Spitze, Glenna, and Linda Waite
  1980   "Young women's early labor force experiences and work attitudes." Sociology of Work and Occupations 7:3–32.
Stafford, Frank, and Greg Duncan
  1979   The Use of Time and Technology by Households in the United States. Ann Arbor: University of Michigan Institute for Social Research.
Stafford, Rebecca, Elaine Backman, and Pamela Dibona
  1977   "The division of labor among cohabiting and married couples." Journal of Marriage and the Family 39:43–57.
Stein, Dorothy
  1978   "Women to burn: Suttee as a normative institution." Signs 4:253–268.
Steinhilber, August, and Carl Sokolowski
  1966   State Law on Compulsory Attendance. Circular No. 793, Office of Education. Washington, D. C.: United States Government Printing Office.
Stern, Bernhard
  1944   "Woman, position in society: Historical." Pp. 442–451 in E. R. A. Seligman (ed.), Encyclopaedia of the Social Sciences 15. New York: Macmillan.

Stevens, Gillian, and Monica Boyd
  1980   "The importance of mother: Labor force participation and intergenerational mobility of women." Social Forces 59:186–199.
Stoddart, Jennifer
  1978   "Feminism in Paris." Canadian Newsletter of Research on Women 7:62–67.
Strasser, Susan
  1980   "An enlarged human existence? Technology and household work in nineteenth century America." Pp. 29–52 in Sarah Fenstermaker Berk (ed.), Women and Household Labor. Beverly Hills: Sage.
Strober, Myra, and Charles Weinberg
  1980   "Strategies used by working and nonworking wives to reduce time pressures." Journal of Consumer Research 6:338–348.
Sturmingher, Laura
  1979   Women and the Making of the Working Class: Lyon 1830–1870. St. Albans, Vt.: Eden Press.
Sudman, Seymour
  1973   "The uses of telephone directories for survey sampling." Journal of Marketing Research 10:204–207.
Sudman, Seymour, and Norman Bradburn
  1975   Response Effects in Surveys. Chicago: Aldine.
Sullerot, Evelyne
  1973   Les Françaises au travail. Paris: Librairie Hachette.
Sullivan, Teresa
  1981   Personal communication.
Suter, Larry, and Herman Miller
  1973   "Income differences between men and career women." Pp. 200–212 in Joan Huber (ed.), Changing Women in a Changing society. Chicago: University of Chicago Press.
Swafford, Michael
  1978   "Sex differences in Soviet earnings." American Sociological Review 43:657–673.
Sweet, James
  1972   Women in the Labor Force. New York: Seminar Press.
Szalai, Alexander
  1973   The Use of Time: Daily Activities of Urban and Suburban Populations in Twelve Countries. The Hague: Mouton.
Szinovacz, Maximiliane
  1977   "Role allocation, family structure, and female employment." Journal of Marriage and the Family 39:781–791.
Tedrow, Lucky, and E. R. Mahoney
  1979   "Trends in attitudes toward abortion: 1972–1976." Public Opinion Quarterly 43:181–189.
Thibaut, J., and H. H. Kelly
  1959   The Social Psychology of Groups. New York: Wiley.
Thornton, Arland
  1977   "Children and marital stability." Journal of Marriage and the Family 39:531–540.
Thornton, Arland, and Deborah Freedman
  1979   "Changes in the sex role attitudes of women, 1962–1977." American Sociological Review 44:832–840.

Tickamyer, Ann
    1981   "Wealth and power: A comparison of men and women in the property elite."
           Social Forces 60:463–481.
Tietze, Christopher
    1968   "Fertility control." Pp. 382–388 in David Sills (ed.), International Encyclopedia
           of the Social Sciences 5. New York: Macmillan & The Free Press.
    1981   Induced Abortion: A World Review. A Population Council Fact Book, 4th edi-
           tion. New York: The Population Council.
Tilly, Charles (ed.)
    1978   Historical Studies of Changing Fertility. Princeton, N. J.: Princeton University
           Press.
Tilly, Louise, and Joan Scott
    1978. Women, Work, and Society. New York: Holt, Rinehart & Winston.
Tilly, Louise, Joan Scott, and Miriam Cohen
    1976   "Women's work and European fertility patterns." Journal of Interdisciplinary
           History 6:447–476.
Treiman, Donald, and Kermit Terrell
    1975   "Sex and the process of status attainment: A comparison of working women and
           men." American Sociological Review 40:174–200.
Tsuchigane, Robert, and Norton Dodge
    1974   Economic Discrimination against Women in the United States. Lexington,
           Mass.: Lexington Books.
Turk, James, and Norman Bell
    1972   "Measuring power in families." Journal of Marriage and the Family
           34:215–223.
Udry, Richard
    1982   Personal communication.
United Nations
    1973   The Determinants and Consequences of Population Trends: New Summary of
           Findings on Interaction of Demographic, Economic, and Social Factors. I. Popu-
           lation Studies 50. New York: United Nations Department of Economic and
           Social Affairs.
United States Bureau of the Census
    1975a Historical Statistics of the United States: Colonial Times to 1970. Part 1. Wash-
           ington, D. C.: United States Government Printing Office.
    1975b Current Population Reports. Series P-20, No. 287. "Marital status and living
           arrangements: March 1975." Washington, D. C.: United States Government
           Printing Office.
    1978   Current Population Reports. Special Studies Series P-23, No. 70. "Perspectives
           on American Fertility," by Maurice Moore and Martin O'Connell. Washington,
           D. C.: United States Government Printing Office.
    1979   Current Population Reports. Special Studies Series P-23, No. 84. "Divorce,
           child custody, and child support." Washington, D. C.: United States Govern-
           ment Printing Office.
    1982   Current Population Reports. Special Studies Series P-23, No. 114. "Characteris-
           tics of American children and youth: 1980." Washington, D. C.: United States
           Government Printing Office.
United States Department of Labor, Bureau of Labor Statistics
    1980   Recent Trends in Labor Force Participation Rates: A Chartbook. Report No. 609.
           Washington, D. C.: United States Government Printing Office.

United States Department of Labor, Women's Bureau
  1928   Summary: The Effects of Labor Legislation on the Employment Opportunities of Women. Bulletin No. 68. Washington, D. C.: United States Government Printing Office.
van den Berg, Axel
  1980   "Critical theory: Is there still hope?" American Journal of Sociology 86:449–478.
van den Berghe, Pierre
  1979   Human Family Systems: An Evolutionary View. New York: Elsevier.
van Es, John, and P. M. Singi
  1972   "Response consistency of husband and wife for selected attitudinal items." Journal of Marriage and the Family 34:141–149.
Vanek, Joann
  1974   "Time Spent in Housework." Scientific American 231:116–120.
Veevers, Jean
  1979   "Voluntary childlessness: A review of issues and evidence." Marriage & Family Review 2:1–26.
Waite, Linda
  1976   "Working wives: 1940–1960." American Sociological Review 41:61–80.
  1978   "Projecting female labor force participation from sex-role attitudes." Social Science Research 7:299–318.
Waksberg, Joseph
  1978   "Sampling methods for random digit dialing." Journal of the American Statistical Association 73:40–46.
Walker, Kathryn
  1979   "Time use in families, a new study." Paper presented to the National Council on Family Relations. Boston.
Walker, Kathryn, and Margaret Woods
  1976   Time Use: A Measure of Household Production of Family Goods and Services. Washington, D. C.: American Home Economics Association.
Walsh, Mary Roth
  1977   Doctors Wanted: No Women Need Apply. Sexual Barriers in the Medical Profession, 1835–1975. New Haven, Conn.: Yale University Press.
Ward, Michael, and William Butz
  1978   "Completed fertility and its timing: An economic analysis of U. S. experience since World War II." Santa Monica, Calif.: Rand Corporation.
Weinbaum, Batya
  1978   The Curious Courtship of Women's Liberation and Socialism. Boston: Southend Press.
Weiss, Nancy Pottishman
  1978   "The mother–child dyad revisited." Journal of Social Issues 34:243–255.
Weiss, Robert
  1979   "Issues in the adjudication of custody when parents separate." Pp. 324–336 in George Levinger and Oliver Moles (eds.), Divorce and Separation. New York: Basic Books.
Weitzman, Lenore
  1981   The Marriage Contract. New York: The Free Press.
Welch, Susan
  1975   "Support among women for issues of the women's movement." Sociological Quarterly 16:216–227.

Westoff, C. F.
  1978a "Some speculations on the future of marriage and fertility." Family Planning
       Perspectives 10:79–83.
  1978b "Marriage and fertility in the developed countries." Scientific American
       239:51–57.
  1980 Comments on a panel, "The Future of Fertility." Presented at the Population
       Association of America. Denver.
Westoff, C. F., and L. Bumpass
  1973 "The revolution in birth control practices of U. S. Roman Catholics." Science
       179:41–44.
Westoff, Charles, and Elise Jones
  1977 "The secularization of U. S. Catholic birth control practices." Family Planning
       Perspectives 9:203–207.
Westoff, Charles, and Norman Ryder
  1977 The Contraceptive Revolution. Princeton, N. J.: Princeton University Press.
Whelpton, Pascal
  1943– 1958 Social and Psychological Factors Affecting Fertility, Volumes 1–5. New
       York: Millbank Memorial Fund.
Whelpton, Pascal, Arthur Campbell, and John Patterson
  1966 Fertility and Family Planning in the United States. Princeton, N. J.: Princeton
       University Press.
Whiting, Beatrice, and Carolyn Pope Edwards
  1973 "A cross-cultural analysis of sex differences in the behavior of children aged
       three through eleven." Journal of Social Psychology 91:171–188.
Wilensky, Harold
  1981 "Family life cycle, work, and the quality of life." Pp. 235–265 in B. Gardell and
       G. Johansson (eds.), Working Life. London: Wiley.
Wilkening, Eugene, and Denton Morrison
  1963 "A comparison of husband and wife responses concerning who makes farm and
       home decisions." Marriage and Family LIving 25:349–351.
Witte, Edwin
  1944 "Labor legislation." Pp. 657–667 in E. R. A. Seligman (ed.), Encyclopaedia of
       the Social Sciences 7. New York: Macmillan.
Wolman, Diane Miller
  1972 "Findings of the Commission's National Public Opinion Survey." Pp. 475–514
       in Robert Parke, Jr. and Charles Westoff (eds.), Aspects of Population Growth
       Policy. The Commission on Population Growth and the American Culture Re-
       search Reports. Washington, D. C.: United States Government Printing Office.
Woody, Thomas
  1929 A History of Women's Education in the United States, Volume II. New York:
       The Science Press.
Wrigley, E. A.
  1969 "Family limitation in preindustrial England." Pp. 157–194 in Michael Drake
       (ed.), Population in Industrialization. London: Methuen.
  1978 "Fertility Strategy for the Individual and the Group." Pp. 135–154 in Charles
       Tilly (ed.), Historical Studies of Changing Fertility. Princeton, N. J.: Princeton
       University Press.
Wulf, Deirdre
  1980 "The Hungarian fertility survey, 1977." Family Planning Perspectives
       12:44–46.

Yinger, Milton
  1974 "Religion, social aspects of." Pp. 604–613 in Macropaedia 15. Chicago: Encyclopaedia Britannica.
Zelnik, Melvin, and John Kantner
  1975 "Attitudes of American teenagers toward abortion." Family Planning Perspectives 7:89–91.

Subject Index

QUANTITATIVE STUDIES IN SOCIAL RELATIONS
(Continued from page ii)

QUANTITATIVE STUDIES IN SOCIAL RELATIONS